T0341363

African Theatre
9

Series Editors
Martin Banham, James Gibbs,
Yvette Hutchison, Femi Osofisan
& Jane Plastow

Reviews Editor
Jane Plastow
Workshop Theatre, School of English, University of Leeds LS2 9JT, UK

Associate Editors
Awo Mana Asiedu
School of Performing Arts, PO Box 201, University of Ghana, Legon, Ghana

Eckhard Breitinger
Forststr. 3, 95488 Eckersdorf, Germany

David Kerr
Dept of Media Studies, Private Bag 00703, University of Botswana, Gaborone, Botswana

Amandina Lihamba
Dept of Fine & Performing Arts, PO Box 3505, University of Dar es Salaam, Tanzania

Patrick Mangeni
Head of Dept of Music, Dance & Drama, Makerere University, Kampala, Uganda

Olu Obafemi
Dept of English, University of Ilorin, Ilorin, Nigeria

Articles not exceeding 5,000 words should be submitted preferably on disk (as a Word file) and always accompanied by a double-spaced hard copy. Typewritten submissions may be considered in exceptional circumstances if they are double-spaced.

Style: Preferably use UK rather than US spellings. Italicise titles of books or plays. Use single inverted commas and double for quotes within quotes. Type notes at the end of the text on a separate sheet. Do not justify the right-hand margins.

References should follow the style of this volume (Surname date: page number) in text. All references should then be listed at the end of article in full:
Surname, name, date, *title of work* (place of publication: name of publisher)
Surname, name, date, 'title of article' in surname, initial (ed./eds) *title of work* (place of publication: publisher).
or Surname, name, date, 'title of article', *Journal*, vol., no: page numbers.

Reviewers should provide full bibliographic details, including extent, ISBN and price.

Copyright: Please ensure, where appropriate, that clearance has been obtained from copyright holders of material used. Illustrations may also be submitted if appropriate and if accompanied by full captions and with reproduction rights clearly indicated. It is the responsibility of the contributors to clear all permissions.

All submissions should be accompanied by a brief biographical profile. The editors cannot undertake to return material submitted and contributors are advised to keep a copy of all material sent in case of loss in transit.

Editorial address
African Theatre, c/o Workshop Theatre, School of English, University of Leeds, Leeds LS2 9JT, UK • j.e.plastow@leeds.ac.uk

Books for Review & Review articles
Jane Plastow, Reviews Editor, *African Theatre*, Workshop Theatre, School of English, University of Leeds, Leeds LS2 9JT, UK • j.e.plastow@leeds.ac.uk

African Theatre 9
Histories 1850–1950

Editor
Yvette Hutchison

Reviews Editor
Jane Plastow

JC JAMES CURREY

James Currey
is an imprint of Boydell and Brewer Ltd
PO Box 9, Woodbridge, Suffolk IP12 3DF, UK
and of Boydell & Brewer Inc.
668 Mt Hope Avenue, Rochester, NY 14620, USA
www.boydellandbrewer.com
www.jamescurrey.com

The publisher has no responsibility for the continued existence or accuracy of URLs for external
or third-party internet websites referred to in this book, and does not guarantee that any content
on such websites is, or will remain, accurate or appropriate.

This publication is printed on acid-free paper

British Library Cataloguing in Publication Data
African theatre.
 9, Histories 1850–1950.
 1. Theater—Africa—History.
 I. Hutchison, Yvette.
 792'.096–dc22

ISBN 978-1-84701-014-8 (James Currey paper)

Typeset in 10/11 pt Monotype Bembo by Long House, Cumbria, UK
Printed and bound in Great Britain by CPI Antony Rowe, Chippenham and Eastbourne

Contents

Notes on Contributors

Cristina Boscolo has a degree in modern languages from the University of Venice, Italy; which included a pioneering study on the English language in Nigeria. Her passion for Nigerian literature, in particular that written in Yorùbá, led to her continuing her research in African studies at the University of Mainz, Germany. She is currently a freelance lecturer. Her most recent publication is *Odún. Discourses, Strategies, and Power in the Yorùbá Play of Transformation* (Rodopi), which analyses the aesthetic features of the Egúngún and Moremi Festival in Nigeria.

James Gibbs taught at universities in Ghana, Malawi, Nigeria, Belgium and the United Kingdom between 1968 and 2007. Now retired from teaching, his 2009 volume of essays on the Ghanaian Theatre entitled *Nkyin-Kyin* and his article in this volume reflect his continued activity as a senior visiting research fellow at the University of the West of England.

Yvette Hutchison is associate professor in the Department of Theatre & Performance Studies at the University of Warwick, UK. Her research area is most specifically Anglophone African theatre and history, and how narratives of memory inform efficacy and advocacy, both for the individual and society as a whole. She is associate editor of *South African Theatre Journal* and *African Theatre* series, and has co-edited books with Kole Omotoso and Eckhard Breitinger. She is currently working on a book entitled *Performance and the Archive of Memory*.

Samuel Kasule teaches drama and postcolonial literatures at the University of Derby. He is a founding member of the African Theatre Association (AfTA) and Reviews Editor of *African Performance Review* (APR). His main research interests are in African popular theatre and performance. His play, *Nannungi*, was recently premiered at the National Theatre (Kampala). Currently, he is the Regional Editor for East and Central Africa, *World Scenography*, a three book and internet database project.

Marisa Keuris is an associate professor in theory of literature and currently the chair of the department of Afrikaans and theory of literature at the University of South Africa (UNISA). Her main field of interest is in contemporary drama and theatre theory. She has published articles on drama and theatre semiotics, dramatic language, ecocritical approaches to drama, as well as translation studies in drama. These articles incorporate discussions of the work of well-known Afrikaans (Deon Opperman, Pieter Fourie, Reza de Wet), as well as English (Janet Suzman, Athol Fugard) South African playwrights.

Christine Matzke has taught African literature and theatre at the Institute of Asian and African Studies, Humboldt-Universität zu Berlin, and at Goethe-University, Frankfurt/Main. Her research interests include theatre and cultural production in Eritrea, and post-colonial crime fiction. She recently co-edited *African Theatre 8: Diasporas*.

Steve Nicholson is currently reader in twentieth-century theatre in the University of Sheffield, School of English. He has published extensively on politics and British theatre in the first half of the twentieth century, and is currently completing the last of four volumes charting a history of theatre censorship by the Lord Chamberlain between 1900 and 1968.

Jane Plastow is a professor of African theatre at the Workshop Theatre, University of Leeds, and director of the Leeds University Centre for African Studies. She has written extensively on African theatre and theatre-for-development, and works practically in both the UK and the Horn of Africa.

Samuel Ravengai is a theatre maker, director, writer and lecturer. He has an MA in theatre and performance and has published several journal articles and book chapters, and presented papers at international conferences including the annual International Federation of Theatre Research and the biennial Dramatic Learning Spaces. He worked as associate director and story consultant of a Zimbabwean pro-development soap opera, *Studio 263* before joining the University of Cape Town drama department, where he is currently a doctoral research fellow. Previously he lectured and was head of department of theatre arts at the University of Zimbabwe.

Owen S. Seda teaches English and theatre studies in the department of English at the University of Botswana. He has also taught at the universities of Zimbabwe, Africa University in Mutare, and California State University, Pomona, where he was a Fulbright Scholar-in-Residence. He is a recent joint-recipient of a Fulbright Alumni Initiatives Awards grant, with Professor William H. Morse II of CSU Pomona, with whom he worked on a trans-atlantic project in community theatre.

Obituaries

Sotigui Kouyaté (1936–2010)

The West African actor Sotigui Kouyaté died in Paris on Saturday, 17 April 2010. Born in Bamako, Mali, to parents of Guinean extraction, Kouyaté was raised in Burkina Faso. The descendent of a long line of *griots*, his early education was firmly rooted in Mandingo culture. Before discovering his affinity for acting, he was a teacher and clerk, and, during the late Fifties, captain of Burkina Faso's national soccer team. In 1966, he made his theatrical début in an historical drama at the behest of his friend, Boubacar Dicko. Shortly thereafter, he established his own, twenty-five strong theatre company, 'The Volta Theatre Company', who wrote and performed their own texts, including Kouyaté's *The Crocodile's Lament*.

In 1982, Kouyaté first appeared on screen, performing in Mustapha Diop's *Le Médecin de Gafiré* (The Doctor of Gafiré) and then in Christian Richard's *Le Courage des autres* (The Courage of Others), a chronicle of the slave trade set in nineteenth-century West Africa. Struck by his screen presence, Peter Brook approached Kouyaté to take a role in his staging of the *Mahabharata*. This marked the beginning of a long and fruitful collaboration. Kouyaté went on to take leading roles in numerous Brook productions, including Shakespeare's *La Tempête* (The Tempest), Can Themba's *Le Costume* (The Suit), and, in 2004, an adaptation of Amadou Hampaté Bâ's novel, *Tierno Bokar* – a source of inspiration that Brook returned to in 2010.

Kouyaté's success on the stage was mirrored in the cinema; he appeared in 60 films over the course of his career. In 2009, he was named Best Actor at the Berlin film festival for his interpretation of an aggrieved father in Rachid Bouchareb's *London River*. At the 62nd Cannes Film Festival (2009), the French Ministry of Culture awarded him the prestigious 'Officier des arts et des lettres' medal in recognition of his lifetime achievements.

Kouyaté also distinguished himself as a tireless advocate of the fledging cultural industry in West Africa. In collaboration with Habib Dembélé and Jean-Louis Sagot-Duvauroux, he founded the Mandéka International Theatre in Bamako in 1997 to cultivate local actors. Later he and his children opened a cultural centre in Bobo Dioulasso (Burkina Faso) to promote and transmit traditional African arts to local youth.

Zara Bennett
St Mary's College of Maryland

Esiaba Irobi, 1961–2010

Esiaba Irobi, poet, dramatist and scholar died in Berlin, Germany, on 4 May 2010 at the age of 49. Irobi studied at the University of Nigeria, Nsukka, and the universities of Sheffield and Leeds. At the time of his death he was working at Ohio University, where he was Associate Professor of International Theatre/ Cinema. He also taught at New York University, Towson University, and Liverpool John Moores University (UK). He will be remembered for his contribution to the knowledge and scholarship of African, African-Caribbean, and African-American theatre and performance. He was widely known for his interdisciplinary work in performance, film and postcolonial studies. Irobi was an accomplished scholar, writer and researcher and will be greatly missed. In 1992, he received the World Drama Trust Award for playwriting for his play, *Cemetery Road*. His creative works include plays and poetry collections such as *The Colour of Rusting Gold; Hangmen Also Die; 'Why the Vulture's Head is Naked' What Song do Mosquitoes Sing?; Nwokedi, Am I Too Loud?; Handgrenades; Gold, Frankincense and Myrrh; The Fronded Circle; A Tent to Pass the Night; Inflorescence: Selected Poems; Why I Don't Like Philip Larkin*. Irobi was one of the founding members of the African Theatre Association (AfTA) and his energy and contributions have helped to shape African performance studies in the diaspora. Among other things, in his provocative and mischievously anarchic style he always energised conferences and these will never be the same again.

Sam Kasule

Introduction

YVETTE HUTCHISON

In the decades following independence for many countries in Africa, and in the
last sixteen years following the end of apartheid in South Africa, politicians, historians and artists have engaged in various revisions of constitutions, curricula,
especially in relation to history. Researchers have been rewriting the histories
of the arts in their respective countries because, it has been argued, one cannot
understand or engage with the present without a clear sense of the past.

Critics have warned of the perils of ignoring history. For example, Ghanaian
poet Kwadwo Opoku-Agyemang has argued that '[h]istory that advances by
denying itself is not history but a pain that perpetually begins anew' (1996: 64),
and the hugely influential French literary theorist, Roland Barthes, has said that
'it is when history is denied that it is most unmistakably at work' (1986: 2).

Re-evaluating how history has formulated national memory and identity
has been central to the post-independence processes of African countries. In
this process great emphasis has been placed on the revision of national and
theatre histories from the 1960s onward, from the perspective of unravelling
these from their previously dominant colonial perspectives. However, in
theatre history, much of the focus of the writing still has been on literary drama
because of the complexities of accessing oral performance linguistically and also
because of the ephemeral nature of performance itself. Furthermore, it is often
hamstrung by being reframed in terms of how 'progress' is defined, and by
whom (Neale, 1985).

It is against this backdrop that the editors proposed that *African Theatre* 9
focus on theatre histories between 1850 and 1950. As issue editor, I was particularly influenced by Diana Taylor's work in theatre in South America where
she explores the relationship between 'the *archive* of supposedly enduring
materials, texts, documents, buildings, bones, and the so-called ephemeral *repertoire* of embodied practice/ knowledge: spoken language, dance, sports, ritual.'
(author's italics, 2007: 19) In her discussion of the archive Taylor traces the
'myths attending the archive': that it is 'unmediated ... that it resists change,
corruptibility and political manipulation'. Here the issues of hegemonic
processes of mediation; those of 'selection, memorization or internalization,
and transmission' (2007: 21), the kind of processes inherent to any archive,

become profoundly significant in relation to issues of contested memories and hegemonies that dominated Africa during colonisation.

Taylor also argues that the repertoire 'enacts embodied memory: performances, gestures, orality, movement, dance, singing – in short all those acts usually thought of as ephemeral, non-reproducible knowledge.' (2007: 20) It is in these embodied memories that one can begin to recover material apparently 'lost' to the formal archive. African historians John Parker and Richard Rathbone succinctly trace how socio-political paradigms have affected the 'writing' of Africa and its history, and how '[r]ecent archaeological research, combined with that by historians, art historians, and anthropologists, has forced a rethink of this [here referring specifically to histories related to the middle Niger region] established narrative' (2007: 19) They also argue that the conflation of the notions of acceptable or reliable 'evidence' or 'sources' with 'document', a western academic perspective, has affected the writing of Africa's histories (ibid: 56). They note, though, that historians are increasingly turning to oral sources and other disciplines, including archaeology, the plastic and performing arts as sources for rewriting histories (ibid: 56-65). This shift in perspective on sources is not exclusive to history as a discipline, but evident also in Theatre Studies, see for example Martin Banham's *A History of Theatre in Africa* (2004), which insisted that the histories included in this collection trace both the oral and written theatre of the continent, including Africa north of the Sahara.

Another advantage to exploring embodied cultural archives is that they require the presence of those in whom the memory and/or form resides, which in turn insists on returning agency in defining histories to individuals and local communities. However, as Taylor rightly argues, the relationship between the documented, material archive and the embodied repertoire is complex and their intersections are not oppositional, easily reduced to a simple binary of repositories of contesting encoded cultural forms. They interact, and affect one another in complex ways. Thus revisiting embodied practices may be a way to begin breaking down some of the old binaries that have existed between oral and literary traditions, and place these in increasing dialogue with one another. Thus the personal, local and above all fictional narratives and memories may challenge dominant histories or singular perspectives on the past.

With these ideas in mind we invited articles that engaged with the following issues and questions:

- How performances, both colonial and indigenous have been documented, whether as texts, reviews, playbills, or which have remained in the oral tradition. Also, how various performance traditions have developed in the context of the complex relationships between colonial and indigenous peoples, including that of missionaries and travellers, between 'collaboration' and 'resistance'?
- The issue of documentation of theatre as an ephemeral form, but made more complex in the African indigenous context because it has been primarily physical, embodied, as opposed to written. Hence, what kinds of

documentation of performances exist (both of colonial and indigenous theatre), and how may this range of documentation have affected, even skewed how we read back into theatre history?

• How have the various performance traditions intersected to create new, complex relationships and forms. Here we include the work of missionaries and travellers. How did 'collaboration' and 'resistance' affect understandings of culture, and was evidenced in the performances that emerged?

The response to this invitation has suggested how great the potential for further research in these areas may be. It has also highlighted serious issues that need to be immediately engaged with if important material is not to be lost forever. Both James Gibbs, who explores Kobina Sekyi's production of the *The Blinkards* (1916), and Christine Matzke, writing about memories of Berhe Mesgun's play *Zehalefe Nebret Ertra* (Eritrea's Past Property), illustrate the many difficulties involved in accessing material, including the physical conditions in which much of the material is kept; at the mercy of heat, dust and insects that may destroy them all too easily, as well as political and economic considerations that affect what may be accessed, spoken about and how events and people are or are not remembered. They also point to the incalculable resources that are literally embodied in a generation that is quickly passing. Matzke particularly highlights the importance of extended research *in situ*, and the importance of developing relationships with the people who hold these memories and experiences. This invokes reflection on the responsibilities of the researcher, and the ethical issues surrounding potential appropriation and misrepresentation of primary research material. It also demonstrates how the political dominance of the present may define, or even skew our reading of the past. Both of these authors draw our attention to the fact that any reading of an event, play or figure of theatre history is provisional, dependent on what is known at the time; and that both the making of theatre and writing of its history are collaborative endeavours.

Almost all of the articles engage with the role of missionaries in the way theatre developed during this period. Whether as facilitators of a new form, as evidenced in Owen Seda's article on 'Medieval morality and liturgical drama in colonial Rhodesia', or in the attempt to impose and control forms, as discussed by Samuel Ravengai in his exploration of 'Contesting constructions of cultural production in and through urban theatre in Rhodesia, c.1890-1950', where he demonstrates the complex relationship between imitation and subversion; the missions' tolerance of some indigenous performance forms and banning of others affected the development of theatre. They consider how the local African populations adapted colonial forms in response to mission injunctions, and even developed new forms in response to the mission schools, adapting these with input from local cultural forms as well as those drawn from the experiences of men who were in the area as migrant workers from Malawi, Zambia and South Africa.

Sam Kasule, focusing on theatre in Uganda, and Cristina Boscolo, focusing on Yorùbá appropriation and resistance, explore missionaries' and administrators' accounts of various performances, and suggest that these both reveal much about the colonial perspective on performances of the period, and have the potential for contemporary researchers to recover material that may perhaps no longer be available. They also insist that this material needs to be reappraised from a more situated perspective. Kasule suggests how the gramaphone recordings of the 1930s may reveal much about oral story-telling and the role of performances that preceded the early twentieth century. Both Kasule and Boscolo highlight the subversive role of these performances, and highlight the way they were being used to negotiate new, multiple identities, as people from various cultures intersected: this included both the colonial and African populations and also the local African and migrant African populations, bringing with them not only differences in language, but also religion and performance forms. These articles suggest a far greater inter- and intracultural level of influence and subtle cultural negotiation than the colonial gaze admitted.

Even the early twentieth-century South African Dutch-Afrikaans dramatic representations of Khoisan characters, as explored by Marisa Keuris, reveal attitudes and ironies which suggest that the relationships between racial groups in South Africa were not as simple as the histories of the time suggest. The character representation and the roles the characters played reveal the 'interferences' in the way people remember the past, particularly in such a divided society (Bartlett, in Sacks, 1995: 173), as well as an interconnectedness with those who appeared to be dominant or subjugated in ways that require a more subtle re-reading. For to understand the past, we also have to understand the reasons for the myths that were made. As Hayden White suggests in *Metahistory* (1987), we need to critically re-evaluate the notions of history as 'empirical' and myth as 'conceptual', and shift the emphasis perhaps, looking at what role memory plays in the (re?)construction of history. This is most important when deconstructing the mythic constructions of the colonial subject, as this reveals the fears and aspirations of the colonizer. However, these mythic constructions and the responses to them by the colonized subject were not simple or one-directional. Many articles in this collection illustrate Homi Bhabha's argument that mimicry is an important counter-hegemonic devise insofar as it is 'constructed around ambivalence; in order to be effective, mimicry must continually produce its slippage, its excess, its difference. ... the sign of a double articulation'(1996: 122). The research illustrates such slippage, or doubleness, and how the mimicry of colonial forms both reveals the constructedness of stereotypes and the ambivalence of them in the colonial discourse. It also exemplifies the extent to which these stereotypes are hybridized and historicized constructs rather than simple states of being.

Steve Nicholson's article 'Images of Africa in early twentieth-century British theatre' is a sharp and witty exploration of these same ideas from the colonial rather than African perspective. It looks at how Africa was 'imaged' and imagined in the early twentieth century. It discusses plays that are no longer in circulation, but can be accessed in the British Library Archive of Lord Chamberlain's Correspondence Files 1900-1968 and the Victoria and Albert

Museum Theatre and Performance Archives, and it includes fascinating photographs of some of the productions.

And finally Jane Plastow traces 'The first African play: Tekle Hawariat's play *Fabula: Yawreoch Commedia* and its influence on the development of Ethiopian Theatre'. This provides a situated contextualization of the translation of the play by Belayneh Abune, which follows.

There seems to be an increasing interest in memory, amnesia and nostalgia that parallels ongoing historical endeavours. Memory Studies is becoming a research field in its own right. With this awareness I return to, and end with, Derek Walcott's argument that the ability to make and remake one's history through the imagination is what gives hope, as the self can be redefined, remade. Baugh quotes Walcott as saying: 'We contemplate our spirit by the detritus of the past' (in Fox, 1986: 337). I would argue that this collection brings together much material that may have lain unnoticed in [cardboard] boxes, or in people who have gradually grown older, but have offered significant material for us to contemplate our spirits, perhaps re-member incomplete histories, and review a period in history that perhaps has been neglected. I also hope that this will inspire more research in the future.

I would like to express my deep thanks to the editorial team, especially Martin Banham, who have supported and advised me with patience and tireless energy in this project. We would also like to note that the team has been strengthened once again by the addition of Patrick Mangeni and Awo Mana Asiedu as associate editors. Many thanks also to Lynn Taylor who has been infinitely patient in advising me on editorial matters.

BIBLIOGRAPHY & FURTHER READING

Banham, Martin (ed.) (2004) *A History of Theatre in Africa*. Cambridge: Cambridge University Press.

Barthes, Roland (1986) *Writing Degree Zero*. (Trans.) Lavers, A. & Smith, C. New York: Hill and Wang.

Benjamin, Walter (1968) 'Theses on the Philosophy of History'. In *Illuminations*. (Trans.) H. Zohn. New York: Harcourt, Brace & World.

Bhabha, Homi (1996) *The Location of Culture*. London and New York: Routledge.

Fox, Robert E. 1986. 'Derek Walcott: History as Dis-ease', *Callaloo*, Vol. 9, No. 2, Spring, 331–40.

Greene, Naomi (1996) 'Empire as Myth and Memory'. In *Cinema, Colonialism, Postcolonialism: Perspectives from the French and Francophone World*. Austin: University of Texas Press.

Hutton, Patrick H. (1993) *History as an Art of Memory*. Hanover/London: University Press of New England.

Kapteijns, Lidwien (1977) *African Historiography Written by Africans 1955–1973: the Nigerian case*. PhD. Leiden: Afrika-Studiencentrum.

Lowenthal, David (1997) *The Past is a Foreign Country*. Cambridge: Cambridge University Press.

Neale, Caroline (1985) *Writing 'Independent' History: African historiography 1960-1980*. Westport/London: Greenwood Press.

Olaniyan, Tejomula (1995) *Scars of Conquest/ Masks of Resistance – the Invention of Cultural Identities in African, African-American, and Caribbean drama*. New York/Oxford: Oxford University Press.

Opoku-Agyemang, Kwadwo (1996) 'A Crisis of Balance: The (mis) representation of colonial history and the slave experience as themes in modern African literature', *Okike*, 32, February, 49–67.

Parker, John & Rathbone, Richard (2007) *African History: A very short introduction*. Oxford: Oxford University Press.

Sacks, Oliver (1995) *An Anthropologist on Mars*. New York: Vintage Books.

Taylor, Diana (2007) *The Archive and the Repertoire: Performing cultural memory in the Americas*. Durham & London: Duke University Press.

Temu, Arnold & Bonaventure Swai (1981) *Historians and Africanist History: A critique – post-colonial historiography examined*. London: Zed Publishers.

Walcott, Derek (1974) 'The Muse of History'. In *Is Massa Day Dead?* Orde Coombs (ed.). Garden City: New York, 1–27.

White, Hayden. (1987) *Metahistory: The historical imagination in nineteenth-century Europe*. Baltimore & London: Johns Hopkins University Press.

Looking for 'Eritrea's Past Property'
Archives & memories
in Eritrean theatre historiography[1]

CHRISTINE MATZKE

In this article I trace various people's memories of Berhe Mesgun's play *Zehalefe Nebret Ertra*[2] – 'Eritrea's Past Property' or simply 'Eritrea's Past' (following its Italian title, *Il Passato dell'Eritrea*) – performed in the Eritrean capital Asmara in 1947. These memories are often shifting, at times contradictory, renderings and are set against the narrative of three periods of 'Eritrea's past' and present: first, the 1940s when the fate of the country was suspended between the remnants of Italian colonialism (1890-1941), a 'care-taker' British administration (BMA, 1941-1952) and a relatively unknown political future, eventually decided by a UN Four Power Commission which opted for the federation with Ethiopia (1952); second, the 1998-2000 Eritrean-Ethiopian 'border war' and its immediate aftermath which marked the end of the first post-liberation period in Eritrea (1991-8); and, finally, the period since the end of 2001 (Reid, 2009: 213) which has been characterised by more overt militarisation and repression, but lately also by a new openness towards exploring Eritrea's theatrical past.

Drawing largely on oral accounts, private archive material and historical scholarship, I will interweave these narratives of Eritrea's past and present with my research experience from 1999-2008. In the process I reflect on what the various archives suggest about contemporary theatre research in a context that is politically complex, partly oral, in cultural style, and thus not focused on the kind of material documentation that often characterises western theatre historiography. I also reflect on the implications of these factors for the researcher trying to make meaning as an outsider from fragments. Finally, this article provides me with an opportunity to revise previously published findings on the first Eritrean theatre association in the 1940s (Matzke, 2002) in the light of ongoing research in Eritrea, rendering this work, as ever, contingent and provisional.

To contextualise the complexities of theatre research in Eritrea, I begin with one of my own memories of meeting the playwright *Ato* Berhe Mesgun.[3] On 29 December 2006, my colleague Yakem Tesfai and I were invited to a sumptuous late breakfast in down-town Asmara. Coffee and *qategna*, were being served, the former prepared in the usual elaborate ceremony, the latter a local delicacy I had rarely tasted: fresh *injeera*, the flat, crêpe-like sourdough

1. *Ato Berhe Mesgun (left) and his son, Dagnew, outside the family villa in Asmara, 29 December 2006. (© Christine Matzke)*

bread, still warm and a little sticky from the *mogogo* or stove, liberally sprinkled with butter and *berbere*, the ubiquitous red pepper spice blend in Eritrea. Dagnew Berhe had invited us to the family villa to meet his elderly father, Berhe Mesgun (see Picture 1). *Ato* Berhe had recently returned from the United States where he had lived with his daughter and where I had managed to telephone him a couple of months earlier. Communication had been difficult at the time, Berhe Mesgun was frail and in no position to sustain a longer conversation. I was therefore happy when he told me he was returning to Eritrea soon, his arrival coinciding with my own travel plans for Christmas.

Ato Berhe Mesgun was credited with writing the first historical play in Tigrinya, the language most widely spoken in the central and southern regions of Eritrea (as well as in Tigray, Northern Ethiopia); *Zehalefe Nebret Ertra – Eritrea's Past Property* (1947).[4] The play had occasionally cropped up in interviews and conversations since 1995, when the Eritrea Community-Based Theatre team conducted the first enquiries into the nation's performing arts (Plastow, 1997b), but so far it had been difficult to trace more detailed information. To my knowledge, there was little, if any, documentation, except for a recently published theatrical memoir by *Memher* (Teacher) Asres Tessema (2006) whose own artistic involvement with the performing arts began in the 1950s. But now I was to meet the man himself and get to know the hows, whys and whens of his drama. This assumption proved to be fallacy. Berhe Mesgun was as frail in person as his voice had sounded on the phone; and he was unable to remember even the basic outline of his play written some 60 years earlier. But as he sleepily rested in the shade, there was a moment when a younger, more dynamic self seemed to surface. *Ato* Berhe might have forgotten about the script, but he had not forgotten the suffering of his people under colonialism. 'The Italians treated us like animals!', he suddenly proclaimed with a forcefulness that belied his age. 'The play just came out of my head one day. I was sitting down, taking an exercise book and writing it all down.' (Field Note (FN) 29/12/2006). Then again he descended into a sleepy silence.

Ato Berhe Mesgun passed away in April 2007, not long after our meeting. Born on 23 March 1919, he had worked as a lawyer for most of his life, retiring as late as 2006 when his strength was finally fading. He had never considered himself a man of the theatre, nor did he believe that his play would be marked in the nation's cultural history. At the time it had been a means to an end, an outlet for voicing a long-harboured anger, a 'writing of history' previously denied to Eritreans under colonial rule. It took such a long time to resurface in the public mind for a variety of reasons, largely to do with the thirty-year liberation war (1961-91) against another occupying force, Ethiopia, and with the trials and tribulations of post-independence Eritrea. In both instances the theatrical moment of the past had been a mere footnote to the drama played out at the time, if it had not been obliterated completely. However, the voyage of *Eritrea's Past* in and out of public awareness can give us insights into the complex processes of documenting and writing (theatre) history – particularly of omission, selection and (re-)construction – and into various modes of archiving the theatrical past. It can also help us understand what is involved in the social production of memory; while illuminating how cultural practices have not only been reflective, but also constitutive of Eritrea's political life.

Theatre research in Eritrea:
Some preliminaries on archives and documentation

Doing historical theatre research in a country that had been ravaged by a thirty-year liberation struggle against Ethiopia (1961-91) and another, more recent, Eritrean-Ethiopian boundary war (1998-2000) is by no means an easy undertaking. Hartmut Quehl is much to the point when he writes that:

> In general, the situation of material, especially primary sources about Eritrea, is extremely difficult. One reason lies in the fact that in the Eritrean culture, narration holds greater importance than the creation of written records. Another reason is related to the monopolisation by authorities, political movements and other organisations in producing written records, selecting what is to be written and, even more importantly, selecting what will be given to the public. (Quehl, 2003: 137-138).

Quehl has carried out very sensitive research on the social history of fighters in the liberation war (2005), and fortunately not all subject matters of theatre research are confidential, or 'off-limits' to the same degree. Yet he is right in pointing out that the flow of written information in Eritrea is tightly controlled, be it in print media or the access to archival files.[5] Quehl's research methodologies (2003: 138) can therefore serve as yardstick for theatre historians; to carefully analyse written sources regarding potential subtexts and their intended audience (particularly with a record of theatre texts that deliberately play with double-entendres; see Plastow, 1997a: 152; Matzke, 2008: 70), and to enquire into the political or institutional background of its author. At times it might also be necessary to ask why a particular source was classified (if we know of its existence) – or why it was published and *not* classified (Quehl, 2003: 138).[6]

Yet the limited presence – not to say virtual absence – of written documentation on many subjects always makes it necessary for theatre researchers to turn to other methodologies, particularly to those of oral history. The debate on the use of oral sources for African(ist) historiography has been ongoing since the 1950s. Initially advocated to recover and valorise the past of African societies without an established literate culture, the discussion has since broadened to include issues such as methodology, critical mediation, modes of interpretation and questions of 'authenticity'. In the given context, these issues can only be dealt with very selectively.[7] It is, however, necessary to distinguish between 'oral traditions' and 'oral history'. Unlike 'oral traditions' which are 'generally stories about the past that local populations produce and reproduce through oral performative transmission, as a means of preserving their own history' (Cooper, 2005: 192), oral history 'is personal reminiscence solicited by the researcher in an interview format, and it may focus on the life history of the person being interviewed, on specific events of interest to the historian, or on the subject's perhaps idiosyncratic memories of a family, neighborhood, community, or movement' (ibid.). Quehl has rightly stressed its importance for the Eritrean context in order 'to compensate for scarcity or even complete lack of written records' (2003: 138). He is not the only one to have stressed the significance of oral sources for the historiography of the Horn of Africa (cf. Taddia 1996; 2008 [2005]), and some writers have already deftly drawn on such sources in their writing practice (cf. Astier M. Almedom, 2006: 110, on Alemseged Tesfai, 2002).

I, too, have often resorted to the 'embodied archive' of living people; not only in terms of verbal memories, but also in the sense of physical recollections of performance. The 'embodied archive' holds its very own problematic to which I will return in due course. The most beneficial approach, however, has always been to access as wide a variety of archives as possible: public, embodied, and those which I call 'private documentation centres', often an old cardboard box or a living room drawer. For the case of *Zehalefe Nebret Ertra* I will give a quick rundown of all the resources upon which I have drawn, while reflecting on the implications and limitations of these various 'archives'.

Public archives
There are few well-stocked public archives and libraries in Eritrea, and in all of them collections on theatre arts are fairly small.[8] The Pavoni Social Centre in Asmara houses a unique library which is particularly useful for sources on Italian theatre activities in Eritrea (cf. Turco, 2003), but less so on Eritrean

performance forms. Cinema Asmara holds the archive of the PFDJ Cultural Affairs – the dominant liberation movement, Eritrean People's Liberation Front (EPLF), turned single party, People's Front for Democracy and Justice (PFDJ), on independence – but again, holdings are limited to the period of the liberation war. Here you find systematic and comprehensive musical records from the 1970s and beyond, but virtually nothing on Eritrean theatre during Italian colonialism and the British administration.

Finally, there is the Research and Documentation Centre (RDC), Eritrea's national archive, which emerged out of the Research and Information Centre on Eritrea (RICE) established in the mid-1970s. Initially based in Italy, it was renamed as RDC after liberation (1991) and relocated to the Eritrean capital where it merged with various collections of the EPLF, particularly their Department of Politicization, Education and Culture, and the Department of Information (http//www.eritreanarchives.org/). Archival collections in the RDC contain records prior to 1950, but again holdings on theatre in the liberation struggle and beyond are more substantial. As you would expect, they too are anything but comprehensive, given the condition of war which made the systematic preservation of theatre records a low-priority task, if not impossible.

Pre-1950s findings are largely limited to announcements in periodicals of the time, or clerical files of the Italian and British administrations concerning the management of expatriate entertainment. Reviews are rare and about European performances only. On the whole documents in the RDC tend to represent official and unofficial viewpoints of the respective power of the time; in our case the British Military Administration (BMA). Occasionally I have found brief censorship notes on Eritrean plays. Despite oral evidence to the contrary, however, censorship notes are a rarity in the RDC — largely because such files are said to be kept in the national police archives, as are presumed to be confiscated plays.

Berhe Mesgun's *Zehalefe Nebret Ertra* is such a case in point. Taken by the British CID (Criminal Investigation Department) after the first performances (Asres Tessema, 2006: 130), the play script – and any written indication at attempted censorship – disappeared permanently. Only oral evidence related to this play remains. While Berhe Mesgun's contemporaries insist that the play is still kept in the police archives, it is doubtful whether it has survived or whether it had been destroyed.[9] Whatever the case, all my previous attempts at accessing the police archive have so far failed.[10] While I have always found initial access to archives in Eritrea difficult, involving various letters of approval or carefully planned personal introductions (with the exception of the Pavoni Social Centre, where I just walked in), the police archive has long remained totally inaccessible to non-law enforcement researchers, no matter their background. Whether this is due to many files being classified or other reasons, I cannot tell; it is also important to note that no law exists which regulates the access to archives or the period of time after which material can, or should, be made public. In September 2008 I was informed that the RDC had put in an official request to use the police archive for its own documentation; by the time of writing this article (in winter 2009), permission had been finally granted. Though in the future this might allow me to access the police archive via the RDC, chances of finding written evidence of the play remain slim.

All this indicates that research solely concentrated on public archives might not lead to tangible results. In the case of *Zehalefe*, without oral testimonies I would certainly have had to abandon the project. Given that the play was developed further in rehearsal, after the confiscation of the manuscript, the play text would have offered only part of the picture, allowing me to trace its evolution from play-script to performance text. However, the awareness of 'embodied' archives allowed me to go on, to search for memories, materials and meanings related to this project. It also turned a very common approach to historical production on its head, namely 'the use of oral materials collected as an appendage or as a complement to written sources or colonial archives' (Fall, 2003: 58). Here, oral history became the principal resource of my research.

'Embodied' archives

African theatre researchers have increasingly become aware of the importance of expanding attention to performance beyond the text, or whatever else 'has been perceived as part of the Written Culture' (Sauter, 2004: 31). This is particularly true when whatever little documentation exists, it is usually of transcriptions of oral history. Conversations with contemporaries and Berhe Mesgun's family suggest that while Berhe Mesgun offered a script, it was during the rehearsal process that the play was given its final shape. One member of the original cast, Alemayo Kahasay, moreover restaged the play with colleagues in 1955 when working as a teacher in Adi Ugri (today's Mendefera, the capital of *Zoba Dubub*, the southern administrative region). It was here that his colleague, *Memher* Asres Tessema first got involved in theatre. He is the only participant of that period who, with the publication of his 2006 memoir, has turned to documenting Eritrean theatre.

The case of *Zehalefe Nebret Ertra* demonstrates that often one's greatest primary sources are multi-layered and complex memories which have undoubtedly changed with each performance and the passing of time. These memories are largely framed through the individual's personal experiences, often previous acting; or visual memories of an audience member that are mixed with general recollections of the period in question.

The embodied archives I accessed were, as primary sources: the playwright, *Ato* Berhe Mesgun; the above-mentioned theatre scribe and 'second-generation' actor, *Memher* Asres Tessema; and an artist who had taken part in the premier of the play, *Ato* Osman Ahmed. My secondary sources included second-hand accounts of first-hand memories, mainly through *Memher* Asres who had interviewed other contemporaries for his theatre memoir; people too frail or too ailing to receive visitors other than those they had known for decades. *Memher* Asres had also been a close friend and colleague of the late Alemayo Kahasay (1925-1991) who had played a key role in the production. Finally, I was kindly given permission to draw on the interviews of the 1995 Eritrea Community-Based Theatre Project (ECBTP), of which two referred to the play.[11]

Yet, as the experience with Berhe Mesgun has shown, memories are by definition idiosyncratic, partial, fragmented, and very subjective. Sometimes they are so few that the absences seem greater than the information gathered. Furthermore, as Donatien Dibwedia Mwembu has shown: 'Memory also finds itself under the yoke of the current political situation' (2005: 447; cf. Taddia, 2008 [2005]: 211). In the case of *Zehalefe*, this proved to be a major challenge with regard to contextualising the play. My initial research on early urban Eritrean theatre history had been carried out during the 1998-2000 Eritrean-Ethiopian war, with everybody but the young and the elderly at the frontline. This situation made people cautious regarding their previous (positive) political standing towards Ethiopia; and crucial contextual information was withheld. While I will go into the historical details in the following section, it is worth noting here that these silences initially made me draw inferences that were inaccurate, thus demonstrating the potential skewing effect the socio-political context can have on oral testimony as a research resource. This is also attested by Quehl, who has candidly addressed particular problems of oral history in Eritrea, especially among the generation of liberation fighters.[12] Quehl speaks of 'standardised' answers among fighters of the liberation war, a phenomenon he calls '"perceptional reality"' which denotes the repetition of 'a collective consensus about what is to be understood as reality' (2003: 139). Although particularly strong among liberation fighters, my own experience suggests that this standardisation of liberation war recollections affects the general approach to any sharing of information in Eritrea, particularly information that might contradict the official version of the historical narrative.[13] More than once I found myself in the situation where people first called the office of the authority which had granted research permission to ensure themselves that my work had been properly 'cleared'. While this had not been the case with *Zehalefe*, there was undoubtedly an initial caution as to what to share with me.

It is worth noting the difference long-term research has made. I have continued my research in this area for over a decade which has allowed me to gradually build up mutual trust; and in some cases genuine friendships, with people I have met in the course of my interviews. This has helped them to both open up, and some of them to engage pro-actively in the research process. My longstanding association with Eritrean colleagues in academia and Cultural Affairs has also been beneficial insofar as we have built on our mutual confidence between ourselves as researchers and with the largely elderly informants we have interviewed.

The last significant factor affecting this research are issues surrounding translation and interpretation, especially in a context such as Eritrea where three different scripts (Ge'ez, Latin and Arabic), and multiple languages are used.[14] David Henige comments that 'it is the rare expatriate Africanist historian who first goes into the field in fluent command of the local language/s' (2005: 176). I experienced this as my first opportunity to work in Eritrea came at short notice. Although I have learnt some basic Tigrinya, I continue to work with translators and interpreters, as my own linguistic skills are insufficient for complex conversations in many of the languages used. Though fully aware that this mediation always also adds additional layers of interpretation, which Henige calls 'inevitably distorted, however unwillingly or unwittingly' (2005: 176), I have become rather pragmatic over the years. While it is the researcher's duty to acquire as much local knowledge as possible, and to work with the best local colleagues available, there will always be 'distortions' through the various boundaries we have to cross, be they race, ethnic, educational or political backgrounds, gender, language and age; and this is equally true for Eritrean scholars.

Finally, I would argue that the person writing up 'his/story' gives it a meaning that is not simply reflective of the sources, but is also shaped by the researcher's culture and history, and the contexts in which the writing is produced. As Cooper perceptively observes: 'History becomes, then, not the past itself, but struggles over the meaning of the past' (2005: 198). It is a history which tells us as much about the present as it does about the past, and as such is an ongoing, continual project.

'Private' archives

Before I turn to my own historical narrative of context and content of *Zehalefe Nebret Ertra*, I want to draw attention to a last, particular important form of archive: the private collections of theatre paraphernalia – such as playbills, advertisements, photographs, audio materials, reviews, or personal diaries – which theatre artists and/or their friends and families have preserved over time, often in a disorderly fashion. In the case of theatre research in war-torn Eritrea, these archives amount to small national treasures and have been my second most important source. Artists have often kept materials as nostalgic keepsakes of a period in their life, of a play, or of friends in the same theatre association. Unlike theatre historical sources in public archives, these items were preserved and taken care of because they were of personal importance to the collector; their historical value for future generations is rarely considered. Even a decade after commencing my work, I still find material I had never dared to dream of: unpublished audio tapes, photographs of people, tours or performances, or theatre programmes. In the case of *Zehalefe*, these were two bilingual playbills, in Tigrinya and Italian, kept by *Ato* Berhe himself, and a couple of photographs of the 1955 Adi Ugri performance tracked down at a colleague's house by *Memher* Asres.

Similar to the oral narratives above, these private archives were often revealed after some time; rarely did anyone volunteer access during the first meeting. It is likely that people have had negative experiences with sharing materials.[15] Under Ethiopian rule, for example, local culture had been considered suspect in Eritrea,[16] while the EPLF had cultivated a 'culture of secrecy' (Pool 2001: 95) during the liberation war which was rooted in the ancient practice of withholding, or rather not recording, one's deeper thoughts and feelings. All this has created a research atmosphere in which hospitality is celebrated, but information and items are not readily shared. One might add to Quehl's aforementioned section on 'What the Tagadelti [Fighters] Don't Talk About' (2003: 142-4), 'what theatre artists don't show'.

Such experiences are an Africanist historian's daily business. To a theatre researcher, who was trained 'on the job', such observations are stepping stones on a continuing learning curve. In 2008 a colleague in Eritrean Studies with whom I shared some of my difficulties replied 'Welcome to History', to which the next phase of this research narrative shifts.

Italian colonialism or 'Eritrea's past property': A (theatre) historical narrative

I begin with the historical narrative of Eritrea which led to the emergence of an urban Eritrean theatre scene from which *Eritrea's Past Property*, *Zehalefe Nebret Ertra*, emerged. Eritrea came into being as an Italian colony on 1 January 1890, after a somewhat piecemeal formation process which began when Italy first gained a foothold through the acquisition of a stretch of coastland in 1869. Historical narratives often divide Italian colonialism into three phases; the first until the battle of Adwa in 1896 when Italy was defeated by Ethiopia in its attempt to enlarge its colonial possessions; the second from 1897 to the mid-1930s when Eritrea was consolidated as a geopolitical and socio-economic entity; and the third from the mid-1930s to 1941 which bore the ruthless stamp of Benito Mussolini's fascism. This period saw the largest influx of white Italian settlers in search of better economic opportunities and the preparation of war, the Italian invasion of Ethiopia in 1935 in the attempt to build an East African Empire (and 'avenge' Adwa), and the eventual demise of the Italian colonial venture. When Italy was defeated in 1941 during World War II, the BMA immediately took custody of Eritrea as 'occupied enemy territory'. (Tekeste Negash, 1987: 1-8; Redie Bereketeab, 2000: 290-92).

For a better understanding of Berhe Mesgun's play – and my own difficulties at (re-) contextualisation – three particulars in Eritrea's past need further elaboration. The first was the physical and intellectual oppression Eritreans experienced during colonial rule, especially during the late fascist period from 1934 when race laws were tightened. The second was the emergence of a 'nascent' urban Eritrean elite during that time, the third a gradual removal of socio-political restrictions for Eritreans under British administration and an increasing politicisation.

Oppression of Eritreans under Italian colonial rule

While the first and second phases of Italian colonisation had been governed by a racism based on the belief of European technical superiority, which resulted in a (no less exploitative) colonial paternalism in which land expropriation and the use of Eritrean manpower as colonial soldiers, *ascari*, played an important role; the 1930s were marked by the introduction of an apartheid-like race segregation which denied Eritreans their humanity (Tekeste Negash, 1987: 108-11; Barrera, 2003a). Inter-racial cohabitation or marriages, tolerated earlier, were now forbidden, and Eritreans were only admitted to the Italian quarter of town for work. 'Eritreans were not even allowed to walk on the main street', eyewitness *Ato* Osman Ahmed described. 'If you did, they would kick you. In buses there were special spaces for Eritreans, with no seats. We had to stand like animals' (I 42; cf. Pankhurst, 1995: 27). Other oral records confirm his account, with the fascist period remembered as beig particularly hostile (Taddia, 1996; Barrera, 2003a: 81). In the capital, Asmara, segregation was more strictly enforced in already separated urban spheres: the first zone for Italians in the imposing centre of town, the heart of political and administrative power; the so-called *zona mista* or 'mixed area' around the market shared by Europeans, Africans and 'others' alike; the third zone the poorer Eritrean quarters at the margins of town, plus an area for industry (Locatelli, 2009: 224-5; Uoldelul Chelati Dirar, 2004: 542-3; cf. map from 1916 in Barrera et al., 2008: 86-7). Performance and entertainment spaces were equally segregated; the Italians were in charge of most purpose-built cinema-cum-theatre houses which hosted films and elaborate variety shows, while – with the exception of Cinema Hamasien, the sole 'native' cinema in Asmara – Eritreans had only informal spaces, such as tea shops (*bet shahi*) or *suwa* houses (*enda suwa*) where home-brewed millet beer, *suwa*, was served and Eritrean music was played (Turco 2003; Matzke 2002).

While significant scholarship exists on Italian racial policies (e.g. Barrera, 2003 a&b), it is the personal accounts of Eritrean eye witnesses that are most illuminating for an understanding of the trials of everyday life. In Irma Taddia's *Autobiografie Africane* (1996), a collection of oral accounts by elderly Eritrean and Ethiopian men, a number of incidents are recorded which also emerge in Berhe Mesgun's play. These include abuse in Italian employment; lack of educational opportunities; maltreatment in public places; inferior, segregated public transport; insufficient pay and the hard life of *ascari* in the colonial army. One scene in *Zehalefe Nebret Ertra*, for example, portrayed parents' futile attempts to get news of their sons serving as *ascari* in Libya, then an Italian colony in North Africa. According to *Ato* Osman Ahmed, the scene revealed the 'Italian arrogance in the administration' (I 1/2007) by showing how badly an elderly man was treated when, with the help of an interpreter, enquiring about the whereabouts of his son. Various versions of this scene are in circulation, but each illustrates the lack of respect for Eritrean relatives. In one case it was a widow (played by Alemayo Kahasay, owing to the lack of female actresses) enquiring about her son; in another it was a father objecting to the conscription of his only offspring. In the play, all were verbally abused and threatened with being sent to Libya.[17]

It is striking, however, that most racist incidents recalled in Taddia pertained to cultural practices and the social sphere, not to military life. One was the prohibition against Eritreans entering most cinemas, which were 'whites-only', thus limiting access to a form of entertainment. The second highest referent to cultural segregation was in connection to treatment at bars – manifest either in a refusal to serve Eritreans, or Eritreans being subject to inferior service (Taddia, 1996: 56, 64, 72, 77, 85, 92, 97, 100, 122). As in Italy, bars have long been local centres of urban social life in Eritrea. They are places where people go to chat and drink coffee or alcohol after work. While it can be assumed that at the time of Italian rule Eritreans tended to frequent *suwa* houses rather than the costlier (and partly off-limits) bars in the Italian and 'mixed' quarters of town, not being served or being given substandard treatment was a grave insult in an indigenous context where hospitality was highly valued. In *Zehalefe Nebret Ertra* Berhe Mesgun developed a whole scene around such an episode. Set in a bar with segregated seating for Italians and Eritreans, it showed a veteran *Shumbash* (also: *Sciumbasci*, the highest rank for an Eritrean colonial soldier, equivalent to a Marshal) enter and order coffee.[18] When the waiter returned, the *Shumbash* was given coffee in a small tomato paste tin, instead of a proper cup. Offended, he complained in Italian, 'Why am I, a very experienced veteran *Shumbash* who has served the Italian government for so many years, given coffee in a tomato paste tin? This is a big insult not only to me but also to the Italian government!' To which a *Sergente Maggiore*, an Italian army officer seated elsewhere in the bar, replied: '*Cosa vuoi pretendere, tu sei un nero* [What do you want, you are black?]' (Asres Tessema, 2006: 133).[19]

The emergence of a 'nascent' urban Eritrean elite during Italian colonisation

Despite the racial discrimination and brutality the Eritrean population suffered, there were developments that were slightly more ambiguous in nature. While oral and written accounts clearly speak of a dominant/dominated dichotomy, there were also alliances between Italians and Eritreans, as Italian colonial rule provided certain Eritreans with some limited opportunities. There were those who benefited as business people, those who were able to learn a vocational trade, and those who were given access to a limited four-year primary schooling to take up lowly white collar positions in the colonial service sector, the army or the economy.[20] While these educational opportunities were extremely restricted and aimed at keeping the locals 'in their place', they nevertheless sowed the seeds for an emerging urban Eritrean middle class, which eventually fought them with their own creative weapons.[21] Uoldelul Chelati Dirar has called for more nuanced analyses of the relationship between Italian colonialism and the emergence of an 'informal' or 'germinal' Eritrean elite (2007: 256), whose existence has often been dismissed or negated. He writes:

> A recurrent theme in Eritrean intellectual discourse on Italian colonialism is the idea that, in deliberately and brutally frustrating Eritrean aspirations, the colonial system militated against the emergence of a local elite able to bridge Eritrea between the colonial and post-colonial eras. While this might be considered a correct assessment in a very general sense, [...] [i]t does not explain the vivacity of the intellectual and political debate in Eritrea in the years following the end of Italian colonial rule. (2007: 267)

This vivacity was also to be found in the emerging Eritrean theatre scene during the BMA which also cannot be explained entirely by better educational opportunities for Eritreans under the British or the latter's love for Shakespeare (Gibbs and Matzke 2005: 26-7). The germ for these cultural activities had been planted prior to the BMA. Given his educational background, which was the highest possible under Italian rule, Berhe Mesgun belonged to this 'germinal'

Eritrean elite and used his intellectual faculties to hold up a dramatic mirror to the one-time rulers.[22] Though penned by a novice to playwriting and theatre, *Zehalefe Nebret Ertra* was ingeniously conceived as a string of loosely connected scenes whose common denominator was Italian racism against Eritreans, not an intricately structured plot. Scenes were not causally linked, even if characters had repeated appearances (such as the aforementioned *Shumbash* and the Italian officer). The play was thus adaptable to the 'poor theatre' conditions Eritreans worked in (in a literal, not a Grotowskian sense), and could easily accommodate a fluctuating cast or changing production conditions. In structure and concept *Zehalefe* is reminiscent of Bertholt Brecht's *Furcht und Elend des Dritten Reiches* ('Fear and Misery of the Third Reich', 1935-1939), a collection of separate scenes which portrayed moments of angst and oppression in Nazi Germany. I doubt that Berhe Mesgun knew of the play, but he certainly used similar theatrical techniques to those of Brecht: individual scenes which could be performed in the given succession or rearranged to the group's personal preferences in a 'montage'; scenes that were based on real-life events, but were often taken to comic (or other) extremes to highlight the absurdity of the situation.

Among the nascent Eritrean elite were also those with practical theatre experience. Though cultural collaborations between Eritreans and Europeans, largely Italians, only started to blossom during the British caretaker regime, a small number of Eritreans had prior access to colonial theatre, mostly backstage. The most prominent case in point is the above-mentioned Alemayo Kahasay, today considered to be the founding father of modern Eritrean theatre,[23] for whom directing and acting in *Zehalefe Nebret Ertra* were early moments in a long performance career. Prior to his engagement in Tigrinya productions, Alemayo had worked as a stage hand for an Italian company.[24] Initially forbidden to perform with them despite his obvious talent (Plastow, 1997a: 146; Asres Tessema, 2006: 93-5), Alemayo acquired his first theatrical skills, which later helped him combine European, modern Ethiopian and selected local performance forms to shape an urban theatre that was genuinely Eritrean.[25] *Zehalefe Nebret Ertra* benefited from this early experience of colonial theatre by drawing on elements of slapstick comedy and naturalistic plays. Having participated in Italian variety shows, especially their *barzellette* (jokes) programmes, Alemayo became particularly famous for his comical skills, and was later widely known as *Wetru Heggus* ('Always Smiling') or the 'Eritrean Totò' (named after the famous Napolitan comedian). In *Zehalefe*, he demonstrated his acting skills by both taking over the role of the elderly woman looking for her *ascaro* son, and also playing an Eritrean stableman taken to task for a grubby horse. As the Italian officer in charge did not understand the groom's explanation why the horse was still dirty despite his orders to the contrary, the latter started rolling around on the floor to demonstrate how the horse behaved after it had been cleaned. The scene was said to have been very popular, with Alemayo, the groom, playing largely for laughs.

It was this mixture of academic and very practical intelligence that characterised the 'emerging' Eritrean elite that ventured into theatre. Humour and slapstick took the edge off a scathing anti-colonial critique, and helped document the play in the audience as an 'embodied archives' because the acting was funny and memorable.[26] According to *Ato* Osman, Berhe Mesgun's initial dialogue was fleshed out in production by Alemayo Kahasay and the rest of the cast, particularly after the script had been confiscated:

> Alemayo was a great manager. He was responsible for the production. Berhe Mesgun only delivered the text. Everything else – the sound, the costumes, etc. – were done by us. [...] Alemayo selected actors for each character. Berhe's play was great because it reached both the older and the younger generation at the time. It moved everyone who had lived through Italian or British colonialism. (I 1/2007)

Eritrean political activism and theatre under the BMA

In this final section I want to outline the profound socio-political changes for Eritreans during the BMA, how it engendered political activism and theatre, and how it was later reflected upon, especially during the 1998-2000 war. To fully appreciate the impact of *Zehalefe*, it is important to understand that the Italian administration was largely kept intact during the British period. Though Italian rule had been officially disposed of with the onset of the BMA, the latter's mandate was that of a temporary 'caretaker', not a colonial government, with insufficient administrative manpower. Certain colonial dynamics between Italians and Eritreans were therefore still existent, as were initially a number of their racist laws (Pankhurst, 1995). Italians might have seceded power to another European force, but they were nonetheless running most daily affairs. This caused great resentment among the contemporaries I talked to. Ato Osman explained:

> We were against fascism. We had strong resentment against the whites. We clashed with them because we were anti-colonialists. Even the English – we never accepted them. But we mainly resented the Italians. Both the British and the Italians allied themselves to re-colonise Eritrea [...] Our aim was not to accept any type of colonialism. (I 1/2007)

Though disliked, the British at least alleviated political and social restrictions for Eritreans, and encouraged a limited policy of 'Eritreanisation' (Trevaskis 1960: 30). Literature in Tigrinya started to reappear, and new local newspapers were published. For literary production, these were 'years of revival' (Ghirmai Negash, 1999: 109, 114-16; Gaim Kibreab, 2008: 102-4), allowing Eritreans to engage in public debates and catch up with the previous lack of opportunity for creative expression. Political engagement was also on the rise. Only one month after Eritrea had been placed under British administration, a heterogeneous group of Moslems and Christians, intelligentsia and elders, was established 'to communicate Eritrean wishes to the BMA'. Above all, they desired an end to Italian domination over Eritrea' (Ruth Iyob, 1995: 65). This association came to be known as *Mahber Fikri Hager Eritrea* (MFHE) or 'Association of Love of the Country of Eritrea' (ibid.: 159, fn. 18). Members initially operated in secret as political parties were banned until 1946.[27] By 1944, however, MFHE had turned into the Unionist Party, *Mahber Andenet* (Gaim Kibreab 2008: 102) which favoured a merger with Ethiopia. Berhe Mesgun and Alemayo Kahasay became members (and eventually leaders) of its youth league, later receiving the honorary Ethiopian title *Grazmach* (military: 'Commander of the Left Wing') for their commitment.[28] In all, two opposing factions came into sight: the aforesaid Unionists, supported by the Orthodox Church and the government of Emperor Haile Selassie (which was known to condone violence against its opponents), and the Independence Bloc at the heart of which were the Moslem League and the Liberal Progressive Party (Redie Bereketeab, 2000: 154).

In 1999-2000 I had found evidence that female singers campaigned on the Unionists behalf, in particular Tsehaitu Berhe Zenar, '*Gual* (daughter of) Zenar', the owner of an *enda suwa* in the 'Eritrean' quarters of Asmara (cf. Matzke, 2002: 34-5). I had also written about the first indigenous theatre association, *Mahber Tewasew Deqqabbat* (Ma.Te.De. or, in their own translation, 'The Native Comedy & Dramatic Association'),[29] which, I believed, had been the first to stage Berhe Mesgun's play (Matzke, 2002: 38). At the time I had difficulties placing Ma.Te.De. politically as evidence was thin and rather contradictory. Some secondary sources declared that Ma.Te.De. had Unionist leanings and that its origins were rooted in a drama production mounted by *Mahber Andenet*; others attributed the play directly to Ma.Te.De. (Plastow, 1997a: 148; Alemayo Kahasay, 1977$_{EC}$ [1985], Yishak Yosief, 1979$_{EC}$ [1986]). Oral accounts from 1999-2000 initially denied any Unionist affiliations. People spoke of the largely 'Italian nature' of theatre, and the lack of Eritrean theatre groups, against which they wanted to set something home-grown. They had also emphasised their 'nationalist feelings' (Matzke, 2002: 38) which I had read as an early desire for Eritrean independence.

With the benefit of hindsight, some of these omissions and half-truths now make a lot of sense. The core phase of my field research was conducted at the height of the so-called Eritrean-Ethiopian 'border war' from 1998-2000. At the time, Unionists links were habitually evaded, if not outrightly denied (cf. Matzke, 2002: 38, 43 fn18) as this could be misconstrued as siding with the 'new-old' enemy, Ethiopia. (Post-independence newspaper articles also did not mention this link, almost certainly for the same reasons.) And though Unionist links were mentioned in some of the rare written primary sources during the Derg regime of Mengistu Haile Mariam (who had ousted the Emperor in 1974), I suspected them to be 'ideologically tainted' by Ethiopian propaganda (Alemayo Kahasay, 1977$_{EC}$ [1985]).

Conversations and further material unearthed after 2001, however, confirmed that Ma.Te.De. had indeed originated in a Unionist theatre group which had been established between 1944 and 1946. When things started to get difficult with the CID, Ma.Te.De. was created to evade any immediate party bonds, even if political sentiments were initially shared. When questioned about this contradiction in 2007, *Ato* Osman wisely replied: 'I think I have explained it before – politics is as dirty as a toilet. At the time we were not mature enough; we had not gone to college. We were just young and sharp.'

ቀዳምን ፡ ሰንበትን ፡ ሰኑይን ፡ ፬ ፡ ፭ ፡ ፮ ፡ መስከረም ፡ ፲፱፻፵ (4–5–6– OTTOBRE 1947)

አብ ፡ ሲ ነ ማ ፡ ሐ ማ ሴ ን ፡

" ዝኃለፈ ፡ ንብረት ፡ ኤርትራ ። ፡ ግአርኮስቱ ፡ ሐደ ፡ ዓብይ ፡ ተዋስኦ ፡ (ኮመድያ ፡) ፡ ብደቂ ፡ ማኅበር ፡ አንድነት ፡ ኪወሃብ ፡ አዩ ፡ ነዚድውን ፡ ንምርኣየን ፡ ባ� ፡ ዘብሳ ፡ ፈላማታት ፡ ኪኸተላእ ፡ አፈን ፡ ንመአተዊኹም ፡ ዚኸውን ፡ ወረቓቅቲ ፡ አብ ፡ "ባር ፡ ነፃነት ። ፡ ጉደና ፡ ማንዞ ፡ ክትዕድጉዎ ፡ ትኽእሉ ፡ ኢ'ኹም ።

ተ ቐ ዳ ደ ሙ ፡ !!

S A B A T O   D O M E N I C A   L U N E D I

4   **5**   **6**

al CINEMA HAMASIEN

verrà data dall'ANDENET una grande commedia in due atti

IL PASSATO DELL'ERITREA

seguono ottimi films

Prenotazioni (BAR NAZENET) Viale Manzoni

AFFRETTATEVI !

2. *Playbill of 'Eritrea's Past (Il Passato dell'Eritrea)' for the performances in October 1947.*
(Playbill courtesy of Dagnew Berhe Mesgun)

3. *Snapshot of the 1955 Adi Ugri performance. According to* Memher *Asres, the colonial officer wears a British, not an Italian, uniform, as these were harder to come by 14 years after Italian colonial rule. (Picture courtesy of* Memher *Asres Tessema)*

[...]. Our main goal was to get rid of the white colonisers and then deal with Ethiopia' (I 1/2007).

In his theatrical memoir *Memher* Asres recalls that performance activities were greatly encouraged by *Mahber Andenet* to help spread their political message. To begin with the theatre group, consisting of male youths, was provided with original and translated scripts by some older members of the association.[30] *Zehalefe Nebret Ertra* was the first play produced entirely by the group itself. Advertised in Tigrinya and Italian (not in English), as *una grande commedia in due atti* ('a great comedy in two acts' - see Picture 2), it not only held up a theatrical mirror to the one-time ruler and its British successor by expressing a deeply anti-Italian sentiment, it also attested to the group's radicalism and youthful vigour. Instead of couching its political sentiment in metaphors and allegories (as became common in later periods), *Zehalefe* openly mocked, criticised and ridiculed Italian colonial rule. This was often done with the help of humour and slapstick comedy. Given how relatively 'voice-less' Eritreans had been in the fascist period, the play came as a shock to many Europeans. Particularly Italians took issue with its bluntness and direct attack on them. According to *Memher* Asres they began to defend themselves by trying to belittle *Ato* Berhe and other Eritrean intellectuals, calling them '*improvvisati politicanti* (politicised amateurs)' (2006: 131).

I have only been able to trace the four individual scenes as described above, though not necessarily in the order of appearance. Each scene was given a slightly different rendering according to the source(s) I have been drawing on. Given the list of the original cast *Memher* Asres provides in his memoir (2006: 132-3), it can be assumed that further scenes were performed.[31] The play was staged to great public acclaim on three weekends in May, June and, by popular demand, in October 1947, in Cinema Hamasien and Cinema Asmara respectively (Asres Tessema, 2006: 131). For years the story of *Zehalefe* remained topical and a favourite with audiences, if only in their recollections; it also became part of Ma.Te.De.'s repertoire when the first Eritrean theatre association was officially formed. In 1955, it was again staged by teachers in Adi Ugri under Alemayo's direction – to my knowledge the only earlier Eritrean play that saw a second production (see Picture 3). By then the European powers had been replaced by a federation with Ethiopia which was already beginning to turn sour. Whether *Zehalefe* was read subversively at the time – not against the Italians but against the rule of Emperor Haile Selassie – is open to speculation.[32] Personally I have my doubts. Eritrean cultural expressions have often been read in terms of 'resistance' against a string of 'colonial successions' – Italian, British and Ethiopian – though, strictly speaking, the term 'colonialism' only applies to the Italian period. A 'subversive' reading of the 1955 performance would neatly fit into the grand narrative of fighting a variety of oppressions, but it jarred with the pro-Ethiopian stance some of the actors still held. Like Eritrean-Italian relations, these interactions cannot be reduced to a dichotomy of oppressed versus oppressors; they were far too complex and multi-layered for that. Official discourses of the present notwithstanding, Eritrean-Ethiopian affairs both then and now require much more nuanced readings.

What the story of *Zehalefe,* however, clearly demonstrates is that in the mid-1940s young people developed and supported a political consciousness with the help of theatre. This made performance not only reflective, but also constitutive of Eritrea's political life. As *Ato* Osman explained:

> We strengthened ourselves through culture. We played drama in areas where we lived. Through this we started convincing the younger generation. [...]
> Sometimes I laugh! I never thought that our work would live that long. Of course, many of them [my theatre colleagues] have passed away, even our supporters at the time. When I look at my wedding picture, only three people are left. We are only a few who are still alive. (I 1/2007)

This underlines the importance of having theatre voices like that of *Ato* Osman recorded and properly archived. 'Embodied' archives are not there forever, and 'private' archives might get lost when the person to whom the collection mattered, departs this life. We, as students of history and theatre, need to find ways to locate 'embodied' and 'private' archives and bring them together with 'public' documentation centres to help make these sources available to future generations. However, as my own research narrative has also shown, we need to be aware that whatever we might 'preserve' are not only (personalised) reflections and reinterpretations of the past, but also of the time and context in which they were produced or collated. We thus need to hone our critical awareness towards different layers of political discourses and similar undercurrents, present and past, and be conscious of how the here and now shapes our own understanding of history in the moment of its interpretation. While the writing of African (theatre) history will continue to remain a terrain of contested readings and representations, it will allow us to come closer to an understanding of the past in all its ambiguity and complexity.

LIST OF INTERVIEWS

Abbreviations: interviewer (int.), recorded (rec.), translator (ttr), transcript (tpt). Christine Matzke (CM), Mohamedsalih Ismael (MSI), Mussie Tesfagiorgis (MT), Yakem Tesfai (YT).
Interviews follow my own reference system.

ECBTP 95/9   Gebremeskel Gebregzhier, author of *Ali in Asmara.*

ECBTP 95/13   Yishak Yoseph, actor, writer, Ma.Te.De.

I 30   Osman Ahmed, Ma.Te.De., with Arefaine Tewolde, Ma.M.Hal., Rec. interview in English/Tigrinya, 27 January 2000, Asmara, Eritrea. Int.: CM, ttr: YT, tpt: MT.

I 42   Osman Ahmed. 2nd rec. interview in English/Tigrinya, 18 February 2000, Asmara, Eritrea. Int.: CM, [no ttr present], tpt: MT.

I 101   Osman Ahmed. 3rd rec. interview in English/Tigrinya, 1 August 2000, Asmara, Eritrea. Int.: CM, tpt: MT.

I 126   Asres Tessema, musician, playwright, Ma.Te.A., Rec. interview in English, 9 August 2001, Asmara, Eritrea. Int./tpt: CM.

I 127   Asres Tessema. 2nd interview, 13 August 2001, Asmara, Eritrea. Rec. interview, in English. Int./tpt: CM.

I 129   Asres Tessema and Osman Ahmed. Rec. conversation in Tigrinya between two theatre veterans, 21 August 2001, Asmara, Eritrea. Tpt: MSI.

I 1/2007	Osman Ahmed, rec. interview in Tigrinya and English, 2 January 2007, Asmara, Eritrea, Int : CM, ttr: YT, tpt: YT, MT.
I 1/2008	Osman Ahmed, rec. interview in Tigrinya and English, 26 August 2008, Asmara, Eritrea, Int.: CM, ttr: YT, notes CM.
I 2/2008	Osman Ahmed, interview in Tigrinya and English, 28 August 2008, Asmara, Eritrea, Int.: CM, ttr & tpt: YT.

Various unrecorded personal conversations with *Ato* Osman Ahmed and *Memher* Asres Tessema. Fieldnotes (FN) 29 December 2006.

NOTES

1   I wish to thank Dagnew Berhe Mesgun and his family for generously facilitating my work, and to *Memher* Asres Tessema and *Ato* Osman Ahmed, my greatest teachers of Eritrean theatre history. Thanks also go to Yvette Hutchison and Uoldelul Chelati Dirar for their invaluable comments on earlier drafts; and to Silvia Scholz of Computing and Media Services at Humboldt-Universität zu Berlin for help with the illustrations. This article would not have materialised without the immense support of my Eritrean colleagues, Yakem Tesfai, Tedros Hagos, Mussie Tesfagiorgis, and Mohamedsalih Ismael. This article is for you. Thank you all.

2   Although consulting a specialist in Semitic languages, I have decided against the usage of a complex linguistic transliteration system for Tigrinya words as used, for example, by the *Encyclopaedia Aethiopica* (http://www1.uni-hamburg.de/EAE/ accessed 14/3/2010). If available, I follow the simplified transliterations most commonly used in English language pub-lications, or those provided by my mother-tongue speaker colleagues (including a trained linguist). In a strictly linguistic sense, this does not do justice to the intricacies of the Tigrinya language. However, I use it as it is more reader-friendly.

3   It is common to address Eritreans by their first name, the second being the name of the father, rather than a surname as in European or North American usage. *Ato* (roughly: 'Mr') is a form of address for an older, respected man.

4   Strictly speaking, *Zehalefe* was not the first Tigrinya-language play to be performed in Eritrea. From around 1942-45 an entrepreneurial teacher, *Memher* Abraham Redda, wrote and staged works of his own, largely in the vein of Christian morality plays. Only two of them were recorded: the first a religious drama, *Lidete Kristos*, 'The Birth of Christ', shown by a student cast in St. Mary's Church; the second, 'New World' (*Hadish Alem*), was noted in 1945 BMA files and possibly mounted in Cinema Hamasien. Abraham Redda (3 November 1945), Alemayo Kahasay (15 February 1977EC [1985]), I 129, ECBTP 95/13, Asres Tessema (2006: 126-7).

5   Print and broadcasting media in Eritrea are solely under government control. In September 2001, following increasing criticism of the government from various circles, private newspapers and magazines which had emerged after independence were shut down. Numerous journalists and editors were arrested, as were prominent government critics, including veteran liberation fighters. None of them has yet been tried; a number are reported to have died in prison.

6   For the sake of comprehensiveness it should also be pointed out that in a multi-lingual environ-ment such as Eritrea, occasionally documents are physically accessible, but remain inaccessible as no one in the research environment is in proper command of the language they are written in.

7   For a useful introduction to the debate see White et al. (2001).

8   To date, I have not been able to look for theatrical evidence in Italian colonial archives. Most written (and also oral) sources were collected in Eritrea itself; some in the United Kingdom and in Germany, due to the presence of a large Eritrean community. The lack of Italian-based sources is obviously a gap that needs to be filled. There are also smaller archives in Eritrea which might potentially hold sources, such as the Archive of the Asmara Municipality, see Locatelli (2004).

9   I was given various explanations, such as a 'ravaging fire in the 1970s' (as alleged by an ex-fighter in Asmara) or the 'pillaging of records' by the Ethiopian military junta, the *Derg* (as noted by a member of the RDC).

10 I have been trying since 2005 in person and via correspondence.

11 For a list of source materials and interviews see Bibliography.

12 While the period of the liberation struggle is of no direct concern for the material discussed here, it gives us a glimpse of the general research atmosphere in Eritrea which is sometimes difficult to penetrate.

13 Quehl provides a detailed list of 'What the Tagadelti [Fighters] Don't Talk About' (2003: 142-4); he also makes a case for 'rumours and gossip as a potential source of information' (144). This is an extremely interesting angle which, however, cannot be dealt with in the given context. See also White (1994).

14 In *Zehalefe*'s case: Tigrinya, Tigre, Saho, Arabic, Amharic, English, Italian and German, as my mother tongue.

15 One Eritrean lady, for example, an actress in a 1960s Italian film, was reluctant to lend me her remaining poster for photographing in 2000 as all other paraphernalia had been borrowed by a local journalist, but were never returned.

16 In the 1960s people were said to have buried records in their back yards for fear of being caught in possession of (often politicized) Tigrinya music. Falceto ([booklet] Ref 82965-2 DK 016:22).

17 All scenes mentioned in this article are reconstructed from Asres Tessema (2006: 128-135) and the interviews listed in the bibliography.

18 It should be noted that in colonial Eritrea *'ascari* as a social category were *de facto* a sort of elite' (Uoldelul Chelati Dirar, 2004: 554). For one this was due to the higher than average pay they received for Eritreans, but also because they served as socio-cultural (and physical) buffers between ordinary Eritreans and Italians. They also received special Italian language training (Uoldelul Chelati Dirar, 2004: 555-60). I wish to thank Uoldelul Chelati Dirar for clarifying the *ascari* ranks for me.

19 This type of racist treatment was also portrayed in a second scene, when the *Shumbash* went to see the *Sergente* in his office and was made to take off his shoes because he was black. Asres Tessema (2006: 134). Even under the British, it took considerable time to 'relax' the so-called 'colour bar' established by the Italians. Pankhurst (1995).

20 Uoldelul Chelati Dirar (2007: 266), Taddia (2008 [2005]: 217). I am largely speaking of men, not women, here. Women had little to no access to formal education, though some of them became very prosperous as proprietors of *suwa* houses or gained financial security as *madamas*, '"comfort wives"' (Ruth Iyob, 2005: 238) to Italians prior to the tightening of race laws. See also Uoldelul Chelati Dirar (2004: 545, fn 37).

21 A recent article by Ghirmai Negash demonstrates how Eritrean intellectuals responded to Italian colonialism in early Tigrinya literature. The texts discussed are a travelogue from Eritrea to Italy by Fesseha Giyorgis (1895), and a novel, *The Story of the Conscript*, by Ghebreyesus Hailu, a Catholic priest. *Conscript* was written in 1927, but only published in 1950, and dealt with the hardships of an *ascaro* in the colonial army (Ghirmai Negash, 2009: 75-6)

22 Berhe Mesgun had received the maximum four years of primary schooling, two of them at Victor Emanuell III School in Asmara, and had done another two years of professional training. During Italian rule he had held white collar jobs – in the Municipality of Massawa, and later in finance, as employee of the *Banca Nazionale del Lavoro* – and from 1943-1956, during most of the BMA into the early days of the Federation, he worked as a teacher before taking up law. Dagnew Berhe Mesgun (2007).

23 In 2009 Alemayo Kahasay was posthumously awarded a certificate for his contribution to Eritrean drama, comedy and acting. The certificate was presented by theatre artists of the PFDJ Cultural Affairs (the cultural department of the single party in Eritrea, Peoples' Front for Democracy and Justice (PFDJ)). Among the recipients was also *Ato* Osman Ahmed, honoured for his acting contribution to *Zehalefe* and subsequent *Ma.Te.De.* plays.

24 Similar to Berhe Mesgun, Alemayo Kahasay had received the highest education possible for Eritreans under Italian rule. At the age of ten he attended an Orthodox Church school and then received four years of Italian schooling. Thereafter Alemayo worked as a messenger for an Italian lawyer and, at the age of 17, found employment as a stage-hand in Cinema Asmara, then Teatro Asmara.

25 It is important to stress the influence of modern Ethiopian theatre on early urban Eritrean theatre work, rather than reduce it to a cocktail of 'modern' European and 'traditional' Eritrean

performance forms. Ethiopia had developed its own type of modern drama in the early twentieth century, largely word-, rather than action-based. It also developed its own form of comedy. Cf. Plastow (2004: 195-202).

26   It can be argued that even today the memory of Alemayo Kahasay's skills is embodied in the work of younger Eritrean comedians, such as (Hagos) Suzinino, who seem to continue to draw inspiration from his line of work.

27   Ruth Iyob (1995: 68). MFHE is not to be confused with 'Ye Ager Fikir Mahber Theatre (The Love of the Country Theatre Association […])' (Plastow, 1996: 55) which emerged in the Ethiopian capital, Addis Ababa, in 1942; a professional theatre group reformed out of 'The Ethiopian National Patriotic Association'. The latter had been a group of *azmaris* (singer-musicians) brought together in 1935 to give 'open air performances […], music and short propaganda plays to inspire the citizens of Addis Ababa to the defence of the motherland' (Plastow, 1996: 54) against Italian occupation. Regarding their initial political motivation, there are certain similarities with later Eritrean groups.

28   Alemayo received his title in 1972, two years before the end of Emperor Haile Sellassie's rule.

29   In earlier publications, Ma.Te.De. has also been referred to as *Mahber Theatre Dekabat* (due to the mixing of Tigrinya and English in conversation) or as the 'Natives' Theatrical Association (NTA). I prefer the Tigrinya abbreviation above as it is widely used and recognised in Eritrea. (Plastow, 1997a: 146); Matzke, 2002: 38).

30   Among them was the writer *Abba* Ghebreyesus Hailu, author of *The Story of the Conscript* (1950). Asres Tessema (2006: 127-128, 172-3, see also Ghirmai Negash (1999: 130-136; here: *The Story of a Conscript*) and (2009).

31   Asres Tessema (2006: 132-3):

Ato Tesfay Ghebrezghis	*Sergente Maggiore* in a bar.
Ato Tikuu Fissehatsion	*Sergente Maggiore* in his office.
Ato Berhe Weldegiorghis	Veteran *Shumbash*
Ato Beyene Weldeghebriel	*Buluqbash* (also: *bulucbasci*, lower in rank than *Shumbash*, but higher than a mere foot soldier, *ascaro*; roughly: Lieutenant) Beyene Aqa
Ato Berhe Tikuabo	*Piantone* (guard) of *Sergente Maggiore* (Tikuu Fissehatsion)
Ato Osman Ahmed Mohammed	*Impiegato* (employee, office worker) Ali
Ato Asefaw Fasil	Religious man, teacher of Geez Fidel.
Ato Tsegai Berhe	*Ascaro, Buluqbash, Carabiniere (police)*
Ato Habtemariam G/zgabher	*Ascaro, Buluqbash, Carabiniere*
Ato Alemayo Kahasay	Butler, groom; also a mother of an only son
Ato Ghebrezgabher Weldemariam	Father of an only son conscripted by the Italian army

32   Ruth Iyob notes that the period from 1958 to 1965 was characterised by the 'politicization of Eritrean culture' (1995: 98), linked to the establishment of the Eritrean Liberation Movement (ELM) in 1958. While songs of later theatre associations can be connected to aspects of the ELM's programme (ibid. 103), especially those of the Asmara Theatre Association (Ma.Te.A.), co-founded, among others, by Alemayo Kahasay and *Memher* Asres Tessema in 1961, I was unable to make a direct connection to any emerging resistance movement in the case of *Zehalefe*. For ELM see also Markakis (1989 [1987]: 104-9).

BIBLIOGRAPHY

Eritrean and Ethiopian authors are listed with their first name first, followed by their father's name ('surname'). Articles published according to the Ethiopian calendar are given with their original date of publication, indicated with $_{EC}$ and followed by the approximate Gregorian year(s) in brackets. Articles originally published in Tigrinya are quoted in the English translation available to the author.

Abraham Redda (3 November 1945) 'To: Political Secretary, Subject: *New World*', unpublished letter. RDC ACC 10690, Box 62, Ref 10/E, 'Clubs & Societies: Cinemas and Theatre Vol. III'.

Alemayo Kahasay (15 February 1977$_{EC}$ [1985]) unpublished manuscript, Ministry of Culture for the Province of Eritrea, English transl. ECBTP 1995.

Alemseged Tesfai (2002 [2001]) *Aynfelale 1941–1952* [*'Let us not be put asunder' 1941-1952*]. Asmara: Hidri.

Asres Tessema (2006) *Te'amot: kab tarikh medrekhawi sne-tibeb Ertra, 1940-1980* [*Tea Time Snack: Stories of the Performing Arts in Eritrea, 1940-1980*], English transl. Tedros Hagos. Asmara: Hidri.

Astier M. Almedom (2006) 'Re-reading the Short and Long-Rigged History of Eritrea 1941–1952: Back to the Future?', *Nordic Journal of African Studies* 15, 2 103-42. Online at http://www.njas.helsinki.fi/, 30/11/2009.

Barrera, Giulia (2003a) 'The Construction of Racial Hierarchies in Colonial Eritrea: The Liberal and Early Fascist Period (1897-1934)'. In Palumbo, Patrizia, *A Place in the Sun: Africa in Italian Colonial Culture from Post-Unification to the Present* (pp. 81–115). Berkeley: University of California Press.

Barrera, Giulia (2003b) 'Mussolini's Colonial Race Laws and State-Settler Relations in Africa Orientale Italiana (1935-41)', *Journal of Modern Italian Studies* 8, 3, 425-43.

Barrera, Giulia, Alessandro Triulzi, and Gabriel Tzeggai (eds) (2008) *Asmara: Architettura e pianificazione urbana nei fondi dell'IsIAO*. Rome: Istituto Italiano per l'Africa e l'Oriente.

Brecht, Bertolt (1970) *Furcht und Elends des Dritten Reiches*. Frankfurt, Suhrkamp.

Cooper, Barbara M. (2005) 'Oral Sources and the Challenge of African History'. In Philips, John Edward (ed.) *Writing African History*. Rochester, NY: University of Rochester Press, pp. 191-215.

Dagnew Berhe Mesgun (January 2007) 'Short life history of Grazmach Berhe Mesgun Tekie', unpublished curriculum vitae.

Falceto, Francis (comp.) (n.d.) *Éthiopiques 5: Tigrigna Music, Tigray/Eritrea 1970-1975*. CD. Buda Musique, Paris. 82965-2 DK 016. Includes booklet.

Fall, Babacar (2003) 'Orality and Life Histories: Rethinking the Social and Political History of Senegal', *Africa Today* 50, 2, 55-65.

Gaim Kibreab (2008) *Critical Reflections on the Eritrean War of Independence: Social Capital, Associational Life, Religion, Ethnicity and Sowing Seeds of Dictatorship*. Trenton, NJ: The Red Sea Press.

Gibbs, James, and Christine Matzke (2005) '"… accents yet unknown': Examples of Shakespeare from Ghana, Malawi and Eritrea". In Schaffeld, Norbert (ed.) *Shakespeare's Legacy: The Appropriation of the Plays in Post-Colonial Drama*. Trier: WVT, pp. 15-36.

Ghirmai Negash (1999) *A History of Tigrinya Literature in Eritrea: The Oral and the Written, 1890-1991*, CNWS Publications 75. Leiden: Research School of Asian, African, and Amerindian Studies (CNWS), University of Leiden.

Ghirmai Negash (2009) 'Native Intellectuals in the Contact Zone: African Responses to Italian Colonialism in Tigrinya Language', *Biography* 32, 1, 74-88.

Henige, David (2005) 'Oral Tradition as a Means of Reconstructing the Past'. In Philips, John Edward (ed.) *Writing African History*. Rochester, NY: University of Rochester Press, pp. 169-90.

Iyob, Ruth (1995) *The Eritrean Struggle for Independence: Domination, Resistance, Nationalism, 1941-1993*. Cambridge: Cambridge University Press.

Iyob, Ruth (2005) '*Madamismo* and Beyond: The Construction of Eritrean Women', In Ben-Ghiat, Ruth, and Mia Fuller (eds) *Italian Colonialism*. Houndmills, Basingstoke: Palgrave Macmillan, pp. 233-44.

Locatelli, Francesca (2004) 'The Archives of the Municipality and the High Court of Asmara, Eritrea: Discovering the Eritrea "Hidden from History"', *History in Africa* 31, 469-78.

Locatelli, Francesca (2009) 'Beyond the Campo Cintato: Prostitutes, Migrants and "Criminals" in Colonial Asmara (Eritrea), 1890-1941'. In Locatelli, Francesca, and Paul Nugent (eds) *African Cities: Competing Claims on Urban Spaces*, Africa-Europe Group for Interdisciplinary Studies 3. Leiden: Brill, pp. 219-40.

Markakis, John (1989 [1987]) *National and Class Conflict in the Horn of Africa*. Cambridge: Cambridge University Press.

Matzke, Christine (2002) 'Of *Suwa* Houses and Singing Contests: Early Urban Women Performers in Asmara, Eritrea'. In Jane Plastow (Guest-Ed.) *African Theatre: Women*. Oxford: James Currey, pp. 29-46.

Matzke, Christine (2008) 'The Asmara Theatre Association, 1961–1974: *Mahber Teyatr Asmera*'. In

22 Christine Matzke

James Gibbs (ed.), *African Theatre: Companies*. Oxford: James Currey, pp. 62-81.

Mwembu, Donatien Dibwe dia (2005) 'History and Memory'. In Philips, John Edward (ed.) *Writing African History* (pp. 439-464). Rochester, NY: University of Rochester Press.

Pankhurst, Richard (1995) 'The Legal Question of Racism in Eritrea during the British Military Administration: A Study of Colonial Attitudes and Responses, 1941-1945', *Northeast African Studies* 2, 2, 25-70.

Plastow, Jane (1996) *African Theatre and Politics: The Evolution of Theatre in Ethiopia, Tanzania and Zimbabwe: A Comparative Study*. Amsterdam: Rodopi.

Plastow, Jane (1997a) 'Theatre of Conflict in the Eritrean Independence Struggle', *New Theatre Quarterly*, 13, 50, 144-54.

Plastow, Jane (1997b) 'The Eritrea Community-Based Theatre Project', *New Theatre Quarterly*, 13, 52, 386-95.

Plastow, Jane (2004) 'East Africa: Ethiopia and Eritrea'. In Banham, Martin (ed.) *A History of Theatre in Africa*. Cambridge: Cambridge University Press, pp. 192-205.

Pool, David (2001) *From Guerrillas to Government: The Eritrean People's Liberation Front*. Oxford: James Currey.

Quehl, Hartmut (2003) 'Oral History on War: Tagadelti in and after Eritrea's War of Independence'. In Bruchhaus, Eva-Maria (ed.) *Hot Spot Horn of Africa: Between Integration and Disintegration*, African Studies 19. Münster: Lit, pp. 136-47.

Quehl, Hartmut (2005) *Kämpferinnen und Kämpfer im eritreischen Unabhängigkeitskrieg 1961-1991: Faktoren der Diversivität und der Kohärenz. Eine historische Untersuchung zur Alltags- und Sozialgeschichte des Krieges*, 2 vols. Felsberg: edition eins. Vol. 1: *Dekolonisierung und Krieg als Staatsbildungsprozess*; Vol. 2: *Das Gesicht des Krieges*.

Redie Bereketeab (2000) *Eritrea: The Making of a Nation 1890-1991*. Uppsala: Uppsala University.

Reid, Richard (2009) 'The Politics of Silence: Interpreting Stasis in Contemporary Eritrea', *Review of African Political Economy* 36,120, 209-21.

Research and Documentation Centre (RDC), Asmara, Eritrea. Online at http://www.eritreanarchives.org/, 30/11/2009.

Sauter, Willmar (2004) 'Theatre Historiography: General Problems, Swedish Perspectives'. In Wilmer, S.E. (ed.) *Writing and Rewriting National Theatre Histories*. Iowa City: University of Iowa Press, pp. 29-46.

Taddia, Irma (1996) *Autobiografie Africane: Il colonialismo nelle memorie orali*. Milan: FrancoAngeli.

Taddia, Irma (2008 [2005]) 'Italian Memories/African Memories of Colonialism'. In Ben-Ghiat, Ruth, and Mia Fuller (eds) *Italian Colonialism*. Houndmills, Basingstoke: Palgrave Macmillan, pp. 209-19.

Tekeste Negash (1987) *Italian Colonialism in Eritrea, 1882-1941: Policies, Praxis and Impact*, Studia Historica Upsaliensia 148. Uppsala: Almqvist & Wiksell International.

Trevaskis, G.K.N. (1960) *Eritrea: A Colony in Transition: 1941-52*. London: Oxford University Press.

Turco, Carol (2003) 'Muse in Africa: Artisti e letterati in Eritrea 1885-1970'. In Bottaro, Luigi (ed.) *Gli Italiani in Eritrea: Esploratori, Missionari, Medici e Artisti*. Asmara: Scuola Italiana in Eritrea, pp. 171-226.

Uoldelul Chelati Dirar (2004) 'From Warriors to Urban Dwellers: *Ascari* and the Military Factor in the Urban Development of Colonial Eritrea', *Cahiers d'Études africaines* XLIV, 3, 175, 533-74.

Uoldelul Chelati Dirar (2007) 'Colonialism and the Construction of National Identities: The Case of Eritrea', *Journal of Eastern African Studies* 1, 2, 256-76.

White, Luise (1994) 'Between Gluckman and Foucault: Historicizing Rumour and Gossip', *Social Dynamics: A Journal of African Studies* 21, 1, 75-92.

White, Luise, Stephan F. Miescher, and David William Cohen (eds) (2001) *African Words, African Voices: Critical Practices in Oral History*. Bloomington, IN: Indiana University Press.

Yishak Yosief (1 October 1979[EC] [1986]) 'Do You Know Much About Asmara? The Indigenous Theatre Association (Ma.Te.De.)', transl. Tesfazghi Ukubazghi, *Voice of Asmara City Dwellers' Association*, publication details unknown, 1-2.

Seeking the Founding Father
The Story of Kobina Sekyi's
The Blinkards (1916)

JAMES GIBBS

Kobina Sekyi's play *The Blinkards* was premiered in Cape Coast during 1916 and was warmly received by the local press. However, the impact of the production was not followed by the establishment of a theatrical tradition or even by any real circulation of the script of the play. When Sekyi died in 1956, obituarists made no mention of either the production or the text, and interest only revived in 1974 when, thanks to the efforts of J. Ayo Langley, Rex Collings and H. V. H. Sekyi, the playwright's son, the text of the play was published. Since then *The Blinkards* has been analysed and celebrated, studied and performed. While it has become a classic text for African drama in English, the circumstances and reception of the first staging have not been described. Errors in the Introduction prepared for the first edition in the early Seventies for the Rex Collings edition have been repeated, and Sekyi's involvement with the production has not been recognized. This paper uses Gold Coast newspapers of the time of the premiere to fill in something of the background to the first production. From research, it emerges, for example, that Sekyi took a major part in staging the play, indeed he was the driving force behind the event. Because of his involvement in the 1916 production, Sekyi must be recognised as an all-round man of the West African theatre.

Students of Ghanaian drama are indebted to the Gambian historian and international civil servant Jabez Ayo Langley for getting *The Blinkards* into print. However, they should approach the influential Introduction he wrote for the 1974 edition with caution. For understandable reasons, that Introduction - reproduced again in the 1994 Heinemann / Readwide or 'Ghanaian edition' - is a flawed document. Langley wrote it near the beginning of his academic career at a time when he was pioneering research on a number of major Pan-Africanists, and when he was campaigning to get a substantial number of important documents into print. The resources he could devote to Sekyi and his research opportunities were limited. However, he was able to visit Sekyi's base, Cape Coast, to pursue research leads there and to interview some of Sekyi's contemporaries. He also corresponded with H. V. H. Sekyi, a member of the Ghanaian Foreign Service. But Langley did not exhaust the research opportunities represented by the newspapers that were being published in

Cape Coast in 1915 and 1916. As a result, he was unaware of the material I examine below, and he reached a number of inaccurate conclusions. For example, Langley's 'Introduction' includes errors about the date of the first production: he has it as being in 1915; it was 1916. He credits the Cosmopolitan Club with the first production, but I suggest it is more helpful to think of the production as having been put on by an *ad hoc* alliance of individuals and of distinct groups. Langley's speculation that the play was initially put on in Fanti runs counter to the evidence.

In the pages that follow, I will share what I have gathered from press reports about the premiere of *The Blinkards*. It will become clear that in telling this story I am deeply indebted to the work of others who have located newspaper items. I would like to acknowledge the insights of the late Adu Boahen and Ray Jenkins, and to express my gratitude to Kofi Baku, Roger Gocking and Stephanie Newell. Of course, I am aware that new information may well come to light, and offer this account as no more than 'a work in progress'. I say this partly because, in the course of researching this article, I have become aware of the existence of relevant 'Sekyi Papers' held in Accra. These were retained by the Sekyi family in Accra after a generous donation to the National Archives. I hope that in due course these, and other sources, will contribute to a full appreciation of Sekyi as a pioneering man of the Ghanaian theatre.

At this point, it is useful to set *The Blinkards* in the context of Sekyi's early life. In compiling the date-line below I have drawn on Kofi Baku's PhD thesis, the outcome of research that was much more tightly focused than Langley's. Baku is particularly good on Sekyi as an undergraduate, on the myths that grew up around him in Cape Coast and on his literary output. With help from him, it is possible to suggest the following outline of Sekyi's early life:

1892 William Essuman Gwira Sekyi, born 1 November at Cape Coast to Gladstone Sackey and Wilhelmina Pietersen. ('Sackey' is an Anglicised form of 'Sekyi' – the form the playwright preferred).
Educated at primary and first stages of secondary school in Cape Coast, including Mfantsipim.

1911 Matriculated, that is to say qualified for entrance to the University of London. Began publishing articles.

1911-1914 Student of Philosophy, University of London.

October 1914 awarded BA Honours degree.
Returned to Cape Coast, exchanged letters with local authorities about the possibility of teaching at Mfantsipim, continued to write articles, completed and was prime mover in preparing to stage *The Blinkards*.

October 21 and 28 1916, *The Blinkards* performed in two parts at the Government School, Elmina Road, Cape Coast.

1917 April, sailed for London on the *SS Abosso*, survived the sinking of that ship, reached London, and subsequently undertook an MA in Philosophy, completed a law degree, and was called to the bar.

Baku made good use of resources that Langley did not investigate, notably the records held by London University. He also spent time in Cape Coast, and consulted the Sekyi Papers that had been donated to the archives there. These, he indicated in his 1991 bibliography consisted of 314 items. However, Baku did not go through the holdings of the relevant newspapers.

One of those who read the newspapers and who emerged with valuable information was Ray Jenkins. In the *Gold Coast Leader* (hereafter *The Leader*) for 21 and 28 October 1916, held at the Newspaper Library in Colindale, North London, he found evidence that the production that Langley had dated 1915 was in fact staged over two Saturdays, October 14 and October 21, during 1916. Jenkins also extracted from the paper the information that a large audience, that included the Provincial Commissioner, had attended the performance of the first two acts and had been 'highly pleased with the play'. A second article in *The Leader* described the drama as 'humorously interesting', and observed that the second part, acts three and four, was 'good entertainment'. The hope was expressed that the performance was a sign of good things to come 'to enliven dull evenings'. Jenkins shared these discoveries with a wide audience in an article entitled 'Sekyi's Formative Years'. This was published in *West Africa* during 1982, and corrected some of the errors Langley had made.

Below, I reproduce *in extenso* the coverage Jenkins drew on in *The Leader*. I also quote from another Cape Coast newspaper, *The Gold Coast Nation*, hereafter referred to as *The Nation*. I am grateful to Stephanie Newell, who also spent long hours at Colindale, for drawing my attention to this source. I have presented the quotations in columns of small print to suggest the lay-out of the newspapers and to suggest something of the difficulty of reading the original documents.

The Nation confirmed the points gleaned from *The Leader* about the dates of the performances and the positive response. It also carried (on 19 October and 9 November 1916), the synopsis of the play that follows:

ACT FIRST
Scene I Mr. Tsiba calls on Mrs. Brofusem, bringing her his daughter to be taught English manners.
Scene II Mr. Okadu calls on My Onyimdzi and begs to be taken on as a clerk and instead of being taught to behave like a white man so as to become as smart as Miss. Tsiba, and thus become eligible suitor for her hand.

ACT SECOND
Scene I At a garden party, Mr Okadu, following advice given by my Onyimdzi in gun [*fun* JG], makes the acquaintance of Miss. Tsiba; and the two become engaged according to the English custom, to the consternation of Mr. Onyimdzi.
Scene II Mrs, Brofusem calls on Mr. Tsiba, and, after some trouble, gets the latter to recognise Mr. Okadu as his future son-in-law. Nna Sumpa, Miss Tsiba's mother, however refuses to admit the validity of such an engagement, and leaves her husband's house.
Scene III Mr Onyimdzi, having heard that Mr. Okadu has taken an unfair advantage of his position as *Fiancé à l'anglais* of Mr. Tsiba, asks him to make the customary amends and marry the girl, or else be dismissed from his office. Mr. Okadu, on leaving, runs into Nna Sumpa, and rushes back to Mr. Onyimdzi who hides him. Nna Sumpa bursts in upon Mr. Onyimdzi, and, while demanding to be shewn where Mr Okadu is, collapses in a paroxysm of rage. A doctor is called in, and the lady is pronounced dead through heart failure.

ACT THIRD
Scene I Mr. Tsiba takes his daughter to Dr. Onveve, and asks him for an operation when he finds out she is in a compromising state. The Doctor refuses.
Scene II A meeting of the 'Cosmopolitan Club" of which Mr. Okada is a member.
Scene III At the reception held immediately after the wedding of Miss. Tsiba to Mr. Okadu, *à l'anglais,* Nana Katawirwa, the mother on Nna Sumpa, and therefore the grand-mother of Miss Tsiba (who has just arrived from a distant town to attend the general custom of her daughter) appears to demand what Mr. Tsiba and his daughter are doing at the festive gathering, one week after the death of her daughter. There she discovers that her grand-daughter is actually the bride. She therefore takes Miss. Tsiba away from the hall, refusing to acknowledge the European wedding ceremony as such, and, moreover, insisting that no man had asked for her grand-daughter's hand.
Scene IV Miss. Tsiba, having, a considerable time afterwards, been given in marriage, according to Fanti Custom, to a man favoured by her grandmother, Mr. Okadu brings about the arrest of the former on a charge of bigamy.

ACT FOURTH
Scene I Mr. Onyimdzi, after successfully defending Miss. Tsiba at her trial for bigamy, is visited by the parson who officiated at the wedding of the separated couple. This parson who misconceives his function and misquotes Scripture to support such misconceptions, informs Mr. Onyimdzi that he is about to suffer the fate of Nebuchadnezzar for bringing ridicule on the marriage ceremony prescribed in Christian prayer-books. Mr, Onyimdzi, is of course, highly entertained by the parson.
Scene II Mrs. Brofusem receives a shock through the strange conduct of Nyamikye, who, having got drunk, begins to behave he has heard her requiring her husband to behave.
Scene III Mrs. Brofusem, cured of her anglomania, there is peace in the household of Mr. Brofusem, who surprised his friends by his open advocacy of Mr Onyimdzi's view on the utter unsuitability of foreign modes of life to those not alien.

From this, it seems that the play presented in Cape Coast in 1916 was substantially the same as the plot of the play which has come down to us. However, I have reason to believe that there may have been minor revisions, and so, perhaps erring on the side of caution, I propose that the text used in Cape Coast in 1916 be referred to as *Ur-Blinkards.*

The synopsis quoted above reveals the loose structure of the play, and the opportunities Sekyi took to incorporate a variety of aspects of Cape Coast life. Although sometimes described as 'Shavian', and despite sharing with Shaw's work an interest in ideas and attitudes, *The Blinkards* rejects conventional European approaches of the time. It is epic, accommodating, uninhibited by narrow narrative concerns or Aristotelian prescriptions. Its point of departure is significantly different. While concerned, like so many comedies – Shavian and other, with 'the battle of the sexes', *The Blinkards* is played out in a gendered context unfamiliar in Europe. The 'battle-field' is totally dominated by the tensions present in Cape Coast as a result of colonial legislation about marriage. It is also significant that, through the White Man who makes an assignation with 'Esi' (III, iv,), Sekyi, the community dramatist, provides a glimpse of a gendered encounter that challenges European rhetoric about conduct.

The 19 October issue of *The Nation* provided further information about the production by naming the actors who appeared in the first two acts. The following partial cast-list is offered with the caveat that the quality of the printing in the paper makes some names barely legible.

Nyamikye	Victor Eminsang
Mrs Brofusem	J. L. Minnow Jr
Mr Brofusem	W. E. G. Sekyi
Mr Tsiba	Jabez J. Thompson
Miss Tsiba	T. M. Bilson
Mr Onyimdzi	K. Ata-Amonu
Half-Crown	F. G. Wilson
Mr Okadu	W. E. Johnson
Boy	T. D. Bentil
Nna Sumpa	T. J. Abraham
Dr Onweyie	J. E. Wood
Ladies and Gentlemen	Schoolboys

Perhaps the name that jumps out most athletically from this list is that of Sekyi himself. It appears that he took a major role in *The Blinkards*. And it is interesting that the part he played was not that of the eloquent lawyer Onyimdzi who often comes across as the spokesman for the playwright within the drama, but that of Mr Brofusem. This is a rewarding role, not only because Brofusem develops in the course of the play, but also because Brofusem delivers the final lines. For the first audience, many of whom must have been familiar with the conventions of moralistic folk-tales in which the 'tail of the tale' is a direct request to reflect upon what has been said, this casting had particular significance. For them, the words that ended the play were spoken by the author. As an actor Sekyi was operating within a radically new performance convention but he carried over residual authority from an indigenous convention that became very clear when he spoke the final lines. In the 1974 edition, Brofusem, we might remind ourselves, concludes the play with the following observation: 'The people of the old days were wise indeed: if only we would follow the customs they left us a little more, and adopt the ways of other races a little less, we should be at least as healthy as they were.' This insight encapsulates the vision, or 'the moral' of the play and had particular weight in Cape Coast in 1916 because it was delivered by Kobina Sekyi, playwright and actor.

The next item on the list that catches the attention is, I suggest, the casting of 'J. L. Minnow Jr' as Mrs Brofusem. The fact that 'J. L. Minnow *Jr*', that is to say a boy, was playing Mrs. Brofusem means that the convention of female impersonation had been employed.[1] There are, of course many precedents in the history of the theatre for boys taking female roles, and the Concert Party tradition that was to emerge from Cape Coast and other Fanti towns continued that tradition in West Africa. Alert playwrights have always relished the extra dimensions of appearance and reality that cross-gender casting opens up. In this instance, female impersonation insinuated into the premiere of *The Blinkards* additional levels of theatricality by highlighting the role-playing dimension. For the audience in 1916, Mrs Brofusem – as portrayed by Minnow Jr – was not only a portrait of a Fanti woman who mimics Europeans in a most exaggerated fashion, but 'she' was also a boy. Put another way, young Minnow the actor was to act on several levels: he had to add 'stage years' to his actual age, he had to present an alienated human being, an 'anglomaniac' and he had to conceal his gender by portraying a female. Near the end Mrs Brofusem's blind imitation of Europe gives way to a more balanced view. This dropping of one level of performance anticipated the final shedding of assumed roles that occurred at the end of the performance when young Minnow Jr stepped forward with a boyish stride to take his bow.

Moving on from the synopsis of the play and the partial cast-list, the next piece of evidence from the Gold Coast press that I want to consider is 'A Card of Thanks'. This was written by Sekyi and sent to the editor of *The Nation* after the production. It was published on 9 November 1916. In it Sekyi expressed his gratitude to those who had made the production 'practicable' – his modest word. The fact that he felt it appropriate to write this Card of Thanks indicates, I think, that he was the prime mover behind the event. I suspect he combined the roles of producer and director.

The individuals and groups he thanked indicate that he had mobilised a wide range of people in order to put on his play. He needed them partly because he had enemies, those who plotted against him the production. I will look first at those who Sekyi thanked and then use the reference in the card to open up discussion about the 'sanctimonious calumniators' who tried to sabotage the event. Printed in the very small font favoured in *The Nation*, the Card of Thanks read:

Aboom,
Cape Coast,
22 October 1916

Dear Mr. Editor,

I should be glad if you could please allow me space in which to express my obligation to all who helped to make the production of my play, "Blinkards" practicable. My thanks are due to: the Lord Bishop Hummel and the Hon. E. J. P. Brown, B.L., who enabled me to get the play typed, thus making it easy to allot the parts in as short a time as possible; to the Hon. E. J. P. Brown, B.L., who secured the boys who took the minor part, and obtained for me permission to use the Govt School for the production of the play; to the heads of the Roman Catholic, the Zion and the Wesleyan Schools who sent boys to take the minor part; to the young men and the schoolboys who filled the important and secondary roles respectively, to the Sisters of the Roman Catholic Mission who provided the clothing for the boys who acted as "frock ladies"; to the Honourable the Acting Commissioner, Central Province, the Tufuhin of Cape Coast, J. F. Thompson Esq., G. H. Savage Esq., B. L., Dr E. Olubomi Becklye and Professor C. E. Graves, who took a kindly interest in the play before its production, whilst sanctimonious calumniators and other unthinking persons were doing their worst to prevent such production; to L. W. Corcoran Esq., the head of the "Our Day" concert committee (Cape Coast), who rendered invaluable aid in facilitating the preparation of the schoolroom for both performances, and especially in bringing about the better lighting of the room for the second performance; to Mr Gardiner, the Provincial Inspector of Schools, who allowed the use of the Govt School; to Mr Wyper of the P. W. D., who furnished the material for the stage, that had to be removed from the Wesleyan to the Govt School; to Mr J. Spio-Garbrah, the Principal Teacher of the Govt School, and those of the other teachers and the boys who assisted in a great many ways; to W. Awoonor Renner, Esq., B.L., for playing selections on the piano during the changing of the scenes at the second performance; and to all the innumerable ladies and gentlemen who came to see the play, and sat patiently through it all.

I have also to thank the Roman Catholic Mission for so kindly printing free of charge all the notices, tickets and the programmes for both performances because the proceeds are to go towards the Red Cross Fund'

Thanking you for space allowed,
I remain, Dear Mr. Editor,
Yours sincerely,
ESUMAN-GWIRA SEKYI

In thanking 'Lord Bishop Hummel and the Hon. E. J. P. Brown B.L.', Sekyi drew attention to, first, Bishop Hummel, that is to say Ignatius Hummel who had become Roman Catholic Bishop of Cape Coast some ten years earlier. Although the Catholic missionaries had arrived in Cape Coast after the Methodists and Anglicans, Hummel was supervising a period of expansion and was in a position to mobilise considerable resources. From subsequent references, it seems the Catholic Sisters of Our Lady of the Assumption were able to provide clothing for the schoolboys playing 'frock ladies'. The Société des Missions Africaines (SMA) put its printing machines and supplies of paper at the service of the production, printing the necessary 'notices, tickets and the programmes'. Although I have not seen any of this theatrical ephemera, I live in the hope that examples will one day be found and their value for students of drama recognized.

In addition to help from the Bishop and the Catholic Church, Sekyi also had the backing of Emmanuel Joseph Peter Brown, a lawyer and a Freemason who enjoyed a very exalted position in the political, cultural and social life of Cape Coast. Evidence of his standing is provided by the fact that, on 11 November 1916, a Masonic Banquet was given in his honour at Hamilton Hall, Cape Coast. The extensive report in *The Nation,* a paper over which he exerted a particular influence, included references to 'sumptuous dishes', loyal toasts and eloquent speeches. In Brown's case the eloquent speech was described as having been delivered in a 'graceful tone'. Shortly afterwards, on the 9 December, the same paper reported that 'officers and members of the Cape Coast Ladies Club [had given] a Garden Party in honour of ... (Brown's) appointment as aboriginal unofficial member of the Legislative Council.' Honours clustered about him thick and fast, and he was the subject of extensive and favourable newspaper comment. (See, for example, *Nation,* 14 December 1916, 1570).

With regard to the production, Brown seems to have been a tower of strength, using his influence with headmasters and school inspectors, and sharing responsibility with Hummel for getting the script of the play typed. As we shall see, he publicly associated himself with the production.

The schools mentioned on the Card show the extent to which Cape Coast had become an educational centre and the way this benefitted the production. I take the reference to the Wesleyan School to be to Mfantsipim that traces its foundations to 1876. The Roman Catholic school referred to may be the first of that Church's educational establishments – set up in 1889. The reference to the Zion School is, presumably, to the institution that dated from 1907 and owed its existence to the Rev'd Frank Ata Osam-Pinanko, M. A., who had responded to a call from the American Methodist Episcopal Zion church and earned a degree in the United States (Ofosu-Appiah, 1997).

Moving on from the schools mentioned to the list of those who took 'a kindly interest in the play before its production', Sekyi names individuals who emerge from different sections of the Cape Coast community. To illustrate this, the *'tufuhin'* can be glossed as the title of the leader, or 'Captain-general', of one of the town's major *asafo* companies. The name 'E. Olubomi Becklye' carries an association with the Yoruba families that could be found in many of the major trading towns along the West African coast. The 'Professor C. E. Graves' mentioned was the Principal of the West African College of Music and Commerce that provided 'comfortable accommodation' under the 'strictest surveillance' for boys and girls who were attending schools in Cape Coast. The reference to L. W. Corcoran as head of the 'Our Day' concert committee draws attention to existing performance traditions of the community. Putting on the play as an evening entertainment meant that there were inevitably going to be difficulties with illumination. Those responsible for the lighting of *The Blinkards* came in for criticism after the first part had been put on, and Corcoran helped address this issue for part two. The reference to 'W. Awoonor Renner Esq. B.L.' playing 'selections on the piano' draws attention to support for the production from another eminent member of the town's professional community. The entertainment he provided reflected the extent to which musical contributions were relished by the West African elite: one of the many ways in which they resembled the Edwardian middle classes in London.

Because some Cape Coast families had taken European, or European sounding, names it is not possible to tell how many of those who contributed to making the production 'practicable' were expatriates. However, Mr Wyper of the P. W. D. (Public Works Department), who 'furnished material for the stage', may well have been a 'European', and Bishop Hummel, who threw his weight behind the production, certainly was. Since we know the (British) Provincial Commissioner attended the first night we can say that both the 'production team' and the audience was integrated.

In the final paragraph of his Card, Sekyi indicated that the proceeds from the performances were destined for 'The Red Cross Fund'. With war raging in France, all elements in the community could unite behind this charity and that that may have been why it was chosen.

Despite the fact that proceeds were going to a good cause, there were those in the town who worked against the production. The Card of Thanks refers to 'sanctimonious calumniators and other unthinking persons (who did) their worst to prevent such production'. This faction prevented the play from being staged at 'the Wesleyan school' and one can well imagine what a blow this was to all those struggling to put on the play.

Insights into the motives of the rumour mongers and the impact of their actions were conveyed in a report of the first part of the production that appeared in *The Nation* on 19 October 1916 under the title 'Mr V. Esuman-Gwira Sekyi's New Play'. Once again I will quote in full:

> The Blinkards (in four acts) was produced at the Govt School-room, Elmina Rd, on Saturday evening the 14th instant at 8.30., with great success. Only the first two acts were performed the other two having been deferred owing to the tardy shifting of the scenes due to the want of proper apparatus which could not permit the entire production at one performance.
>
> Before the production, certain wild rumours had been circulated by some person or persons to the effect that the play was of an impious nature which ultimately led to the changing of the place of production. However, all who attended were convinced that there was not the slightest tinge of impropriety in the play and the lessons it taught were wholesome and they brought some valuable home-thrusts to those who overstep the boundary of propriety in engrafting foreign customs on their own.
>
> The stage which was ingeniously got up was an admirable improvement on any we have seen out here and the scenic effect was simply grand. The only defect (if such it was, for it was amply compensated for by the all-round completeness and perfection of the general get-up) was the lighting arrangement which was due to the failure to obtain sufficient lights for the room.
>
> The actors one and all did well, and the clever acting of the principal characters in the play was too realistic for words; we offer them our congratulations. It is the first attempt by a native and the effort has been crowned with marvellous success. We should encourage and not hamper home article, especially where it is original, and Mr Sekyi's talent and effort show the latent ability of our people in the dramatic art. When the curtain was rung down on the last scene, the Honourable E. J. P. Brown introduced Mr Sekyi as the author of the play to the audience who loudly cheered and applauded him. The continuation of the performance takes place next Saturday the 21st instant at the Govt School-room and we bespeak for it a full house. The proceeds will go towards the Red Cross Fund, and our people should see to it that a generous sum is raised. We give below the programme.

In these columns, the anonymous journalist brought the motives of the saboteurs before us by referring to rumours that 'had been circulated … to the effect that the play was of an impious nature.' This reminds the reader that Sekyi, the philosophy graduate with a degree from London University and the critic of Anglomaniacs, was certainly at odds with elements in the religious establishment in Cape Coast. While in London, he had moved away from the Methodism of his parents and abandoned the church-going habits that were engrained in the lives of an influential section of the Cape Coast community.

On his return, he had ruffled feathers at Mfantsipim by making it clear that he would not accept any teaching post in which he had to answer to a European (Boahen, 1996: 212). Sekyi's clash with the Mfantsipim hierarchy may have contributed to the saboteurs' suspicion of him and may have strengthened their determination to deny him the use of the school premises.

Whatever the calumniators' motives, the resulting disruption of the production can easily be imagined. It must have been especially trying because the production was a pioneering venture and because it meant moving the stage from one school-room to another, from, I take it, Mfantsipim to the Government School in Elmina Road. The reference to a curtain ('When the curtain was rung down') may indicate that those responsible may have felt it incumbent upon them to erect a proscenium arch.

In the event, the performance, scheduled to start at 8.30, moved slowly because of 'tardy scene shifting'. A glance at the text of the play shows that the first two acts require several scene changes, and some substantial items of furniture (including a piano!). If, as was almost inevitable in a school-room, the wing-space was limited and the staging improvised, one can imagine that set changes took time. At some point during the evening, the decision was taken to postpone Acts three and four until the following week. Reading this, one inevitably wonders how the dress and technical rehearsals had gone! Indeed, one wonders if there had been time to have a dress rehearsal. However, our speculation about shortcomings in staging *The Blinkards* should be set against the comment in the quotation above that the 'stage was ingeniously got up … and the scenic effect was simply grand'.

The reviewer was also very impressed by the acting, affirming that 'The actors one and all did well, and the clever acting of the principal characters in the play was too realistic for words'. At this distance, it is difficult to know quite what was meant by 'realistic'. Some of the writing, such as that for the inebriated Nyamikye who provides a grotesque parody of Brofusem in the penultimate scene, calls for daemonic exaggeration. However, I think we can take the word of the reviewer that the actors 'did well'. The histrionic court-room performances of the mature Sekyi have been attested to by Joe Appiah, and it may also be relevant to note that Ata-Amonu, who took the role of lawyer Onyimdzi, went on to occupy a position, that of 'barrister member' for Calabar (1923-28), that called for thespian talents (Appiah, 1990 and Okafor, 1972).

The reviewer drew attention to the action of Brown and the response to Sekyi at the end of the first half. We learn that 'The Honourable E. J. P. Brown B.L.', filling, assuming or usurping the role of Master of Ceremonies, introduced Sekyi to the audience, and that Sekyi received loud cheers and applause. By taking the initiative described, Brown associated himself with the production in a strikingly public way – and, by the same gesture, ensured that he shared the young writer's glory. One wonders, however, what thoughts went through Sekyi's mind as people clapped him with Brown standing beside him. Sekyi had already given signs of independence of thought and action, and, while he was undoubtedly obliged to Brown for support in many ways, he was not his protégé.

The plaudits continued, and may have been the louder because of the opposition that had been overcome. In *The Nation* for 9 November 1916, the production was declared to have been a 'great success' (1537) and this approval was backed by thoughtful recognition that the play taught 'wholesome lessons' to 'those who overstep the boundary of propriety in engrafting foreign customs on their own'. Sekyi's 'talent and effort' were acclaimed and, in a manner beloved of the Cape Coast press of the period, presented as 'showing the latent talent of our people' – in this instance for 'the dramatic art'.

Subsequent newspaper coverage gave further insight into the way people felt about the play, and into Sekyi's plans for it. *The Leader* for 10 February 1917 expressed the following wish: 'We should like to see the brilliant author of "The Blinkards" render the drama into the vernacular for the edification of Fanti speaking folk.' (4) This is disconcerting because, as Newell, who drew attention to this item, has pointed out it implies that the play was initially presented in English. Can this have been the case? Was *Ur-Blinkards* a monolingual text? I am reluctant to accept this because the play makes such very effective use of Fanti and because so much of its humour derives from the switching between one 'code' and another. I think 'the jury must remain "out" on this'. In the meantime, we should note that Langley speculated that 'the play may well have been performed entirely in Fante' (Langley in Sekyi, 1974:11). There is no evidence for that.

The paragraph on Sekyi in the February paper, contains another revelation in a reference to the possibility of 'an early publication of that work…'. This hope was not, of course, fulfilled and we had to wait fifty-seven years for the text to appear. One can only suppose that Sekyi discussed plans for publication, and ponder what his plans might have been. Did he, one wonders, toy with the idea of publishing the play in *The Leader* or *The Nation*? Or did he hope he could interest one of the mission presses in the work, perhaps the one that had printed the programmes for the production? Had he, perhaps, expectations of using the London contacts he had made when an undergraduate? Whatever his hopes they were not realized, and it is possible that experiences on his voyage to England affected his plans.

At the beginning of April 1917, despite German attacks on British shipping, Sekyi embarked for England on the *SS Abosso*, to take forward plans to qualify as a lawyer. However, on 22 April, when west of Fastnet the *Abosso* was torpedoed and went down with the loss of sixty-five lives.[2]

Sekyi was among those who survived and he went on to London. His theatrical success in West Africa followed him, and, at the end of the month, *West Africa*, a new publication, carried an item headed 'A Play by a Fanti Author'. In it 'A Correspondent' described *The Blinkards* as an 'A drama of Anglo-Fanti life in four acts'. The Correspondent continued: 'the author does not shrink from holding up to ridicule a section of his own people who think that racial character can be acquired by a few externals' (*West Africa,* 28 April 1917; quoted in Whiteman, 1995: 618).

From this point on, *The Blinkards* disappears almost completely from view until the 1970s, though one can imagine that readers of *West Africa* asked about it and that those who had seen it in Cape Coast talked about it. Perhaps some kept alive the hope of more plays from the pen of the 'brilliant author'. In fact, Sekyi did try to get it published. During October 2007, I followed in the footsteps of Langley, Baku, and Asiedu Yirenkyi by making my way to the Cape Coast archives. By then the Sekyi's papers were in the hands of the Public Record and Archives Department (PRAAD). When I asked to see the Sekyi Papers, I was presented with a few cardboard boxes, with far fewer items than on the list compiled by Baku. The boxes contained carbon copies of articles and distressingly fragile manuscripts of poems. However, they also contained some page-proofs of *The Blinkards* that had been prepared in the early 1940s by the British publisher Allen and Unwin. Their existence indicates that Sekyi had followed up his intention to find a publisher for his play, had nursed the hope of seeing it in print and had made some progress towards that end. Sadly the proofs I saw in Cape Coast were not accompanied by correspondence and a subsequent search among the surviving Allen and Unwin Papers held in Reading did not produced any indication of the negotiations about the publication. For some reason that I have not been able to determine the project was abandoned.

During his lifetime, Sekyi slipped the text prepared for Allen and Unwin and page-proofs into a 'bottom drawer, where they remained, forgotten, along with Sekyi's reputation as a man of the theatre'. When he died in 1956, he was celebrated as an intellectual and a nationalist, lauded as a lawyer and as political writer, but his achievements as a playwright – and short story writer and poet – were not mentioned. Even in 1967, when K. A. B. Jones-Quartey contributed a biographical article on Sekyi to the Legon *Research Review* and the name of Bernard Shaw was invoked no mention was made of Sekyi the dramatist. Like the obituarists of 1956, Jones-Quartey did not mention *The Blinkards*.

Sekyi's recognition as a playwright came over a decade after his interment. It came with the awakening of new interests and from the happy collaboration of an enthusiastic scholar (Langley), an enterprising publisher (Collings) and a 'literary executor' (H. V. H. Sekyi) who was prepared to take responsibility. Publishing is a complicated process at the best of times and in the case of *The Blinkards* there were particular difficulties. These included the fact that the author was long since dead, and because his text was in two languages. A bilingual edition of a play by a long dead writer carried risks that any small publisher, such as Collings, would have hesitated to shoulder. Collings considered the risks and then proceeded to spread them by involving James Currey at Heinemann, UK, and Donald Herdeck at Three Continents Press in Washington D. C. Involving all three meant delays and the possible erection of further hurdles. In fact, Currey solicited a 'Readers' Report' on the text from P. V. A. Ansah, who propelled the publishing process forward by arguing that the play's relevance had, if anything, increased, rather than diminished, in the decades since it was written. When *The Blinkards* emerged, it was a Rex Collings hardback in the UK, a Heinemann paperback (Number 136 in African Writers Series) and a Three Continents Press (3 Cs) title in the US. World rights were divided up in the manner in which UK and US publishers had become accustomed.

In December 1975, a little more than a year after publication, *The Blinkards* was given its second 'outdooring' on the Ghanaian stage. The occasion was an ambitious 'season' of performances to mark the gathering of African Ministers of Culture in Accra. The producer was George Andoh Wilson, the venue an open-air stage in Ridge Park, Accra, and the group responsible the Ghana Playhouse. There have since been other productions in Ghana. In February 2007 for example, a production by Derek Sewornu, that made use of University of Ghana students, opened a programme of plays to celebrate Ghana's 50th Anniversary of Independence. By that time the play had attracted the interest of academics, notably Asiedu Yirenkyi who had delivered a conference paper on it at the University of Ibadan in 1976. Since then, Sekyi's reputation as a playwright has spread and his native land has honoured him with the establishment of a series of Memorial Lectures named after him. The series was inaugurated in November 2009 by Professor George Hagan.

Sekyi's star has also risen outside Ghana. In Nigeria, his works found a champion in Ghana-born Joel Yinka Adedeji, head of the Theatre Arts Department at the University of Ibadan, and in the United States Roger Gocking encouraged undergraduates studying Ghanaian history to read the play. (Personal communications from Femi Osofisan and Roger Gocking, May 2009.) In London, Adjoa Andoh presented a rehearsed reading at The Drill Hall in Bloomsbury during September 2004.

Conclusion

Not surprisingly, given the time that has passed since 1916, I have not been able to speak to anyone who had first-hand knowledge of the first production. Sadly, death has also removed those who were involved in publishing the 1974 editions. That list includes Paul Ansah, Rex Collings, Donald Herdeck, Ray Jenkins, Ayo Langley and H. V. H. Sekyi. I have also failed to locate any relevant research notes or records of interviews. Only in PRAAD and the Reading University Archive among the papers related to the Heinemann African Writers' series was I able to see relevant written material.

I wish I could say that the 2007 production and the 2009 establishment of the Kobina Sekyi Memorial Lecture series had swept aside all the ignorance about Kobina Sekyi as a creative and intellectual giant. Sadly, it did not do so. Many Ghanaians remain ignorant about much that Sekyi undertook. The level of ignorance was exemplified by the Ghana Broadcasting Corporation (G.. B. C.) News items, carried on the web in November 2009, referred to 'a public memorial lecture in honour of the late Kwamena Sekyi'!

Ignorance about Sekyi can be partly traced to the fact that he has not been the subject of an adequate biography – Kofi Baku's excellent PhD thesis remains unpublished – and it may also stem from the poor state of Ghana's archives. It was much easier to work with the collection of Gold Coast newspapers in North London that those in Legon, Cape Coast or Accra. Effective arrangements for the cataloguing and preservation of vital documents must be put in place, and archivists trained at the national university must be encouraged to devote themselves to operating in a functioning public sector.

The state of the Sekyi Papers is an indictment of the state's attitude to the nation's written heritage. I remain haunted by the memory of my encounter with the Sekyi Papers in Cape Coast. There, I experienced both delight at finding the page-proofs of *The Blinkards* and distress at feeling that material the Sekyi family had entrusted to the nation disintegrating between my fingers. As I touched them, fragile, neglected, potentially death-defying documents were reduced to dust.

NOTES

1   For many in the original audience, J. L. Minnow Snr would have been a well-known personality. He features as a school teacher in Adu Boahen's history of Mfantsipim.
2   In addition to an inaccurate rendition of what happened, Langley has been shown to be mistaken about the ship Sekyi sailed on: he has the *Falaba* for the *Abosso*, and the year in which he travelled, 1915 for 1917. Baku (1991) sets the record straight.

BIBLIOGRAPHY

Note: The focus of this bibliography is Sekyi's *The Blinkards*. However, I have included some material that refers to his creative writing generally and to the Ghana National Archives. Baku should be consulted for general matters relating to Sekyi and for an extended bibliography (1987 and 1991).

Anon. 'General News', *Gold Coast Leader,* 21 October 1916. (Refers to the performance of the first part of *The Blinkards*).

Anon. 'General News', *Gold Coast Leader*, 28 October 1916, 2. (Refers to the performance of the 'remaining part' of *The Blinkards*).

Anon. 'A Play by a Fanti Author'. *West Africa* (London), 28 April 1917.

Anon. 'Editorial Comment '. *Gold Coast Leader,* 10 February 1917, 4.

Anon. 'Kobina Sekyi is Dead'. *Daily Graphic*, 23 June 1956, 4.

Anon. '*Blinkards,* a drama that kept the crowds coming'. http://www.myghanaonline.com/ morenews.php?id=878&type=%91Blinkards%92+a+drama+that+kept+crowd+coming

(Review of production, signed 'Showbiz. Refers to 'Kwamina Sekyi'. Posted 1 March 2007.)

Appiah, E. E. (pseud.) (1967) 'William Esuman Gwira Sekyi - Popularly Known as Kobina Sekyi'. *Legon Observer*, 24 November: 21-22.

Appiah, Joe (1990) *The Autobiography of an African Patriot*. Westport, Conn.: Praeger.

Baku, Kofi (1987) *An Intellectual in National Politics: The Contribution of Kobina Sekyi to the Evolution of National Consciousness*. Unpublished PhD thesis, University of Sussex.

Baku, Kofi (1991) *Kobina Sekyi of Ghana: An Annotated Bibliography of his Writings*. Working Papers in African Studies, 151, Boston: African Studies Centre, Boston University. Also (1991) *International Journal of African Historical Studies*, 24, 369-81.

Boahen, A. Adu (1996) *Mfantsipim and the Making of Ghana: A Centenary History, 1876-1976.* Accra: Sankofa.

Danquah, J. B. (1956) 'Obituary: Kobina Sekyi'. *Daily Graphic,* 22 June, 7.

Danquah, Moses (1956) 'Kobina Sekyi – Defender of Ghana'. *Daily Graphic*, 27 June, 5.

Doortmont, Michael R. ed. (2005) *The Pen-Pictures of Modern Africans and African Celebrities by Charles Francis Hutchison*, Leiden: Brill.

Dumett, R. E. (1974) *Survey of Research Materials in the National Archives of Ghana*. Basle: Basler Afrika Bibliographien.

'GBC News', Ghanaians charged to project Culture, GBC News: Art & Culture | Mon, 16 Nov 2009. http://www.modernghana.com/music/10504/3/ghanaians-charged-to-project- culture. html Accessed 12 01 2010.

Gocking, R. (1981) *The Historic Akoto: A Social History of Cape Coast, Ghana 1843–1948,* PhD Dissertation, Department of History, Stanford University.

Gocking, Roger (1986) 'Creole Society and the Revival of Traditional Culture in Cape Coast during the Colonial Period'. *International Journal of African Historical Studies,* 17, 4: 601-6.

Gocking, Roger S. (2002) *Facing Two Ways: Ghana's Coastal Elite Under Colonial Rule.* Lanham: University Press of America.

Gocking, Roger S (2005) *The History of Ghana.* Waterford, Conn: Greenwood.

Henige, David (1973) 'The National Archives of Ghana: A Synopsis of Holdings'. *The International Journal of African Historical Studies,* 6, 3: 474-86.

Jenkins, R. G. (1982) 'Sekyi's Formative Years.' *West Africa,* 6 September: 2270-72.

Jenkins, R. G. (1985) 'Gold Coasters Overseas, 1880-1919: With Specific Reference to their Activities in Britain'. *Immigrants and Minorities,* 4, 3: 5-52.

Jones-Quartey, K. A. B. (1967) 'Kobina Sekyi: A Fragment of a Biography', *Research Review* (Legon), 4, 1: 74-8.

Kimble, David (1963) *A Political History of Ghana, The Rise of Gold Coast Nationalism 1850-1928* , Oxford: Clarendon Press.

Langley, J. Ayo (1970) 'Modernization and its Malcontents: Kobina Sekyi of Ghana and the Re-Statement of African Political theory.' *Research Review* (Legon), 6, 3: 1-61.

Langley, J. Ayo (1973) 'Introduction to Kobina Sekyi's Play *The Blinkards.' Ndaanan* (Bathurst), 3, 1: 10-18. (Reprinted in Sekyi, 1974 and 1994).

Langley, J. Ayo (2002) 'William Esuman-Gwira Sekyi (Kobina Sekyi) of Ghana, (1892-1956): Theory of politics, development and cultural identity'. *Tinabantu,* 1, 1: 81-103.

Newell, Stephanie (2002) *Literary Culture in Colonial Ghana: How to play the game of life.* Manchester: Manchester University Press.

Newell, Stephanie (2009) 'Newspapers, New Spaces, New Writers: The First World War and Print Culture in Colonial Ghana.' *Research in African Literatures,* 40, 2: 1-14.

Ofosu-Appiah, L. H. (1977) 'Sekyi, W.E.', in *Dictionary of African Biography, Vol. 1.* New York: Reference Publications, 315-17.

Okafor, Samuel O. (1972) 'Ibo Chiefs and Social Change', *The Journal of Modern African Studies* 10: 128-9.

Sekyi, Kobina (1974) *The Blinkards.* London: Collings. (A Heinemann African Writers' Series edition (number 136 in Series) of the play came out in the same year, as did a US edition from Three Continents Press, Washington DC. Foreword in all cases by H. V. H. Sekyi, Introduction by Ayo Langley.)

Sekyi, Kobina (1997) *The Blinkards, A comedy, and The Anglo-Fanti, A short story.* London: Heine-mann with Accra: Readwide. (This reprints H. V. H. Sekyi's Foreword and Langley's intro-duction from the Collings 1974 edition. The Fanti sections of the text and the names of charac-ters have been rendered using current orthography.)

Shaloff, Stanley (1972) 'Controls and Sedition Proceedings in the Gold Coast 1933-39.' *African Affairs,* 71 (July): 241-63.

Whiteman, Kaye (1995) 'The Sekyis, Father and Son.' *West Africa,* 24 April: 618.

Yirenkyi, Asiedu (1977) 'Kobina Sekyi: The Founding Father of the Ghanaian Theatre.' *The Legacy* (Legon), 3 2 (September): 39-47. (Part of a conference paper presented in Ibadan during 1976.)

I would like to acknowledge the help of those who have responded to enquiries. These include James Currey, J. L. Bartels, Roger Gocking, the late Ray Jenkins, Stephanie Newell, and members of the Sekyi family, I would like to express my gratitude to archivists in Accra, Cape Coast, Colindale and Reading.

Extensive enquiries have been undertaken to try to identify the holder of the copyright to the picture of Kobina Sekyi used on the cover of this volume. Lack of success in this matter provides an insight into the state of visual resources archives in West Africa, and draws attention to some of the problems encountered in trying to recover historical source material. Anyone claiming the copyright is invited to contact the editors.

Medieval Morality & Liturgical Drama in Colonial Rhodesia
Early Christian martyrs dramatized

OWEN S. SEDA

This article attempts to analyze the documentation, influences and practice of early Christian drama in colonial Rhodesia by examining the documentation and what it reveals about the way church dramas were used in Christian prose-lytizing by the Catholic Church, the Wesleyan Methodist Church and the Anglican Church. One of the examples selected is an adaptation and translation of Father Pedro Calderon de la Barca's *El Gran Teatro del Mundo*, a medieval morality play from Spain. Others include various dramatizations of the lives and martyrdom of two of Zimbabwe's best-known Christian martyrs of the early colonial period, namely Bernard Mamiyeri Mizeki of the Anglican Church and Modumedi Moleli of the Wesleyan Methodist Church.

As forms of drama that were used in colonial Rhodesia in the conversion and maintenance of African converts, the article will examine affinities between these plays and some aspects of medieval morality plays and liturgies. It is also a scholarly attempt to throw light on an aspect of colonial Rhodesian drama that has not been written about extensively in the past.

Christianity in colonial Rhodesia – a brief historical background

The first European contact with Zimbabwe dates as far back as the sixteenth century with the arrival of Portuguese traders and missionaries on the east coast of Africa (Gann, 1965). At that time the geographical area now known as Zimbabwe (then colonial Rhodesia and Southern Rhodesia) was the seat of power for the Empire of the Mwene Mutapa or Munhumutapa. According to Gann, one of the very first Europeans to call at the court of the empire of the Mwene Mutapa was Father Goncalo da Silveira, a Catholic missionary from Portugal.

The arrival of Father Silveira and many other European missionaries after him was to lead to the gradual and steady Christianization of Southern Rhodesia through the establishment of Christian mission stations across the country. Although the biggest wave of Christian proselytizing began around 1890 following the arrival of the Pioneer Column, some missionary organizations had already set up in Southern Rhodesia during the mid-nineteenth century and earlier. These included the Catholic Church, which arrived in the kingdom of the Mwene Mutapa as early as the sixteenth century, and the London Missionary Society which commenced work in Matebeleland in 1859. The Church of England had also arrived at Lobengula's capital in Matabeleland in 1876. The Wesleyan Methodist Church opened its first mission in 1891 at Fort Salisbury under the stewardship of Reverend Owen Watkins and Reverend Isaac Shimmin. Notably, the establishment of the Wesleyan Methodist Church was strongly linked to the colonizing process insofar as it was able to begin its work in Southern Rhodesia following a small grant from Cecil John Rhodes's Chartered Company (Gann, 1965). By 1900 there were up to ten missionary organizations operating in Southern Rhodesia.

As a branch of European colonialism in Africa the spread of Christian missionary ideas was sometimes accompanied by strong sentiments of cultural and religious prejudice on the part of the early colonialists. Some of these prejudices were evidently predicated on the philosophical ideas of nineteenth-century Europe, particularly Georg Hegel's *Philosophy of History* in which Africa was considered to be a continent that was trapped in time, without a soul or a legacy. In the words of Hegel:

> Africa proper as far as History goes back, has remained – for all purposes of connection with the rest of the world – shut up, it is the Gold-land compressed within itself – the land of childhood, which lying beyond the days of self-conscious history, is enveloped in the dark mantle of Night…
>
> The negro as already observed exhibits the natural man in his completely wild and untamed state… there is nothing harmonious with humanity to be found in this type of character…
>
> At this point we leave Africa never to mention it again. For it is no historical part of the world; it has no movement or development to exhibit.
> (Quoted in Ashcroft, Griffiths and Tiffin, 1995: 15)

For instance, while writing back to his principals in the London Missionary Society in England in 1860, Robert Moffat who set up a mission station at Inyati in Matebeleland is quoted as having said:

> I am among a people living in Egyptian darkness… In beastly degradation, everything in their political economy is directly opposed to the will of God.
> (Quoted in Zinyemba, 1986: 17)

Proceeding from such religious and cultural prejudice, the early missionaries and their African disciples such as Bernard Mizeki and Modumedi Moleli consequently saw their task as one of spreading the word of the Christian god, while simultaneously suppressing and eventually eliminating indigenous ancestor worship, rituals and the practice of African medicine. In the words of Ranga Zinyemba, the early missionaries 'preached not a modification of African rituals and ceremonies but a complete uprooting' (ibid.). Indeed it is this very quest which was to lead to the martyrdom of Modumedi Moleli and Bernard Mizeki during the Mashona Uprising of 1896.

It is also in the above context that the establishment of the Christian church in colonial Rhodesia was accompanied by significant cultural work some of which involved drama. This will form the basis for the analysis that follows.

Medieval liturgies in colonial Rhodesia?

The practice of early church drama in colonial Rhodesia bears a striking resemblance to the religious liturgies of medieval Europe. Dramatic performance in medieval Europe was strongly influenced by the Catholic Church. As the only church at that time, the Catholic Church also played a central role in people's lives. Although the church had been in the vanguard of closing secular Roman theatres in the sixth century (Worthen, 2000), it was to revive later and sponsor the theatre through what came to be known as liturgical drama. Robert Cohen (2000: G7) defines liturgical drama as 'dramatic material that was written into the official Catholic Church ... and staged as part of regular church services in the medieval period' Similarly Wilson and Goldfarb (2004: G6) define liturgical drama as 'any religious drama, usually sung or chanted, that relates to the Bible, and is presented ... inside a church sanctuary'. Oscar Brockett (2000) makes the point that with time, some religious plays began to be performed outside the confines of the church.

The present article would argue that to the extent that the plays under analysis were developed and performed in religious (church) contexts, with the deliberate purpose of reinforcing the Catholic, Wesleyan or Anglican faiths, they may be considered to be a form of liturgical drama in a contemporary context.

Perhaps Cohen's definition as cited above also alludes to the archiving of these dramas as plays which existed mainly in an oral form, i.e. in religious performance contexts rather than in written and published form, something which is the case with Mizeki and Moleli's plays.

The three examples cited in this article are used to support the argument that early religious drama in colonial Rhodesia may be read as liturgical drama to the extent that it was developed and presented in commemorative contexts of devotion and religious worship.

Early religious drama in oral archives

A survey of the documentation of early religious dramatic activity in colonial Rhodesia indicates that much of what is known about early Christian drama largely exists in the form of oral traditions.

Although the first missionaries to arrive in Southern Rhodesia found the indigenous people to be generally hospitable and receptive towards strangers they were puzzled as to why they (i.e. the indigenes) did not readily accept

Christianity and convert to Christianity in large numbers. Missionaries soon discovered that for their message to strike a chord with the indigenous people, they had to infuse emotional life into their sermons to make Christianity appeal to a people whose own traditional religion included much ritual dramatization with virtually no preaching in the 'accepted' Christian way.

The use of drama to aid missionary work dates back to the early days of the establishment of Christianity in Southern Rhodesia. The earliest dramatizations of issues not directly stemming from the Bible was begun at Inyati and Hope Fountain Missions in Matabeleland when dramatizations of how Christianity had taken root in Matebeleland were presented. According to D.G.H. Flood (1973), pageants were held at the London Missionary Society's Inyati Mission in Matebeleland depicting the 'pacification' of the Ndebele nation. These performances, which were presented by Ndebele converts, emphasized firstly Ndebele war dances, then threatening and aggressive attitudes towards missionaries, which changed to or were followed by ostensibly orderly Christian choirs.

Besides the early dramatizations at Inyati and Hope Fountain missions in Matabeleland, there is substantial oral evidence of Christian religious drama taking place at mission stations such as Tekwane and Cyrene in Matabeleland Province, Gokomere and Morgenster in Masvingo Province, Dadaya in the Midlands Province, Chishawasha, St Albert's and Kutama in Mashonaland Province, and Mt Selinda and Chikore in Manicaland Province (Chivandikwa, 2010)

Since the education of nearly all black people in Southern Rhodesia was pioneered by missionaries, it can be said that school pupils were exposed to religious drama at least during the time that they were in school. It may also be argued that religious drama was the first introduction to formal drama that many Africans had. It was only when the provision of education was secularized through the establishment of government schools in the colony, or when non-mission educated teachers came into the school system that most school pupils were exposed to non-religious dramas by Shakespeare and other western canonical playwrights. The introduction of published western canonical play texts may be considered the point of transition from the production of oral texts to published play scripts in Zimbabwean theatre history.

African Christian martyrs dramatized

Although Christian missionary denominations in colonial Rhodesia largely operated independently of each other, parishioners, especially school pupils, frequently interacted with one another at various forums leading to the spread of Christian ideas. One such idea was the spread of the dramatization of the lives and activities of African Christian martyrs such as Bernard Mizeki of the Anglican Church and Modumedi Moleli of the Wesleyan Methodist Church.

With the upsurge in African nationalist politics after Ian Smith's Unilateral Declaration of Independence (UDI) in November 1965, African congregations were assailed by a need to approach the Christian faith from the perspective of the black people of Southern Rhodesia who had dedicated their lives in the service of the church, thus following closely the example of Christ and some of the biblical prophets. It is against this background that the Wesleyan Methodist Church has celebrated the martyrdom of Modumedi Moleli around 24 June each year as part of celebrations held in honour of the church's founder John Wesley. These commemorative performances constitute a festive and devotional celebration of the life and martyrdom of Modumedi Moleli, which includes theatre, song and dance.

Modumedi Moleli was an African Wesleyan Methodist convert and evangelist. Originally from the Transvaal in South Africa, Moleli arrived in Southern Rhodesia in August 1892 as an assistant to Reverend Owen Watkins, having agreed to come to Southern Rhodesia to work as a missionary and teacher in Mashonaland. Upon arrival in Southern Rhodesia, Modumedi Moleli opened a school in Chief Nenguwo's area but soon found himself in conflict with Shona customs, culture and beliefs on issues to do with polygamy, sorcery and ancestor worship. The traditionalists among his hosts were soon agitating for the closure of Moleli's school and calling for his expulsion from their midst (Graaf, 1988). Moleli was subsequently murdered on 21 June 1896 during the Shona and Ndebele uprising by forces loyal to Mbuya Nehanda and Sekuru Kaguvi.

The life and martyrdom of Modumedi Moleli has inspired dramatizations in memory of Moleli's pioneering Christian missionary work among Wesleyan Methodist converts in the Mashonaland province. The Moleli play is not a published play script. People's sense of the play is based on drama performances which are presented by secondary school children from Wesleyan schools. These plays are produced with the assistance of school teachers and church elders. The performances are based on a series of scenarios which seek to approximate the historical circumstances immediately surrounding Moleli's teachings and his martyrdom. Worshippers from Wesleyan Methodist centres converge on Waddilove Mission near Marondera to celebrate the life and martyrdom of this early Christian martyr. The Moleli play is a depiction of how saintly white missionaries and their surrogates became targets of 'dark' forces of the Shona and Ndebele uprising in 1896 following pronouncements sent out by Sekuru Kaguvi and Mbuya Nehanda who were the spiritual leaders of the Shona uprising.

Being a play which is not published but is presented by a number of different school groups, the Moleli play adopts a basic framework which goes along the following broad outline; Chief Mashayamombe and Headman Chizengeni heed the call by Sekuru Kaguvi pronouncing that all white people and their supporters are to be eliminated because they have desecrated indigenous religion and culture. Headman Chizengeni assigns Chiriseri, one of his subordinates and also a supporter of the uprising, to eliminate all local missionaries and whites who are based near Waddilove Mission in Chief Mashayamombe's area. Chiriseri's first task is to eliminate a white farmer by the name of James White. According to historical records, James White and

Modumedi Moleli were close friends (Graaf, 1988). When James White is attacked, Moleli sets out to assist him, whereupon he is also waylaid, attacked and fatally wounded by Chiriseri's men. Although Moleli is in possession of a rifle at the time of the attack, he refuses to use it in self-defence saying that guns were not meant to kill fellow humans. After they have murdered Moleli, Chiriseri's party heads for Moleli's homestead which they ransack before murdering some members of his household.

From the scenarios outlined above and from our encounter with actual performance, the Moleli play dramatizes forces of evil and darkness against forces of Christian enlightenment and salvation. It pits forces of meekness against forces of darkness and blind retribution. The performance of the play in a devotional commemorative context is what informs our analysis of the play as a latter day example of medieval liturgies.

Bernard Mamiyeri Mizeki of the Anglican Church was another early Christian martyr whose life and work is commemorated through drama. Originally from Mozambique, Bernard Mizeki moved to Cape Town where he later converted to Christianity. In 1891 Mizeki volunteered to accompany Bishop Bruce, a white Anglican missionary, to Mashonaland to help to establish the Anglican Church. Bernard Mizeki was murdered in 1896 by forces loyal to the uprising. The life and martyrdom of Bernard Mizeki is commemorated annually through worship, song, dance and drama by members of the Anglican Church on the weekend closest to 18 June at the Bernard Mizeki shrine near Marondera in Mashonaland East Province (see Fig. 1). The shrine is located at the site of Bernard Mizeki's homestead where he is believed to have been murdered. According to Reverend T. Mutongomanya (2010), the commemoration of the life and martyrdom of Bernard Mizeki has been taking place every year since 1905.

The unpublished Mizeki play is presented under the title of *The Life and Martyrdom of Bernard Mizeki*. Having evolved over a considerable period of time, the script is presented as a one act play of six scenes. With an elaborately presented cast list, clearly written dialogue and extensive stage directions, the Mizeki play comes across as a modern realist play that has enjoyed critical and stylistic inputs spanning a long period of performance. The performance of the unpublished script evidences a play which has been put together by a group of people with a professional knowledge of scripted drama though the actual authorship remains anonymous. According to T. Mutongomanya (2010) the same script is used each year for the annual performances. Preparations and rehearsals for the play are conducted at the Harare Anglican Cathedral and these are led by a church drama group consisting mainly of church youths who work with the assistance of the Mothers' Union and interested church elders. Each year the main festival, which incorporates commemorative worship and performances of the play is organized by the Bernard Mizeki Guild, which is led by Reverend J.C. Gada according to whom (2010), the play enjoys two performances. The first performance takes place on Friday night and the second on Saturday afternoon at the end of the main service. Reverend Gada says that the two performances are the main attraction for the parishioners.

1. *Signpost indicating the route from the shrine to the open air theatre space where* The Life and Martyrdom of Bernard Mizeki *is performed annually* (*All photographs with the kind permission and courtesy of the Anglican Diocese of Harare*)

2. *The rock from which actors in the Mizeki play simulate the booming sound and brilliant flash of lightning which preceded Bernard Mizeki's mysterious disappearance.*

3. *The glass frame outside the main entrance to the Bernard Mizeki Shrine. It contains photographs and information about the life and times of Bernard Mizeki.*

4. *Rev. J.C. Gada co-ordinator of the Bernard Mizeki Guild stands in front of the rock where Bernard Mizeki used to pray for his converts.*

Although the written script for *The Life and Martyrdom of Bernard Mizeki* is very short, the performance lasts on average over one-and-a-half hours. The disparity between the written script and the actual performance can only imply that the written script serves as a guideline and a road map to a performance enhanced by improvisation. This is easily done, given the fact that the play script spans a considerably long period of time in Bernard Mizeki's life and ministry in Chief Mangwende's area.

The following is an overview of the key events dramatized in *The Life and Martyrdom of Bernard Mizeki*; having entered Southern Rhodesia through Mozambique, Mizeki decides to settle among Chief Mangwende's people near Nhowe in Mashonaland Province. Mizeki quickly learns Shona, and immediately sets out to achieve his evangelical work. Among the first converts to Christianity is Zvandiparira, Chief Mangwende's head wife. Unfortunately however, Muchemwa, one of Chief Mangwende's sons, deeply resents the conversion of Zvandiparira as he also sympathizes with the cause of the 1896 uprising against missionaries and colonialists. As a result he deeply resents Mizeki's presence in Chief Mangwende's area. Muchemwa and his brothers are joined in their hatred and resentment for Mizeki by Denha, who is the local *n'anga* or traditional medicine man. According to the script and information brochure posted at the shrine, Denha deeply resents Mizeki for preaching against 'polygamous marriages, child murder, witchcraft, spirit worship, animal sacrifices and drunkenness'. Mizeki is also accused of being responsible for 'the rinderpest, the drought and famine, the plague of locusts, the slaughter and branding of cattle and the imposition of a hut tax' (undated).

When the spiritual leaders of the 1896 uprising send orders to their followers to eliminate all whites, missionaries and their surrogates, Mizeki obviously becomes one of Muchemwa's targets. When the uprising breaks out, Mizeki is advised to go and seek refuge with his principals in Umtali (present-day Mutare) but he steadfastly refuses. Muchemwa's forces then lay siege to Mizeki's homestead. Everyone in the household escapes into the night except Mizeki, the prime target, who has been fatally wounded. At end of the attack, members of Mizeki's household return to the compound and are surprised not to find him. He is eventually found at a water spring not far from his homestead, weak with pain and the excessive loss of blood. He refuses their assistance, insisting on being left alone to die.

His wife and the rescue party decide to go back to the homestead to prepare food and medicine for Mizeki, but on their return to the spot where they left him lying injured, there is a dazzling flash of light and a booming sound similar to the roll of thunder. These phenomena emanate from the spot where Mizeki lay (see Fig 2). Moments later when they have recovered from the shock, they realize that Mizeki has disappeared. This mysterious disappearance and the circumstances surrounding Mizeki's murder have led many adherents of the Anglican Church from far and wide to canonize him. They are convinced that he is a local saint of the Anglican Church who was transported to heaven in a chariot of fire, reminiscent of Elijah in the biblical account.

The commemorative events at his shrine are coordinated and organized by the Bernard Mizeki Guild and hosted by students, teachers and priests from the nearby Bernard Mizeki College. Representatives of Bernard Mizeki's descendants come from Mozambique, and other participants come from Europe as well as southern Africa. (Gada, 2010)

Earlier I argued that early religious drama in colonial Rhodesia may be read as liturgical to the extent that it was performed in contexts of devotion and worship, incorporating aspects of biblical teachings. Here the script for *The Life and Martyrdom of Bernard Mizeki* may be read as liturgical drama to the extent that it contains recitations drawn from Anglican Church sermons, which is an indication that besides chronicling Mizeki's life, one of the chief purposes of the performance is worship rather than mere entertainment. This is particularly evident in Scene III, entitled 'The Gospel is Brought to the Mangwende People'. In this scene Mizeki leads his congregation of new converts in a call and response prayer saying:

Bernard: *Mwari iwe wakadzidzisa moyo yavanhu vako vanotendeseka, nokutumira kwavari rujeko rwoMweya wako unoyera: Ipa kuti nouyo Mweya mumwoyo tive norushananguko rwakanaka muzviro zvese, nokuzofara nariini mukunyaradza kwako kunoyera; pamusana pokufanira kwa Jesu Kristu, Muponisi wedu, uyo agere nokutonga newe, muuhumwe hwomweya mumweyo, Mwari mumwe nariini nariini. Amen* (All repeat the phrases of 'the Lord's Prayer' after Bernard) ... (undated)

Our dear heavenly father who sent us the Holy Spirit, grant us the good grace to repent and live in righteousness in everything that we do, to have eternal happiness within the Holy Spirit, knowing that you sent your son Jesus Christ our saviour who sits by your right hand side in the oneness of the Holy Spirit forever and ever. Amen. (All repeat the Lord's Prayer after Bernard)...

In Scene IV, entitled 'Bernard's Marriage at Rusape' biblical vestments are similarly chanted by Father Mtobi when he pronounces Mizeki and Mutwa married, saying;

Fr Mtobi: *Vadikani kwazvo, taungana muno pamberi paMwari nepamberi peChechi yake kuzokumbanidza munhurume nouyu munhukadzi mumuchato unoyera, uru ndirwo rugaro rwakafanira kuremekedzwa rwakarurwa naMwari pachake.* (undated)

Dear all who are present, we are gathered here today to join this man and this woman in holy matrimony, for this is what god has ordained for all men, and to which we give respect in the name of our heavenly father.

In actual performance, the audiences participate, joining the call and response sequences in such a way that the division between performer and spectator becomes blurred. Audience participation also comes in the singing and dancing of Anglican Church hymns which accompany the action, opening and closing some scenes. The incorporation of biblical vestments as illustrated above with religious song and dance further underlines the play's performance as belonging primarily within religious rather than a secular context.

That *The Life and Martyrdom of Bernard Mizeki*'s authorship is anonymous and that it only serves as a working script which is used to guide actual performance may be read as an indication of the absence of pressure to conform to canonical styles of play production with their insistence on individual authorship and slavish adherence to the written script. It also shows the hybridity of form, with Christian religious ideas being presented in pre-colonial indigenous performance forms.

Medieval *Everyman* in colonial Rhodesia

I now turn to more formal examples of contemporary African productions of religious drama in a published form. There are various instances of contemporary African productions of the medieval morality play *Everyman*, either in the original version or in translation. Martin Banham (1998) cites the Ghanaian playwright Efua Sutherland's *Odasani*, P. Mbaya and Albert Mongita's *Bisa Batu (Mister Everybody)* in the then Zaire (Democratic Republic of Congo) and the Nigerian playwright Duro Ladipo's *Eda*.

In colonial Rhodesia the closest example of a dramatization of the medieval morality play *Everyman* is the scripting and performance of a play entitled *Mutambo wapaNyika* at the Catholic Church's Gokomere Mission. It was published in 1958 by Mambo Press, a printing press owned by the Catholic Church, and it stands out as one of the earliest scripted performances to take place at a mission station in Southern Rhodesia. *Mutambo wapaNyika* is a direct translation of Father Calderon de la Barca's *El Gran Teatro Mundo*, which was written in Spain in the seventeenth century. Calderon's play largely approximates the original version. Unlike the original, in Calderon's play as translated at Gokomere, Tenzi (God) summons Nyika (Earth) to prepare a play in his honour:

Tenzi: *Zvandiri musiki wako nomuumbi woumiro hwako undiombere nokundigadzirira mutambo... Uyezve hupeny hwose hwomunhu mutambo chete. Saka zviunga zvedenga zvinoda kuona nhasi mutambo panyika. Iwe Nyika chiita dariro romutambo vanhu vagoita vatambi.*

Nyika: *Mambo wangu mukuru naTenzi wangu, ndozarura dariro rangu rakaita ndandanda kuti vanhu vagoedzwa mumutambo. Handingarambi. Ndinoita senhumbi dzebasa muruoko rwemhizha* (1958).

God: As creator and giver of life to all men, I hereby summon you and instruct you to prepare a play in my honour... The play's cardinal lesson be 'life is but a process.' All the angels in heaven would like to see this play and I hereby instruct you to set the stage and bring all my subjects as performers.

Earth: Almighty lord and my master. I am now setting the stage for you so that the people may audition for the play. I cannot but obey your command, I am no more than a tool in the hand of an expert craftsman, Your wish is my command. Whatever command you give, I will obey.

Calderon's play, like its Gokomere version, differs from the original in that besides the living, Tenzi (God) also summons the souls of all the unborn in order that they are able to witness the process and meaning of life before Nyika assigns some of them to various roles in the play. In addition, Calderon's play also includes choirs of angels, Mother Mary, Innocence, and a king and his subordinates. The other characters such as Death, Beauty, Goods, Five Wits, Good Deeds and Angel Michael largely approximate those in the original version of *Everyman*. By introducing Mother Mary and the concept of purgatory in his play Calderon firmly locates his version within a Catholic context.

Unlike Calderon's play, *Mutambo wapaNyika* has a collective authorship, having been written and translated by Catholic fathers, teachers and students at Gokomere, one of the country's oldest Catholic mission stations, in the southern part of the country in present-day Masvingo Province. Whereas in the medieval period morality plays may have existed mainly as oral performances or liturgies in Catholic churches, *Mutambo wapaNyika* enjoys a dual existence in both the oral and the written forms through the aegis of the Catholic Church owned Mambo Press. This has allowed the play wider propagation and performance to a much larger Catholic community.

Mutambo wapaNyika, The Moleli Play and *The Life and Martyrdom of Bernard Mizeki* as medieval morality and liturgical drama in a contemporary context

Like its medieval forerunners *Everyman* and *El Gran Teatro del Mundo, Mutambo wapaNyika* has a strong leaning towards a biblical lesson. It reads like a sermon whose cardinal lessons are the biblical commandments 'love thy neighbour' and 'live and work in the service of god your one and only creator'. The play continually exhorts its audiences to keep in mind the fact that human life is no more than a process which should be lived solely in the service of God: 'Rupenyu rwomunhu mutambo chete' *(Life is but a process)*. The presentation of the play within a religious context of devotion and worship is introduced right at the beginning when a chorus of angels sings a hymn in Latin, reminding us of the play's strong Catholic influences. The rest of the play's dialogue is also interspersed with numerous choral songs of worship. This sustains the notion of the play as a performance which is presented within the context of religious worship. It also places the performance in a local Zimbabwean context where music, song and dance are an integral part of religious worship.

Both the plot and theme in Father Calderon de la Barca's play, and its Gokomere translation, closely resemble the medieval classic *Everyman*. Like the original it is a Christian allegory based on the Christian doctrine of righteousness and redemption. The play depicts man as a sinner who can only be redeemed through repentance while God is depicted as a force which is omnipotent, infinitely patient and merciful. When the play opens, the narrator announces the play's theme as one which is based on the cardinal biblical injunction 'Ida mumwe wako sokuzvida kwaunoita iwe. Itai zvakarurama. Kumusoro kwenyu kuna Mwari' (*Love thy neighbour. Live in righteousness. Remember your one and only God almighty*).

Like the characters in *Everyman*, the characters in *Mutambo wapaNyika* are embodiments of abstract values, mainly vices and virtues. The characters are confined to the roles defined for them by their names and their identities. Having been assigned to create a play in honour of God, Nyika (Earth) creates a moral allegory with the following as some of the characters: Mupfumi (Wealth), Murimi (Bounty), Ungwaru (Wisdom), Unaki (Beauty), Mucheche (Innocence), Rufu (Death) and Mupemhi (Poverty or Meekness). Each one of the main characters is invited to request just one thing from God and they each choose in accordance with their names or character's identities. Mupemhi (Poverty or Meekness) who is the main character then goes around begging for assistance from the other characters. They all decline to assist him except Ungwaru (Wisdom) who pities him and provides him with food and shelter. Just when all the characters are at the peak of happiness in their respective roles, following their various endowments, a new character, Rufu (Death) arrives. He makes the inescapable demand of death on all the characters. The only character who welcomes Rufu is Ungwaru because he is assured that when he dies he will go to heaven where he will continue to lead a happy and prosperous life on account of his virtuous earthly deeds.

The play ends with Nyika marching all the characters to the throne of God for judgement where they are all condemned to eternal punishment. Only Mupemhi and Ungwaru are admitted to heaven on account of their good earthly deeds. The condemned characters subsequently repent their sins before they are cleansed by Maria Mutsvene (Mother Mary) after which they are happily admitted to heaven.

If read as a form of liturgical drama, The *Moleli Play* and *The Life and Martyrdom of Bernard Mizeki* display considerable affinities with medieval moralities in so far as the two plays also teach biblical lessons. Greenwald, Schultz and Pomo have written that 'Moralities dramatized the battle between good and evil for the soul of an ordinary person on life's pilgrimage towards eternity' (2001: 43). In line with lessons of the Bible, characters and their actions belong to two distinct groups, that of the heathen villains led by Chiriseri, Muchemwa and others and that of the Christian saints led by Modumedi Moleli and Bernard Mizeki. Chiriseri and Muchemwa's men are portrayed as unreasonable, cold-blooded murderers while Moleli, Mizeki and their Christian converts are portrayed as virtuous, saintly, and innocent souls who lived and died trying to convert the heathens to Christianity. It is clear that the characters in these two plays belong to two distinctly opposing sides; that of the saints and that of forces of evil led by the leaders of the uprising. Also in line with biblical teachings, these characters represent the vices of hatred and cruelty, or the opposite virtues of meekness, obedience, and selfless devotion correspondingly.

The virtues of meekness and devotion and the biblical injunction to 'turn the other cheek' are particularly reinforced in both plays. In the *Moleli* play, Modumedi Moleli steadfastly refuses to use his rifle in self defence even in the face of a mortal attack by Chiriseri's men. Similarly, in *The Life and Martyrdom of Bernard Mizeki*, Mizeki not only refuses to escape and take refuge in Umtali, he also refuses members of his family to carry him back to the safety of his compound. His last words to his wife Mutwa are quoted below:

Mizeki: *Madzibaba ako andiuraya. Ndavakufa. Asi ndinoda kuti iwe nemwana ari mudumbu mubhabhatidzwe. Usafunge hako kuti nekuti madzibaba ako zvavandiuraya, basa ravafundisi nevadzidzi rapera. Kwete, ini ndafa kuchaya vamwe vakawanda uye richava zuva rimwe chete iro hama dzako dzese dzichaita maKristu.* (undated)

Your uncles have attacked me and I am dying. However, I want you and our unborn child to be baptized. The work of the priests and the teachers is not ended. When I am dead more priests will come and one day all your people will be Christians.

In both instances, the sense of self-righteousness of the two martyrs assumes messianic dimensions in much the same way as Christ steadfastly declines to call upon the might of his heavenly father to save him from the crucifix.

Conclusion

This article has attempted to analyze the documentation, influences and context of performance of early religious drama in colonial Rhodesia. It has attempted to analyze two plays based on the lives, ministry and martyrdom of Modumedi Moleli of the Wesleyan Methodist Church and Bernard Mamiyeri Mizeki of the Anglican Church. It has also attempted to analyze a local translation and adaptation of Father Pedro Calderon de la Barca's medieval play entitled *El Gran Teatro del Mundo* which was translated and produced by teachers and students at a Catholic mission in colonial Rhodesia under the title of *Mutambo wapaNyika*.

From reading these plays it is evident that they were used in Christian proselytizing. What is interesting is that these dramas seem to demonstrate strong affinities with liturgical drama and medieval morality plays which were used in earlier European Christian worship and education.

In the case of the *Moleli Play* and *The Life and Martyrdom of Bernard Mizeki*, these scripts appear in the form of anonymous working scripts whose main purpose is to provide a guideline of action and scenarios surrounding the lives of the two martyrs. This, together with the incorporation of song and prayer book invocations, particularly in the case of the Bernard Mizeki play, locates these dramas within an oral context of devotion and worship that is not dissimilar to many forms of African oral performances. Gokomere mission's *Mutambo wapaNyika* also incorporates choral music and numerous biblical injunctions taken directly from the scriptures, thereby locating the play within a similar context.

In terms of plot, theme and character all three plays reinforce biblical teachings in which characters clearly stand for the abstract notions of good which is pitted against forces of evil. To that extent the three plays may be read respectively as medieval moralities and liturgical drama set within a contemporary context.

An analysis of the three plays also indicates that there is an interesting hybridity of form, with religious ideas being presented in pre-colonial indigenous performance traditions, which incorporate orality, improvisation and audience involvement. The marriage between African cultural norms of orality with earlier European forms clearly demonstrates that in spite of the time and spatial divide between the two continents there are striking similarities between the forms of medieval moralities, liturgical drama and traditional African performance. The compatibility between the two forms made it easy for the former to be easily incorporated within a colonial cultural context.

Finally, the article has attempted to throw light on an aspect of Zimbabwean or colonial Rhodesian drama which has previously not received much scholarly attention. From the above analysis, it may well be that there are other hybrid forms of early Zimbabwean drama which have failed to attract critical scholarly attention on account of their being archived in oral rather than in written and published forms. This could form the basis of further interesting research.

BIBLIOGRAPHY

Primary Sources
Anonymous (Undated) *The Life and Martyrdom of Bernard Mizeki* (Unpublished)
Anonymous (Undated) *The Moleli Play* (Unpublished)
Calderon de la Barca, Pedro (1958) Trans. of *El Gran Teotro del Mundo Mutambo wapaNyika* (Gweru, Mambo Press)

Interviews
N. Chivandikwa Personal Interview, 10 March 2010
J. C. Gada. Personal Interview, 3 March 2010
T. Mutongomanya. Personal Interview, 2 March 2010

Secondary Sources
Ashcroft, B., Griffith, G. & Tiffin, H. (1995) *The Post-colonial Studies Reader*. London: Routledge
Banham, M. (1998) 'Notes on *Eda*: A Nigerian Everyman' in Catherine Batt (ed.) *Essays in Honour of Peter Meredith, Leeds Studies in English* New Series XXIX. Leeds: School of English.
Brockett, O. (2000) *The Essential Theatre (7th Ed.)* Belmont, Thomson: Wadsworth.
Cohen, R. (2000) *Theatre*. Mountain View California, Mayfield.
Flood, D.G.H. (1973) 'The Contribution of the London Missionary Society to African Education in Ndebeleland 1859–1959'. In Anthony J. Dachs (ed.) *Christianity South of Zambezi*. Gweru: Mambo Press, pp. 97–107.
Gann, L.H. (1965) *A History of Southern Rhodesia; Early Days to 1934*. London: Chatto & Windus.
Graaf, B. (1988) *Modumedi Moleli*. Gweru: Mambo Press.
Greenwald, M. L., Schultz, R. & Pomo, R.D.(2001) *The Longman Anthology of Drama & Theatre: A Global Perspective*. New York: Longman.
Snell, M. L. (1986) *Bernard Mizeki of Zimbabwe*. Harare: Kensington Consultants.
Weller, J.C. (1980) *Anglican Centenary in Zimbabwe 1891-1991*. Mutare: Zimpapers.
Wilson, E. & Goldfarb, A. (2004) *Living Theatre: A History*. Boston: McGraw Hill.
Worthen, W.B. (2000) *The Harcourt Brace Anthology of Drama (3rd Ed.)* New York: Harcourt.
Zinyemba, R. (1986) *Zimbabwean Drama: A Study of Shona and English Plays*. Gweru: Mambo Press.

Contesting Constructions of Cultural Production in & through Urban Theatre in Rhodesia, *c.* 1890–1950

SAMUEL RAVENGAI

In this article I attempt to analyse three urban African performances; *Nyawo*, the tea party, and *Beni*. I employ the socio-historical analysis model which attempts to understand the relationship between the field of cultural production and the field of power. Historically the ascendancy to power of the bourgeoisie in Western Europe facilitated the assimilation of its culture and taste by virtually all of Western civil society. Colonisation in Rhodesia (in its blue print form) intended to use the same principle of extending English rulership and influence with the goal of transforming Rhodesia to be like the metropolitan state in manifesting the nature and will of the English in lifestyle, actions, activities and culture.[1] As evidenced by the nature of these urban African performances, domination does not necessarily result in absolute collaboration. Rhodesian discourse was both collaborated with and resisted by African cultural producers. I look at this element of collaboration and resistance through Ranajit Guha's (1997) frame of the articulation of power where domination implies subordination. In the case of colonial administrations, coercion seems to outweigh persuasion in the articulation of domination thereby denying absolute assimilation of colonial culture by Africans as was the case of civil society in Western Europe.

Rhodesian discourse and power

According to Michel Foucault (1976) discourse is an institutionalised way of thinking that intrinsically erects a cordon to define what can be written, performed or said about a specific topic. In theorising about the discourse on language, Foucault (1976) argues that the production of discourse is controlled, selected, organised and redistributed according to clearly defined procedures. It, therefore, follows that a discourse is an invented truth manufactured by a dominant group in a society and peddled as the only acceptable way of thinking and doing things as Foucault adumbrates '[e]ach society has its regime of truth...that is the types of discourse which it accepts and makes function as true...' (1980: 131). Rhodesian discourse was a collection of 'truths' manufactured by European scholars (such as Hegel, Charles Darwin, Sigmund Freud, De Gobineau, Linnaeus, Blumenbach and others) who formulated cultural frames that were applied by various European empires. Their ideas are often grouped together in postcolonial criticism as colonial discourse, which is/was a framework sometimes used by Europeans living in Africa and/or diasporic Europeans to represent Africans[2] as pathological or the inferior other. Rhodesians[3] were influenced by philosophical and (pseudo-)scientific works of these scholars in their dealings with Africans. The whole vision of colonialism in Rhodesia was summed up by Cecil John Rhodes, the proprietor of the Chartered Company (British South Africa Company) that ran the country until 1922, who declared '[e]qual rights for all civilised men' (Mamdani, 1996: 17). The 'uncivilised' African would be subjected to a process of tutelage in order to enjoy the privileges of citizenship.

Rhodesian discourse covered a whole spectrum of intellectual activity including the field of cultural production (theatre, literature, drama, film, music, dance and fine art). Pierre Bourdieu provides a framework that postcolonial theory has appropriated to explain the relationship between the coloniser and the colonised, and in our case between the dominant white Rhodesians and the dominated black Africans. The struggle in the Rhodesian cultural field over the imposition of the legitimate public imagery is inseparable from the struggle between white Rhodesians and African cultural producers to impose principles or definitions of human accomplishment. Bourdieu offers an explanation that is equally applicable to the Rhodesian field of cultural production, where he argues that:

> The field of cultural production is the site of struggles in which what is at stake is the power to impose the dominant definitions of the writer (artist)... In short the fundamental stake in literary struggles is the monopoly of power to say with authority who are authorised to call themselves writers ... it is the monopoly of the power to consecrate producers or products... (Emphasis added, 1993: 42)

This struggle to impose the dominant discourse is explicable in terms of what Foucault calls 'power' which resonates with Antonio Gramsci's (1971) concept of 'rule', although the two terms are not necessarily synonymous. Rule constitutes the coercive apparatus of the state established according to law in order to exclude, blockade and repress those groups who do not agree to the various forms of domination by the coloniser. Even where there is no evidence of non-compliance Gramsci (ibid.) argues that this apparatus is proactively put in place in anticipation of moments of crisis. However, power and rule would be fragile phenomena if they worked on the level of force, or to put it in Foucauldian terms, 'exercising itself only in a negative way' (1980: 59). Hegemony and discourse come in to supplement power and rule. Gramsci defines hegemony as 'the spontaneous consent given by the great masses of the population to the general directions imposed on social life by the dominant group' (ibid.: 12). This consent given to Europeans by Africans comes 'naturally' due to the perceived accumulated prestige of the white cultural producers. This consent was given grudgingly in Rhodesia after both the

Ndebele and the Shona were defeated in the 1893 Anglo-Ndebele war and the 1996-7 Anglo-Shona war. Although force was occasionally used to recruit local labour and suppress black workers' strikes, colonialism proceeded in Rhodesia through the soft power of a discourse that persuaded Africans to view themselves as inferior to the white race. This came through a discourse embedded in a skewed education curriculum (Rodney, 1989; O'Callaghan, 1977) which promoted such values. This was reinforced by processes of economic and cultural undermining by the imposition of European systems in most aspects of life. Persuasion, however, was by far outweighed by coercion.

In order to get that spontaneous consent Rhodesians had to produce knowledge that justified the domination of Africans. It seems to me that power cannot exist without the knowledge which justifies it. Power, therefore, insists upon the production of discourses of a particular 'truth', which it forces cultural producers to speak and write about. Power will continually renew, recreate and modify itself until it is capable of institutionalising and professionalising every field including rewarding producers who further its pursuits. In a way, power, far from denying knowledge produces knowledge to serve it. Power and knowledge support and imply one another.

The Bourdieusian diagram representing the field of cultural production and the field of power can be reinterpreted and modified to dramatise the power relations between the Rhodesian field of power and the artistic field with its sub-fields of European theatre and African theatre. It will explain how African cultural producers resisted and collaborated with colonial authorities by demonstrating centres of sameness, difference and resistance.

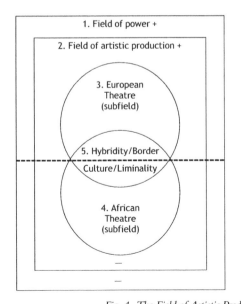
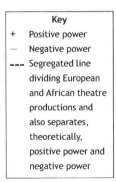

Fig. 1. The Field of Artistic Production

The field of power (1) is the one that generates the laws for social engineering as well as the ideology and discourse to justify its power. However, the field of power is weak on its own. It must depend on cultural structures for its coherence and justification. Something needs to supply an explanation for colonialism and this is the field of artistic production (2) which subsumes a variety of subfields within it. For our purposes, I have singled out two subfields (3) and (4) representing European and African theatre respectively. The imaginary broken line represents a racially segregated artistic field and also divides all fields into two polarities – the positive (+) and powerful pole which is occupied by whites and the negative (-) less powerful pole which is occupied by mostly black cultural producers. The artistic field is a site of struggle since agents who occupy available positions 3, 4 and 5 are in a perennial competition for two things – public imagery which must be allowed to float in the minds of people and symbolic and cultural capital. This is an unfair competition, particularly during the colonial period because agents occupying positions 4 and 5 (blacks) lack adequate power to decide on spaces where they can show their images as well as power to consecrate their artistes. The power to give these resources lies outside the field of African theatre. It lies with academics, publishers, critics and producers who are conduits of colonial power. As the black artist moves from the bottom of position 4 to position 5, the more capital s/he gets in terms of recognition, consecration and prestige. Because of the subjectivity and agency of the black playwright, there is a limit to which the artistic and political field can exert force on her creativity. The intersecting area represents the point of contact, sameness, and at the same time difference. This is the point of entanglement where hybrid texts are formed.

Even if blacks occupying positions 4 and 5 are subjected to the same pressures they resist them in different ways. Agents occupying position 4 have largely refused to succumb to the external structures and continue to produce traditional theatre. This explains the phenomenon of the co-habitation of both modernity and tradition in the same geopolitical space. These agents have customs and laws of their own that preserve them even against the harshest external conditions, for example ceremonial performances (weddings and coronations) continued to be performed. Ritual performances that had to do with the survival of the community such as the rain-making ceremony (*doro romukwerera*) continued even with stiff opposition from resident missionaries (McCulloch, 2000). However, for many communities, maintaining a positive relationship with nature was more important than obeying colonial laws such as the African Affairs Act and the Witchcraft Suppression Act which forbade such practices.

Sally Moore (1978) has provided anthropological theories of resistance that are useful to explain the production and maintenance of black performances in the early days of the colonial city. She argues that the process of regularisation of society through ideologies, social systems, laws, rules and force or the threat of it do not always produce what she calls 'situational adjustment'. This is as a result of continuous struggle between pressure to establish or maintain order or regularity and the attendant counter-activities and complexity that make life unsuited to absolute ordering. Imposed rules, customs and frameworks that operate in a community, she argues, work in the presence of areas of 'indeterminacy', 'ambiguity', 'uncertainty' and 'manipulability'. Social relationships and processes are in their nature mutable and to impose laws is an attempt to fix their mutability. She argues that order never fully takes place. Moore's theoretical position aptly explains the existence of African performances in the then Salisbury and other mining towns even though both missionaries and colonialists had banned some of them. Bans and prohibitions did not always result in compliance, as can be seen in the following examples. On 18 August 1899 the British South Africa Company passed the Witchcraft Suppression Act which defined witchcraft as 'the throwing of bones, the use of charms and any other means or devices adopted in the practice of sorcery' (Statute Law of Zimbabwe, 1899: 295). This ordinance was used to ban *mhande*, a Shona traditional dance (Plastow, 1996). *Nyawo* was banned in the mid 1920s (Parry, 1999). The courtship dance (*mbende*), danced by the Zezuru (a sub-group of the Shona) was banned in 1910, but continued under an undercover name (*jerusarema*) (Asante, 2000: 44). Missionaries had the power to ban a dance which they thought was not consistent with Christian values and this had been the fate of *mbende*. The same missionary, however, reinstated the dance after a plea by the local chief in Mrewa[4] (ibid.).

Ranajit Guha (1997) while talking about Indian experiences of colonialism concurs with Sally Moore and goes further to give his own reason for the failure of the colonial administration to achieve absolute assimilation of colonial subjects as had happened between the Western bourgeoisie and its civil society. He argues that colonialism relied on autocracy (instead of democracy), coercion and force in order to subjugate its subjects. In this kind of domination coercion far outweighed persuasion for there could be no colonialism without force. Guha calls this condition 'non-hegemonic' (where the term hegemony is used to describe a system of domination where persuasion outweighs coercion) and argues that domination cannot be absolute where force is applied more than persuasion. He proffers the argument that in this particular case the articulation of domination is followed by subordination which is characterised by both collaboration and resistance. This seems to be true when applied to the Rhodesian field of cultural production as evidenced by performances that reflect this condition of collaboration and resistance. Early African migrant workers did not become bewildered and passive aliens in a white world. Neither did they jettison their cultural baggage upon entering a predominantly white city.

Oral performance as collaboration and resistance

Rhodesia (now Zimbabwe) between 1890 and 1930 did not have a standard Shona orthography.[5] Missionaries translated the Bible and wrote books and pamphlets using dialect systems that they had independently developed in their areas of jurisdiction. It follows that there is no known written play that has survived to provide evidence of written drama during this period.

However, this is not to suggest that there were no African performances during the period 1890–1950, nor that the history of performance began with the arrival of Europeans. Since I am interested in how African theatre and performance responded to given socio-political conditions and experiences, it follows that I draw examples from the historical trajectory influenced by colonialism. Another interesting dimension of this oral performance period is that there is a general absence of Shona and Ndebele people from the repertory of urban performances, which is where real contact between Europeans and Africans was more pronounced.[6] The urban space, therefore, presents a fertile case study of African cultural responses to colonial discourse. Paradoxically, a large proportion of the urban African population was drawn from outside Rhodesia. Most of the immigrants came from Malawi, Zambia, the DRC and Mozambique. While for towns located in drought prone areas like Bulawayo, the population of local Ndebele people was relatively higher, Salisbury (now Harare) was marked by a relative scarcity of Shona people.[7] The significance of this is that the cultural life of the early urban dwellers in Rhodesia was dominated by northern ethnic groups. The lingua franca of most of the mining towns, settlements and cities was Chinyanja – the urban language of northern ethnic groups. It follows that performances, music and other forms of recreational culture had a northern flavour. According to Yoshikuni (1999) this trend began to change after 1950 when large numbers of Shona migrants settled in the towns – especially Salisbury. Before 1950, according to Yoshikuni, the Shonas in Salisbury were less than 40 per cent of the African population, however, he demonstrates that '[t]he proportion of Southern Rhodesian Africans rose from 41 per cent in 1951 to 72 per cent in 1962 and 83 per cent in 1969' (Yoshikuni, 1999: 120). It is thus not surprising that from 1968, we see an exponential growth of drama written in African languages as well as oral performances from the increasing numbers of urban Africans in Rhodesian.

Kirby (1974) has argued that African oral performances can be broken down into the following seven categories. They consist of simple enactments (such as *mahumbwe*/child role playing), ritual enactments (such as *doro romukwerera*/rain making ceremony), story-telling performances (*ngano*), spirit-cult enactments (*bira*/ancestor worship), ceremonial performances (weddings, coronations, *Beni*) and comedies (*ndyaringo*). However, the missionaries tolerated some of these, and banned others, particularly any performance modes that praised or worshipped what they perceived to be 'heathen' gods, like ritual enactments and spirit cult enactments. With a few possible exceptions, these remained banned in areas under full control of missionaries.

How then did oral performances collaborate with and resist colonial discourse? Going back to Figure 1 above, I would argue that there were oral performances that appropriated Western styles and mocked Rhodesian discourse from within by refusing to be wholly Western. These include tea parties and *Beni* performances. The other category of dances such as *Nyawo* were refused entry into the arena accepted by colonials. When *Nyawo* performances were banned they went underground and continued to be performed once at the start of each new moon out in the secluded darker areas of the city. The

banning, according to Parry (1999) took place in 1920. What is known, however, is that it was brought by immigrants from Malawi who came to Southern
Rhodesia looking for work at the beginning of colonisation in the 1890s and
throughout the early twentieth century. The other variation of *Nyawo* came
from Northern Rhodesia (Zambia) via Zambian job seekers. According to
Sambo (2002) Zambian immigrants brought what he calls the 'social Nyawo
performance' while Malawian immigrants brought what he calls the 'mysterious type'. The mysterious *Nyawo* is a ritualistic performance played once a
month. Although it is entertaining, its main purpose is efficacy achieved by
initiating neophytes, giving supplication to the spirits of the dead and maintaining cosmic order. For this reason it is a religious institution only welcoming
those who are born into it: the Chewa. The social *Nyawo* is non-ritualistic. It
can be performed at social gatherings, dance festivals and galas for entertainment. There is no religious motif to it. Historical explanations, for example
Rangely (1952) as cited by Sambo (2002) offer Tanzania and the DRC
(formerly Belgian Congo/Zaire) as the origin of *Nyawo*. The performance
moved further south into Malawi and Mozambique through intermittent
migrations. Sambo, relying on the work of Rangely (ibid.) mentions that
Nyawo or *Gule WaMkulu*, as it is known in Chewa language, was brought into
Malawi by the Maravi people from Lubaland in the DRC. Oral tradition
indicates that the performance was invented in Malawi during a famine as a
way of getting food from villagers who came to watch this dance. A character
called Phiri was later joined by dignitaries of the village wearing masks as they
did not want to be seen as partaking in a somewhat demeaning way of getting
alms from equally starving people (Sambo, ibid.). The performance developed
into a masked dance. This is the performance that was brought to Rhodesia
(Zimbabwe) by young Malawians seeking for fortune from about 1900.

In the early 1900s *Nyawo* performance absolutely refused to collaborate with
colonial demands. These early *Nyawo* performances were embellished with
skin paintings, masks made of animal skins and feathers as a way of constructing
characters. They put on masks of animals such as cows (*chimombemombe*) zebras
and ostriches. With time, an element of collaboration with colonial discourse
crept into the *Nyawo* performance, as evidenced by how the costumes changed
from skins and feathers to cotton and synthetic fabric. Some characters were
constructed from colonial and Catholic religious figures that were popular
during the early days of colonialism to both emulate and mock them. In order
to be larger than life, they developed masks that took on certain characters.
Sambo (ibid.) has included a list of characters that *Nyawo* dancers played.
Colonial figures that were satirised included the Native District Commissioner,
the colonial figure who was authorised to interact with Africans in Tribal Trust
Lands, as well as popular white characters in Western films and novels like
James Bond. The dancer playing James Bond was adorned in a suit and put on a
white mask to suggest a white person. The masked dancer playing the Native
District Commissioner would be clothed in appropriate uniform complete
with uniform, helmet and baton stick. Catholic figures that were satirised
included Maria (the Virgin Mary, mother of Jesus) who was dressed in white

apparel decorated with all kinds of ornaments and a white faced mask to suggest her white race. The Pope (Papa) was also another character played by the *Nyawo* dancers costumed in appropriate robes and papal emblems. Biblical characters like Simon were created with white or yellow paint on the face with a brunette wig to suggest a white person.

Never would a *Nyawo* dancer reveal his identity as a masquerade character. Performers rarely spoke to each other as this might reveal their identities to members of the audience who might recognise their voices. They made muffled sounds and sang, and the small apertures in the masks further distorted their voices beyond recognition. Owing to the aspect of violence in the *Nyawo* ritual, during the colonial era, a *Nyawo* dancer was a 'criminal' in a mask – never to be discovered because he committed crimes incognito and never admitted to them after the ritual was over. The mask offered another opportunity for resistance insofar as some masks presented white personas, often figures central to the Catholic faith. A *Nyawo* performance was a ritual dance where characters interacted with spirits from the graveyard, indeed, preparations for the dance originated from a *makolo*, a graveyard or a bush which gave the audience the impression that performers were not real human beings, but spirits visiting the human world, and for initiations the dance was performed in a bush clearing called *dambwe* in the case of male initiates and for the same space *tsimba* in the case of female initiates.

Thus for Catholic characters to emerge within such an intensely 'heathen' practice was an affront to Catholicism and Christianity. *Nyawo* dancers took turns to dance randomly and spontaneously according to the tempo and rhythm of the drum. To present a white persona (religious or political) amongst other mystical beings dancing in the most grotesque of patterns to an African drum was standing Rhodesian discourse on its head and exploding the 'preferred' and politically correct transparent image of whiteness. European bodies that came to Rhodesia carried with them a lot of cultural baggage. In other words they were cultural bodies that were supposed to radiate manners, values and comportment of what Shilling (1997) has called 'civilised' bodies. Throughout the medieval times and the court societies the European body became subject to expanding taboos transforming it into a site for an expression of behavioural codes (see Shilling, ibid.: 63–103). The Victorian and Edwardian body that came to Rhodesia embodied those values. To enact this 'civilised body' giving up its taboos and adopting the Bakhtian grotesque body in an intensely African ethnic dance was an insult to Victorian values. It was both tragic, shattering the preferred image, and comic, as it brought relief to Africans who played and/ or watched Europeans being satirised. It was affirming the European image through emulation and at the same time mocking it by caricaturing it. A white person in Rhodesia could not be created in a work of art through the agency of a black person. Who says a black man cannot play white? Look at what I can do to this white figure once I have become him. It seems like a form of Brechtian *gestus* where the actor while playing the character is offering a commentary on the character he is performing.

There were oral forms that also mimicked Western cultural productions.

Records of earliest urban African performances in Rhodesia (McCulloch, 2000; Makwenda, 2005; Parry, 1999) indicate tea parties and *Beni* dances as performances that celebrated and mocked Rhodesian discourse through mimicry. The tea party as a cultural production was appropriated from white Rhodesian elites. According to Robert Cary (1975) Lady Rodwell, wife of the Governor of Southern Rhodesia in the early 1930s was particularly fond of tea parties, and wives of white Rhodesian elites normally held tea parties in the morning where they congregated at the house of one of their colleagues to drink tea and dance to music from the gramophone (ibid.).

The earliest performance of a tea party held by Africans in Southern Rhodesia was in 1904 and it was organised by Tom Loiswayo for elite Africans of the Salisbury town. He also invited a white *Herald* editor (Parry, 1999). In Gwelo (Gweru), the capital of the Midlands province, the tea party dates back to 1905 when, according to Chimhete (2004), an irritable *Gwelo Times* correspondent complained of Africans hiring unoccupied houses in the townships 'when they wish to indulge (in drinking) under the pretext of tea meetings at 2s 6d per head – ladies 1s 6d' (ibid.: 54). When the Native Commissioner of Inyathi investigated whether there was prostitution and debauchery at these tea parties he discovered that African 'tea meetings there resembled the cabaret favoured by Europeans' (McCulloch, 2000: 136). Women put on the latest urban costumes copied from white ladies and the men put on the best suits money could buy. The Master of Ceremonies gave the whole event structure by introducing each performance which varied from sketches, song, and dance to theatre. These were performed in the living room of a house which more often than not proved to be too small for African audiences resulting in the party spilling over into the yard of the house, or in the case of lower class tea parties, a bush clearing adjacent to the house. The arena always took the form of a circle with guests sitting on chairs or benches or standing. Guests dined and drank non-alcoholic beverages while watching performances or while they danced themselves. The Master of Ceremonies addressed guests as ladies and gentlemen as opposed to the colonial terms 'boys' and 'girls' or African Male and African Female.

These descriptions suggest that the tea party was an ambivalent performance which both affirmed colonial culture and challenged it. In its various manifestations in most early Rhodesian urban and peri-urban centres the tea party was not a homogenous phenomenon. Black communities, inspired by the class structures of early white Rhodesian society separated themselves socially on the basis of their own class positions which were reflected in these tea parties.

There were two classes of tea parties – the African elite[8] tea party and the African lower class tea party which also mutated into two types. The first African elites, who identified themselves with the white middle and lower classes, were South African immigrants (better known as 'Cape boys') who came together with the Pioneer Corps in 1890. These people earned better money because they had skills 'in leather working, transport riding, smithing, building and market gardening' (Parry, 1999: 55). For political reasons these black South African immigrants were not allowed to live in local Shona homesteads through a Company[9] ordinance passed in the mid 1890s (ibid.: 57). Apart from their skills they also brought what Parry calls 'a complex array of cultural baggage' which on the negative side comprised alcoholism and violent recreation and on the positive side social order and Christian values inculcated by mission stations in the Cape (ibid.: 56). Nowhere was this social order displayed as in the African elite tea parties. As time moved on African elites grew in number and formed associations to lobby for equal rights with whites, for example the 1914 Native Vigilance Association which demanded equal status with whites (ibid.), the 1920 Southern Rhodesia Native Association which petitioned the government to open special bars selling European liquor (Chimhete, 2004) and the 1923 Bantu Voters Association which represented the interests of thirty or so African elites who qualified to vote (Parry, ibid.).

After the Second World War in 1945, the manufacturing and tertiary sectors of the economy expanded and there were a greater number of African elites with disposable income. However, according to Weinrich (1973: 34) this class became powerless because its members competed for positions, money and even prestige; '... forces dividing them [were] stronger than forces uniting them'. It never became a strong political force. Ironically the strongest bond uniting its members was the aspiration to European lifestyles and the attendant frustration sparked by a caste barrier which denied them access to privileges enjoyed by Rhodesians. Both the aspirations and the frustrations are evidenced in the forms these tea parties took.

The Christianised African elite tea parties were held 'under the auspices of a white controlled religious body (often the Wesleyan church)...' (Parry, 1999: 58), however, those not held under the auspices of a colonial organisation served alcohol to participants and audiences. They played European music and ate and drank European food (fat cookies, cakes, rice, salads, roasted/fried chicken and beef) and beverages, often European Liquor.[10] Makwenda (2005) recounts that African elites favoured Township jazz 'as this type of entertainment was associated with Western or "modern culture"' (ibid.: 28). Makwenda goes on to argue that during the 1940s elite tea parties often hired a one man band musician called a *Masiganda* (Shona) or *Omasiganda* (Ndebele) which is a corruption of the Afrikaans word *musikant* for musician. Popular musicians in the 1940s included Josaya Hadebe, George Sibanda, Sabelo Mathe, Jacob Mhungu and John White. Their music imitated Western country following trendsetters of the period like Jimmy Rogers, Louis Armstrong, Elvis Presley and others. Chimhete (2004) cites the musician Friday Mbirimi on the elite tastes of the 1940s and 1950s: 'it was the norm to go West ...local music was frowned upon, except for the manual worker' (ibid.: 39). When holding a tea party in a public hall like Mai Musodzi, which African elites called a concert, they played Western music from a gramophone and did ballroom dancing and a man usually paid a fee for dancing with a woman (Chimhete, 2004; Makwenda, 2005).

Lower class tea parties were patronised by lower-class Africans. They manifested in two slightly different ways. The first type was the house tea party which hired neighbouring houses near the tea party or adjacent compound[11] to act as retreat zones for men wanting to have sex with hired girls (Chimhete, 2004). The second type of lower class tea party was affectionately labelled a 'speed bar' because of its associations with running at great speed if police raided the party. This was operated in a bush on the outskirts of a black township. The dance arena was a temporary enclosure constructed in the bush. According to a 1949 government report, to take a hired girl for a dance in the dance arena cost 3s 4d per record (ibid.). Both these types of tea parties served the traditional brewed beer mostly from a tea pot to disguise the contents (Makwenda, 2005). According to Chimhete conspiracy theories doing rounds in the 1940s popularised the view that municipal brew contained birth controlling chemicals and this endeared lower class Africans to the traditional brew. Instead of the tea and European food, music and European dances, these parties included traditional beer, African popular music and traditional dance as well as Afro-contemporary dance. Prostitution was also rife. The name tea party was a covert name for a beer party. From 1950 lower class tea parties transformed their name to *mahobho* parties after a popular musician composed a song entitled '*Aya Mahobho Andakuchengetera*' (These breasts I have kept for you). At big tea parties organisers hired bands to attract maximum performers and audiences at a cost of about £6-£10 (Chimhete, ibid.). Fully fledged music bands that were popular during this period were the Bantu Actors formed by Kenneth Mattaka in 1932 and the De Black Evening Follies who broke away from Mattaka in 1943 under the leadership of Mphahlo Mafusire (Makwenda, ibid.).

Although the obvious influence and aspects of collaboration with colonial culture is clear, one may ask whether these tea party performances resisted the colonial culture in any way? I would argue that these parties were not slavish imitations of the white elite tea party, but had their own customs included. However, it is in the lower class tea parties that one sees resistance most clearly – the music played was African pop – usually rumba from the Belgian Congo, traditional *mbira* music and a ghettoised version of Western Jazz called *tsavatsava*. According to Claire Jones (1992) the jazzy sound intrinsic to *tsavatsava* was derived from the music of the rural social dances. Jones singles out August Musarurwa as a *tsavatsava* musician who entertained lower class Africans at their tea parties in the late 1940s eventually recording his *skokiaan* in 1951, which was later adapted by Louis Armstrong and became a hit in the USA in 1954. The dances were improvised contemporary movements to suit the rhythm of rumba and *tsavatsava* music.

As Bhabha puts it, mimicry is 'an exaggerated copying of language, culture, manners and ideas' (cited in Huddart, 2006: 57) and that it subverts in its slippage, in the way it differs from the source. This is a form of resistance to colonial discourse in a number of ways. While the production responds to colonial notions of respectability by copying Western values, it refused to be wholly assimilated, as seen by the exaggeration in the copying in the lower class African tea parties.

The second dimension of resistance lies in the ways in which the production refuses the fixedness of the African stereotype. Rhodesian discourse fixed the

African in one place as a savage and understood that savage on the basis of prior knowledge. When the 'savage' refused this position of stasis by being able to do what the colonial master could do, Rhodesian discourse created new stereotypes in order to maintain the status quo. For example, the Rhodesian Ministry of Information put together a booklet entitled *The Man and His Ways* (as an guide to understanding Africans in Rhodesia) which was distributed to white school children, tourists and members of the police force and army. Through that booklet the African was understood not through lived experience, but through prior knowledge. University sociologist M.F.C Bourdillon complained about the African myths it contained:

> ... [it] allows the status quo to be maintained, with whites preserving their privilege. That's what's behind the development of this mythology: the instinctive realisation that if the mythology is exploded, the position is no longer justified. Therefore the mythology must be maintained at all costs (cited in Frederickse, 1982:16)

However, mimicry is a powerful challenge, as it breaks the stereotype causing anxiety in the coloniser. When the African refuses the fixed stereotype by being able to do what the European can do, then the coloniser is made anxious and must manufacture new stereotypes to once again fix the new African, otherwise colonialism would collapse. This search for respectability and acceptance into the colonial ruling order by blacks in Rhodesia caused much anxiety among early colonialists as evidenced by the *Herald* editor in 1904 who after watching an African elite tea party, wrote:

> The black must remain the servant of the white and if such gatherings as these are permitted, the Tom Loiswayos and the rest of this race will ere long refuse to submit to the white, the dire consequences of which cannot be foreshadowed. (Parry, 1999: 58)

The Master of Ceremonies addressed audiences as ladies and gentlemen, thus promoting African 'girls' and 'boys' to the status of their European counterparts. The official titles for professional Africans were AM for African Male and AF for African Female. These appellations were dropped in 1953 when Garfield Todd ascended to power and replaced them with the European titles Mr or Mrs or Miss.

To add to that not all European theatres admitted African audiences or performers during this period (1890-1960).[12] The only social spaces available for Africans were council beer halls, opened only on weekends. Tea parties offered an alternative space for relaxation, performance and entertainment which did not respect colonial policy on African socialisation. Furthermore, if the colonial government did not want to acknowledge and respect African elites, elite tea parties, even if they were European in form and style became one of the many ways that African elites 'tried to shape their own sociability and determine how they spent leisure time' (Chimhete, 2004: 53). At some lower class tea parties especially those that took place in the bush (speed bars), participants performed traditional dances and drank traditional brew. This could be taken to mean that even if Africans were uprooted from their natal origins by relocating to the

European city, they tried to recuperate their culture in an urban context using an art form appropriated from English culture.

Another important aspect of resistance, especially after the Second World War, was 'the winds of change' that swept across Africa as nationalism. As municipal beer halls were seen by Africans as an extension of white hegemony they, according to Chimhete (2004) started to boycott council beer halls and patronised tea parties and later shebeens. This was a form of passive resistance to white domination. Related to this was the Africans' response to laws banning them from drinking what was classified as 'European beer' (wines, brandies, whiskies, spirits, lagers and all clear beer) under the African Beer Act and the Liquor Act until 1957. Tea parties were an opportunity to usurp colonial authority by transgressing the law through drinking prohibited substances.[13]

The *Beni* dance is another example of oral performance that resisted Rhodesian discourse through mimicry. This dance still survives today in Zimbabwe, but it has its roots in Germany East Africa/Tanganyika (now Tanzania). The version that was brought to Rhodesia is the *Beni Arinoti*, (from *Harinoti*, meaning the perspiring or unclean ones) which was a friendly competitor of the Dar-i-Sudi which formed the Marine Band known in local language as *Beni Marini*. According to Ranger (1975) membership to the *Beni Marini* was restricted to free born Swahili *Khassa* while that of *Beni Arinoti* was open to all foreigners not originally belonging to the coast freemen. It is less likely that *Beni Marini* could have moved beyond its catchment area of Swahili freed slaves. *Beni Arinoti* was brought by ethnic groups from Malawi who took part in the King's African Rifles that fought the Germans. When this military unit was disbanded at the end of the First World War in 1918, as was traditional in the early 20th century, the demobilised soldiers together with other young Nyasas, thirsty for opportunities in the more prosperous south, moved to the present day Zimbabwe and carried with them this cultural form.

Originally *Beni* was created by slaves rescued by the British Marines (navy) and put under the supervision of missionaries at Freetown. Earliest records (Ranger, 1975) indicate that when freed slaves tried to celebrate their freedom by playing African drums and dancing African rhythms, the hosting missionaries were riled by this behaviour and banned the drums which they perceived as 'wicked'. If their own drums and dances were not allowed, then they could resort to playing and copying European ones and the closest ones were that of the military band which played in ships that had rescued them and continued to play after docking at the east coast harbour. Missionaries supported this shift by offering gymnastics and games alongside this music and rewarding those who excelled with a red coat with big buttons. The values of cleanliness and pride in a uniform thus encroached into the *Beni* dance. Ironically these symbols of European naval power – drums, music, the uniform, guns, and drills – served as an example of acceptable performance to the culturally starved freed slaves. According to Ranger (1975) *Beni* also grew out of traditions of dance competition in eastern Africa. The freed slaves chose what they wanted to include from African traditions. These traditions had undergone what Ranger (ibid.: 20) calls 'intensive Arabisation' in the late nineteenth century. Being close to Zanzibar, these traditions also had strong Indian overtones. These diverse influences introduced new instruments, costumes and dance forms. The Arab elements were to become a cause for concern for colonialists and missionaries as will be explained below.

When *Beni Arinoti* moved to Southern Rhodesia in 1918 the 'quasi-military atmosphere of the compound endowed with its own emphasis on discipline, status, uniforms and barracks' (Phimister and Van Onselen, 1997: 8) provided a fertile hosting culture for its development. It moved down with the same European characteristics – military drills with dummy guns made from wood, dances which took the forms of a parade, procession or a march past and sometimes a platoon form. The songs were in Chewa or Nyanja. *Beni Arinoti* had a hierarchy of office bearers who wore uniforms and had titles of honour that replicated the British navy. The Port Herald Burial Society which hosted these dances, for example had the following titles of office bearers: King, Governor, Prince, General, Commander, Doctor, Bishop, Lord and King's Servant (Parry, 1999; Phimister and Van Onselen, 1997; Ranger, 1975). Although they were honoured during the performance, these office bearers performed administrative roles for the welfare of members. Organisation of this nature was normally discouraged by the colonial authorities as it didn't fit the frames of the African stereotype. However, as in other similar cases where an African performance or organisation had been banned, Africans responded by emulating the establishment of philanthropic organisations like the Red Cross which Europeans had founded. Phimister and Van Onselen (ibid.: 7) recount that in 1918, seven per cent of all black workers died during the Spanish influenza epidemic. Rhodesians during the same period started a number of voluntary organisations to make a contribution to the war and this capacity for organisation struck Africans who used the crisis as a reason to form their own voluntary organisations such as the Loyal Mandabele Patriotic Society 1915, Nyasaland Boys Club 1917 and Port Herald Burial Society 1918. It would have seemed ridiculous to stop Africans organising the burial of their society members during such a critical moment.

A number of things in the *Beni Arinoti* acted as a challenge to both mission-aries and colonialists. First, even if the missionaries could see that most of the *Beni* elements were aping European models, they opposed African autonomy to choose what they wanted to appropriate from European styles and what they did not want. Choosing from African performances and Arab dances as was evident in *Beni* was taken as exercising too much freedom of choice. What Ranger (1975) has called the 'intensive Arabisation' of *Beni* was interpreted as a way of trying to spread Islam in a British Christian colony. Just as in Tanganyika, *Beni* in Rhodesia was met with bitter missionary hostility to the extent that the Southern Rhodesia Missionary Conference of 1930 recom-mended the banning of African dances in their areas of jurisdiction (McCulloch, 2000: 137). While they might have admired European styles, the secular innovations were unpalatable to their spiritual sensibilities. Both O'Callaghan (1977) and Jones (1992) agree that early missionaries in Rhodesia required African assimilation into European culture. They acknowledged nothing of value from African culture. Converted Africans had to drop their tunes and style of singing to assimilate the European *a capella* style in four part harmony. All dances, including *Beni*, which brought innovations from elsewhere were despised. However, according to Jones (1992) missionaries in Rhodesia 'repented' from this notion of assimilation in 1954 with a programme which required the incorporation of African instruments and melodies in worship. This has become an annual event run under the auspices of the Ecumenical Arts Association still run today (Jones, 1992). Missionaries in eastern Africa had long changed their attitudes from the 1920s and 1930s relating to African performing arts. According to Ranger (1975) missionaries supported traditional dances which they found to be consistent with morality.

Second, colonial industrialists and mine owners also felt challenged by *Beni Arinoti*. The capacity for organisation by Africans was interpreted as a recipe for industrial action, particularly in the congested compounds. In Tanganyika this capacity for organisation in the form of *Beni* dance had produced strikes. A warning had been cabled to Southern Rhodesia that such organisations were 'eminently capable of misuse for propaganda purposes' (Phimister and Van Onselen, 1997: 9). The Compound Manager at Shamva confirmed fears from Tanganyika by viewing the Port Herald Burial Society formed in 1918 as 'liable to lead to a great deal of trouble' (ibid). In fact in 1927 a strike broke out at Shamva mine. Although some scholars attempted to link the strike to the Port Herald Burial Society, Ranger, depending on studies by Clyde Mitchell has concluded that the strike had no connections with *Beni* (1975: 138). The Chief Native Commissioner wrote a circular instructing that the leadership of *Beni* should be put under surveillance. The Chamber of Mines was perturbed by these reports of organised drill of *Beni* performances, and they 'expressed the fear that the dance societies might become "the basis of labour movements"' (Ranger, ibid.). Those fears were not unfounded as it later proved that the first labour movement the Industrial and Commercial Workers' Union (ICU) was formed through the structures provided by African voluntary organisations (Parry, 1999).

Lastly, colonialists linked *Beni* dances to the rise of nationalism. This fear was given impetus by a Belgian rightwing journalist, Daniel Thwaites, who in 1936 wrote that *Beni* and its mutations constituted

> ... a cancerous growth of racial hatred deliberately cultivated on modern lines by a mastermind well versed in native lore with a profound knowledge of how to make the complicated appeal to native psychology... (Ranger, 1975: 138)

The use of military titles was interpreted as a preparation to take over the colony. To use them, according to the journalist, was a way of understudying Europeans for the inevitable takeover. For this reason, *Beni* was banned in the Belgian Congo in 1934 (now DRC), but there is no record of its being banned in Rhodesia. It simply caused anxieties in the missionaries and colonial administrators. There is no systematic study at the moment that has documented the number of *Beni* societies that existed between 1890 and 1950. What can be said with certainty, however, is that with the closure of mines in Zimbabwe and the invasion of farms by ZANU PF militias and war veterans as well as displacement of workers of mostly Malawian origin, cultural life revolving around *Beni* dances has been emasculated. There are still *Beni* societies that perform at social and political galas in Zimbabwe. While in eastern Africa the dance died a natural death in the 1960s, in Zimbabwe it still exists. Some of the movements like the 'borrowdale' dance popularised by the *sungura* artist Alick Macheso have been incorporated into *Beni*. Probably what exists now is its mutation rather than *Beni* as it was in its 1918 form. However, it played a particular role in black Zimbabwean (peri)-urban culture in the early twentieth century as a form of cultural resistance to European performance forms.

Conclusion

In staging the various performances, Africans both submitted to and resisted Rhodesian discourse resulting in hybrid ambivalent works that both mocked and celebrated colonialism. The notion of hybridity which characterises urban performances was a way of survival and negotiating new identities in an otherwise hostile world which attempted to suffocate some African traditional performances. The contact between Europeans and Africans was not only physical, but cultural and in the latter allowing cultural transmission, less in the direction of the coloniser and more in the direction of the colonised owing to unequal power relations. Cultural criticism in Zimbabwe has tended to apply the 'dominant hypothesis' which portrays the coloniser's power as absolute and having the propensity to dislocate and denature African culture. Critics have failed to notice spaces of resistance where they were apparent in African performances. This necessitates an academic endeavour to return to social and cultural history to investigate forms that emerged during colonial rule and this article has attempted to illuminate sites and spaces in urban African performances where Rhodesian discourse was resisted and appropriated. I have tried to avoid the now tired debate about what constitutes theatre and what is not theatre. Our culture-specific values enter into our description of the social world, thereby affecting ideologically statements that we make, regardless of how factual or sincere we are. The notion of theatre and how it is understood in different discourses has been dealt with at length in my earlier work (1994), as well as by Schechner (1994) and Hauptfleisch (1997), to name but a few scholars. While articulating the performance features of the above urban African performances I argued that Rhodesian discourse was not absolute.

NOTES

1 Although direct rule (where Africans would be subjected to a single legal order defined by European law and native institutions would not be recognised) was the official administration policy in the nineteenth century, it was abandoned for Lugard's policy of Indirect rule by the 1920s which rested on three pillars: a native court, a native administration, and a native treasury. Colonialism's capacity for absolutism was checked (see for example Mamdani, 1996).

2 I am aware of the many layers of meaning around the term African(s) to a point where it is almost criminal to use the term carelessly without clarification. There are three types of Africans – black Africans, Arab Africans and European Africans. In this article the term African is used to refer to black Rhodesian Africans. This is also the sense in which 'African' was used by Rhodesians to refer to blacks. The terms African(s) and black(s) are used interchangeably for stylistic reasons in appropriate circumstances to refer to blacks residing in Rhodesia.

3 The term is deployed here as a descriptor of whites. The terms 'Rhodesian(s)' and 'white(s)' are used interchangeably in this article. Rhodesianness is not a singular category which accommodates only English white people. Everybody who according to law was white and resided in Rhodesia was a Rhodesian. Although the country began as Southern Rhodesia, it became Rhodesia from 1970 to 1979 and changed to Zimbabwe-Rhodesia after the internal settlement in 1979.

4 According to one version of recorded evidence, the chief went to the missionary and told him that he had dreamt the baby Jesus being born in Jerusalem (sic) and had seen a vision where all chiefs were coming to Jerusalem with presents singing and dancing *mbende* (which from then became *jerusarema*). The missionary was impressed and allowed the dance to be performed to commemorate the birth of Jesus.

5 Shona orthography was established in 1931 when the Doke report was adopted by the House of Assembly. Although the Ndebele alphabetic system was developed by the London Missionary Society in 1863, there is no record of written plays till the second half of the twentieth century.

6 Urban Africans were more exposed to Western values as they interacted with whites at workplaces and even lived with them (in the case of domestic servants). The urban space was under direct rule while the rural space was under indirect rule. The rural people were relatively less exposed to Western influence. The difference though was a matter of degree.

7 The reasons for this anomaly are varied and have been dealt with at length by Yoshikuni (1999) and Ranger (1985).

8 African elite is used here to refer to Africans who were Western educated, wealthy and practised a combination of Western and Judeo–Christian values (even if in some cases they were not religious). Weinrich (1973) has suggested an annual salary of £250.00 as a marker of elite economic life. This class of Africans included priests, pastors, doctors, nurses, social workers, lecturers, teachers, headmasters, school inspectors, clerks, traders and artisans.

9 Rhodesia was colonised by a chartered company – the British South Africa Company under a Royal Charter. After a white referendum, Company rule ended in 1922 and the Responsible Self Government took over power in 1923.

10 Only Africans with university degrees could drink European liquor according to the 1957 amendment of the African Beer Act. All other Africans were not allowed to drink it, but they used this tea party opportunity to evade the law. Since the 1920s the law on liquor was honoured more in breach than in compliance.

11 Compounds were tiny housing units in mining towns to house large numbers of African labourers. Phimister and Van Onselen graphically describe a typical compound. Large compounds were typically three-tiered: the inner or square compounds were used to house either short-term workers or recruited labourers. ...The huts of single workers surrounding the inner compound housed longer-term miners. ...Finally separated from both these tiers were the huts of married workers and their families – fully proletarianised workers, semi-skilled with above average wages – the group least likely to desert (1997:4).

12 City by-laws did not allow Europeans and Africans to use the same ablution facilities and in a sense the same theatres. This was successfully challenged in court by the Salisbury Repertory Theatre and the by-law was set aside. Reps theatre through a secret ballot in 1960 voted 419 for and 196 against admission of black audiences (see Cary, 1975). Admission of blacks from 1960 onwards depended on individual theatre houses.

13 Tea parties started to decline from 1962 when the African Beer Act was amended and removed all restrictions on beer consumption, allowing Africans to buy any type of beer. There was no need to disguise the drinking of beer under a tea party, but the economic benefit could not be ignored. According to Makwenda (2005) the tea parties slowly transformed themselves into shebeens, but carrying with them the same class tags – elite shebeens and lower-class shebeens.

REFERENCES

Asante, Kariam Welsh (2000) *Zimbabwe Dance: Rhythmic Forces, Ancestral Voices – An Aesthetic Analysis*, Asmara: Africa World Press.

Bourdieu, Pierre (1991) *Language and Symbolic Power*, Cambridge: Polity Press.

Bourdieu, Pierre (1993) *The Field of Cultural Production: Essays on Art and Literature*, Cambridge: Polity Press.

Cary, Robert (1975) *The Story of Reps: The History of Salisbury Repertory Players 1931-1975*, Salisbury: Glaxie Press.

Chimhete, Nathaniel (2004) *The African Alcohol Industry in Salisbury: Southern Rhodesia c. 1945-1980*, Harare: unpublished MA Dissertation, University of Zimbabwe, Department of Economic History Library.

Fischer-Lichte, E. (1992) *The Semiotics of Theatre*, Indianapolis: Indiana University Press.

Foucault, Michel (1976) *The Archaeology of Knowledge and Discourse on Language*, New York: Colophon Books.

Foucault, Michel (1980) *Power/Knowledge: Selected Interviews and Other Writings 1972-1977*, New York: Harvester Wheatsheaf.

Fredrickse, Julie (1982) *None But Ourselves: Masses versus Media in the Making of Zimbabwe*, Harare: Zimbabwe Publishing House.

Godwin, Peter and Hancock, Ian (1993) *Rhodesians Never Die: The Impact of War and Political change on White Rhodesians c. 1970-1980*, Oxford: Oxford University Press.

Government of Zimbabwe (1899) Statute Law of Zimbabwe, Volume 2, Harare: Government Publications.

Gramsci, Antonio (1971) *Selections from the Prison Notebooks*, New York: International Publishers.

Guha, Ranajit (1997) *Dominance without Hegemony: History and Power in Colonial India*, London: Harvard University Press.

Hauptfleisch, Temple (1997) *Theatre and Society in South Africa*, Pretoria: J.L.van Schaik Publishers.

Huddart, David (2006) *Routledge Critical Thinkers: Homi K. Bhabha*, London: Routledge.

Jones, Claire (1992) *Making Music: Musical Instruments in Zimbabwe – Past and Present*, Harare: Academic Books.

Kaarsholm, Preben (1999) 'Si ye pambili – Which way Forward? Urban Development, Culture and Politics in Bulawayo'. In Raftopoulos, Brian and Yoshikuni (eds) *Sites of Struggle: Essays in Zimbabwe's Urban History*. Harare: Weaver Press, 227-256.

Kirby, E.T (1974) 'Indigenous African Theatre', *The Drama Review*, 18: 4, 22-35.

Makwenda, Joyce-Jenje (2005) *Zimbabwe Township Music*, Harare: Storyline Promotions.

Mamdani, Mahmood (1996) *Citizen and Subject: Contemporary Africa and the Legacy of Late Colonialism*, New Jersey: Princeton Press.

McCulloch, Jock (2000) *Black Peril, White Virtue: Sexual Crime in Southern Rhodesia, 1902-1935*, Bloomington: Indiana University Press/Oxford: James Currey.

Moore, Sally Falk (1978) *Law as Process: An Anthropological Approach*, Reprinted (2001), Oxford: James Currey Publishers.

O'Callaghan, Marion (1977) *Southern Rhodesia: The Effects of a Conquest Society on Education, Culture and Information*, Dorset: UNESCO.

Parry, Richard (1999) 'Culture, Organisation and Class: The African Experience in Salisbury 1892-1935.' In Raftopoulos, Brian and Yoshikuni (eds) *Sites of Struggle: Essays in Zimbabwe's Urban History*. Harare: Weaver Press, 53-94.

Phimister, Ian and Van Onselen, Charles (1997) 'The Labour Movement in Zimbabwe: 1900-1945.' In Raftopoulos, Brian and Phimister, Ian (eds) *Keep on Knocking: A History of the Labour Movement in Zimbabwe 1900-1997*. Harare: Baobab Books, 1-54.

Plastow, Jane (1996) *African Theatre and Politics: The Evolution of Theatre in Ethiopia, Tanzania and Zimbabwe – A Comparative Study*, Amsterdam: Rodopi.

Ranger, Terence (1975) *Dance and Society in Eastern Africa*, Ibadan and Nairobi: Heinemann.

Ravengai, Samuel (1995) *Towards the Redefinition of African Theatre*, Harare: unpublished BA Honours Dissertation, University of Zimbabwe, Department of Theatre Arts Library.

Rodney, Walter (1989) *How Europe Underdeveloped Africa*, Nairobi: Heinemann Kenya.

Sambo, Kudakwashe Shane (2002) *The Functions of Costumes within Urban Nyau Dances*, Harare: unpublished BA Honours Dissertation, University of Zimbabwe, Department of Theatre Arts Library.

Schechner, Richard (1994) 'Ritual and Performance.' In Ingold, Tim (ed.) *Companion Encyclopaedia of Anthropology*. London: Routledge, 613–47.

Shilling, Chris (1997). 'The Body and Differences.' In Woodward, Kathryn (ed.) *Identity and Difference*. London: Sage Publications, 63–107.

Taylor, Charles. T. C (1968) *The History of Rhodesian Entertainment 1890-1930*, Salisbury: M.O Collins (Pty) Ltd.

Weinrich, Anna Katharina Hieldegard (1973) *Black and White Elites in Rural Rhodesia*, Manchester: Manchester University Press.

Yoshikuni, Tsuneo (1999) 'Notes on the Influence of Town-Country Relations on African Urban History before 1957: Experiences of Salisbury and Bulawayo.' In Raftopoulos, Brian and Yoshikuni (eds) *Sites of Struggle: Essays in Zimbabwe's Urban History*, Harare: Weaver Press, 113-28.

'Don't Talk into my Talk'

Oral narratives, cultural identity
& popular performance in colonial Uganda

SAMUEL KASULE

Introduction

Performance in colonial Uganda was dominated by dance and song, although individual technical mastery of dance, song, and instrumentation was a prerogative of the professional performers and court musicians who played at the royal courts, beer parties, and market places. There are limited written materials available on indigenous performances of the colonial period in Buganda. However, the existence of a corpus of archival Luganda musical recordings, going back to the 1930s, and oral narratives of aged people, gives us an insight into performance activities of this period. Old musical recordings help us to understand various forms of performance about which we know little, and contribute to aspects of performance that have shaped contemporary Ugandan theatre. Popular performances of the colonial era allowed the Baganda indigenous culture to indulge itself, therefore, they have become a memory bank where everything, economic, social and political is presented. Ian Steadman in his article, 'Towards Popular Theatre in South Africa', insists that any evaluation of archived indigenous performances 'must be sensitive to the complexities of performance which are inscribed therein, complexities in which surplus meanings are produced and often subvert the meanings intended for the reader of the printed text' (1990: 208).

It is from this approach to an embodied archive, with performance central to the analysis, that I am approaching the following examples of colonial theatre in Uganda. In orientation and performance, Serumaga's *Majangwa* (and Kawadwa's *Oluyimba lwa Wankoko* (1975)), offered re-interpretations of indigenous theatre in order to challenge oppressive systems whose policies impinged on people's freedom. At the same time, these plays drew upon specific forms of indigenous theatre known for their cryptic defiance of authority, through, for instance, folk and solo songs, dance, recitation, and story telling. In *Oluyimba lwa Wankoko* for example, Wankoko is hailed by the people as the 'liberator', and he responds with a defiant song, which, apart from mocking the palace administration, draws the workers' attention to the tyranny in the palace, and asks them to stand for their rights: '*Ani asobola atyo? Nze banange kye ngamba: Ffena Twenkana!* / Who wants to go on living like this? This is my proposition: We are all equal!' (Kawadwa, 1975: 9) Once again, this draws applause from the workers (and the audience) and immediately Wankoko invites them to learn his song of resistance, *Ffena Twenkana*.

Kawadwa in his plays, *St Lwanga* (1969) *Makula ga Kulabako* (Kulabako's Beauty, 1970), and *Oluyimba lwa Wankoko* (Song of Wankoko, 1971), appears to suggest that musical narratives are central elements of traditional Baganda popular performance that continues to attract audiences and performers alike. Kawadwa's death by torture at the hands of Amin's government pundits, who seem to have understood the play's message and been threatened by it, reminds us of the potential subversive power of indigenous popular performance. I use this post-independence example as a preamble to explaining the power of entertainment and critical aspects of indigenous performance that were embedded in dance, choral/solo folk songs, recitation, story telling, and ritual performances during the colonial period.

In this article, I explore ritual, folk songs, the travelling musician, and the changing context of traditional performance of the colonial period in Uganda up to 1950. This selection may not be comprehensive but it is indicative of the theatre performances of the period, and highlights their popularity, as practices that are archived within embodied memory and culture. Because many of them are 'musical or dance oriented', we have to rely on a limited number of physical recordings of solo folk performers and written records of these dramatic activities. Therefore, my analysis will draw on a selection of recorded song performances, eyewitness accounts of early European travellers, and personal observation of embodied performances as an attempt to provide as comprehensive a picture of cultural creativity of colonial Uganda as is possible.

Many early records of Uganda's indigenous performance came from European missionaries and administrators' witness accounts. Roscoe (1911), for example, whose work gives a eurocentric interpretation of the customs and beliefs of the Baganda, blends his observations with statements on (im)moral issues:

> Dances, among the young people, took place nightly amidst the plantain groves during the time that the moon was nearing the full, and especially on the night of full moon. The mixed dances ended frequently in immoral conduct.
> (Roscoe, 1911: 24)

Roscoe's contemporaries extensively developed this European (moral) gaze, for instance Lugard, the first British Imperial Company representative in Uganda,[1] describes the theatricality displayed in the greetings between King Mwanga and Prince Mbogo's entourage:

> The meeting was a curious spectacle. They held each other's hands and gave vent to a long drawn O——Oh in a guttural; the Ah——Ah in higher note; then long low whistles, as they gazed into each other's faces; this went on for a very long time, and became ludicrous to a European conception, for at times while giving vent to this exclamation indicative of intense surprise, their eyes would be roaming round in a

very inconsequent manner. Then they fell on each other's necks and embraced, and then again began the former ceremony. Then Bambejja – princesses who had followed Mbogo – fell on Mwanga's neck, and princesses of Mwanga's suit fell on Mbogo's neck. Meanwhile the same performances were going on between chiefs, and chieflets, and common people on every side on a more compressed and not quite so long-drawn-out a scale till the crush became greater and greater, and *it was hard work to preserve one's dignity or even one's balance, among the crowd of performing monkeys.* (Lugard, ed. Perham,1959: 266 – my emphasis)

Lugard's description, in addition to Roscoe's quoted before, reveals significant European attitudes towards the Baganda and their performance; that 'they' are the binary opposite of the European, their greetings mirror the behaviour of monkeys and that these people are easily given to immorality, with an implicit comparison to animal behaviour. Indeed, their 'wild' gesticulations, vocalisation, mimicry and movements communicate a different message for a different/potential audience in colonial Uganda. The interjections of 'guttural noises' contribute to the theatricality. Arguably, in Roscoe and Lugard's view, these native performers are the 'other' (Said, 1979) and 'the space on which the battles for truth, value, and power' (Taylor, 1998: 162) will be fought by missionaries and colonial administrators. Notably, by re-presenting these performances in their diaries, Europeans force us to be the voyeurs of aesthetics, cultural codes, and styles displayed in various indigenous performances. Nevertheless, this writing offers descriptions of forms that are otherwise lost in contemporary history, outside embodied contemporary residual forms; hence, if one can unravel the colonial gaze and values, one can 'read back' to some extent into these older performances.

Folktales and dramatic performance

Story telling was an intrinsic communal form of theatre in Buganda. In this theatre form, knowledge of performance skills and texts was internalised, or as Taylor argues in relation to similar forms in South America, it was 'learned and transmitted through the embodied practices that are termed as the repertoire. Through formal and informal techniques of incorporation, people memorized and rehearsed stories and the accompanying music' (Taylor, 2004: 358). These dramatised narratives encapsulate and transmit not only performance forms, but also primary values of the community including 'theatrical, verbal and non-verbal components of performance' (Irobi, 2007: 270). Predominantly communal in orientation, this theatre was 'integrated' and everyone could take part in 'the performance of […] song, dance, mime, and drama' (Mbowa, 1999:228). Performances were shaped by the need to engage with issues of identity marginalisation, opportunity, and community. I now turn to a few specific examples to illustrate these ideas.

Olugero lw'Akakookolo' (The Leper and The Pretty Girl), is a common story learnt by children in Buganda and its content and style of presentation evolves and expands as they reach adulthood. The plot is simple but it has characteristics of indigenous performance, for instance, it includes elements of mimicry, music, and dance. In this context, *akakookolo* may mean a mask or someone with a blemish on his nose therefore, the protagonist's name is generic, suggesting someone who is marked.[2] In the story, suitors, including Akakookolo, dressed in colourful costumes came to the village to woo the girl. During the narration, the storyteller used verbal and physical means to impersonate the suitors. For instance, he blocked his nose with his fingers in order to produce the nasal sound generally associated with the character of Akakookolo. The latter, dressed in strips of dirty bark cloth, was presented as uncouth, and in addition, he was treated as an outcast. Despite his physical appearance, his musical performance that included singing and playing the bowl-lyre, amused the people. Finally, attracted by the virtuoso performance, the girl followed him off stage singing:

Girl:	*Kakookolo gwe, Kakookolo*
	Kakookolo kwako eddiba lyo
Akakookolo:	*Ndetera Maama, ndetera*
	Agenda n'omulungi talaga…
Girl:	Kakookolo, please, Kakookolo
	Kakookolo here is your mat (animal skin)
Akakookolo:	Bring it to me, my dear, bring it
	He who elopes with a pretty one never says any farewells.[3]

The dramatic action was realised through dance, music, and spectacle. The narrator may have had props such as a smoking pipe and a bowl-lyre, which he used to enhance the dramatic presentation. It is normal practice in indigenous theatre for the performer to ask the audience to applaud the performance and in addition, to direct them to be quiet and orderly. Hence, Akakookolo contrived comedy by his cynical remarks directing the audience to control their excitement:

Nze bwemba nnyimba saagala anyumya.
Don't talk into my talk/song.

This always created potential for a dynamic interactive process between the performer and the audience. It demanded and encouraged audience participation as well as critical reflection on the performance act. 'Don't talk into my talk/song' was a phrase used by the performer to contrive humour and create rapport with the audience and/or to control an excited audience. In this context, the performance charmed the audience and at the end, they rewarded the narrator and Akakookolo with beer and food. The narrator invested the story with his own meaning hence the depth of his performance and thought identified him as a person with a vision. Often this excited the audience further, giving the actor/performer/singer a chance to terminate his show and name his price, usually a gourd of beer, for a repeat performance.

Knowledge of both the performance skills and the stories was 'learned and transmitted through the embodied practices that are the repertoire' (Taylor, 2004: 358), and thus come down to us in embodied forms today. The dramatic presentations of these narratives, accompanied by audience verbal interjections, loud drumming, and singing marks the beginning of drama. These types of stories have continued to be popular and their style of narration provides us with insights into the performance styles popular in colonial times.

Ruganda's *The Burdens*, was inspired by this story and he uses it to highlight the attitude of Tinka to Wamala, her husband, and to comment on the deteriorating relationship between the politicians and the electorate in Buganda. Retelling her own version of the story to Kaija, her son, Tinka compares her plight to the chief's daughter, Nyenje, who married a leper (Wamala):

Tinka:	Ngoma, Paramount Chief ... sent word round that whoever wanted her beautiful hand had to prove his prowess by climbing a very tall tree and bringing down, in one piece, the gourd containing her umbilical cord ...
Kaija:	And Nyenje's beauty dazzled their [the suitors'] eyes.
Tinka:	You have it. Then came the leper. A common leper stinking with leprosy and commonness. Dragging misery behind him...
Kaija:	People ran away in horror.
Tinka:	But Ngoma was a fair man. He let him try his luck.
Kaija:	Nyenje was tucked away in a corner drenched in tears...
Tinka:	As the leper climbed the tree he sang his song.
Kaija:	The tune...let's have the tune mother.
Tinka:	The night, too, has ears, son.
Kaija:	Just this once, mother.
Tinka:	He climbed higher.
Kaija:	Nyenje's heart sunk low.
Tinka:	You have it... He climbed higher and higher still.
Kaija:	Ngoma regretted his fairness.
Tinka:	[T]he gourd was now an arm's length from him.
Kaija:	Ngoma bid his subjects tie a band around his tired loins. (*Wamala's voice can be heard faintly from without*)
Tinka:	To cut the long story short, the leper brought down the gourd.
	(Ruganda, 1972: 14-17)

Arguably, through Tinka, the memory of the pretty girl is conveyed through this embodied retelling of the tale. The story presents a symptomatic representation of how dramatic folk tales shape contemporary theatre. More especially, it foregrounds the concept of *abadongo*, travelling musicians who either played instruments as solo artists or performed as an ensemble. Their strength is marked by the 'conscious' exploitation of their socio-political role as the voice of the community, which collectively makes this perhaps the most dynamic form of traditional entertainment to be adopted by later formal theatre in Uganda. The political aspect of the performer's role is illustrated by the public performances of Majangwa and Nakirijja, the last surviving travelling musicians described by MacPherson in her article, 'What happened to Majangwa?' (1976: 68-70). From 1940 to 1975 Majangwa was part of the life of the people in Kampala, the capital of Uganda, and Nakulabye, one of its suburbs. His importance as a performer was the manner in which the people related to him. Majangwa was an exhibitionist who played his *ngalabi*, long drum, and sung at different open markets while his wife, Nakirijja, performed dances to the crowds. Their performances took place in the open markets and/or sometimes in drinking places (*ebinywero*). In a jovial mood, surrounded by a crowd, Majangwa would move around, persuading people to join the performance or to pay him for the show. Macpherson notes that Majangwa was

> Frightening ... challenging... [and] ...pathetic ... a little piece of Kampala's social history, something a little out of the ordinary, someone who reminded us all that there was a little bit more to life beside a job for the day light hours, a bit of social oblivion in the evening and a dead night's sleep. (MacPherson, 1976:69)

Majangwa refused to conform to modernity – he had no permanent job so he lived on donations of food and money from his audiences. His dance music contained sexual innuendos mirroring a society that had become impotent, both literally and metaphorically. His performance also displayed the specific exhibitionistic performance style of folk musicians that underlined solo performance.

Archived performances

Global developments, specifically the gramophone, had a direct impact on popular performance in Uganda. Vernon states that companies concentrated on 'Native music' records because they were a 'cheap' product that would boost their sales of gramophone machines (Vernon, 1997: 3). Since archived recordings of the indigenous performances that date back to colonial times are limited in number, we cannot know the exact details of the performances and what they meant to the audience and the performers. This section offers an analysis of a selection of archived performances that document knowledge of sociopolitical changes in Uganda, namely, the Baganda contributions to Ugandan theatre. By analysing the performances we uncover important aspects of Ugandan culture, politics, and theatre that were expressed in songs composed in the *abadongo* style. We know that these songs were performed in Kampala, but there is also enough evidence to suggest that they were performed outside that town as well.

In indigenous settings, performances were interactive, however, with the introduction of 'studio' recording where artists performed without live audiences, folk songs were more focused on performance rather than on communcation with the audience. It would be interesting, therefore, to know how musicians responded to performing to or in an empty room. Early recordings of popular indigenous music were made in the 1930s with performers like Ssekinoomu and Sumoni. In spite of the unfamiliar space in a recording room, these performers used the performance occasion to make politically engaged statements on themes particularly to do with their sociopolitical position within a colonised country. In the songs discussed below, performers weave the theme of colonisation into their songs, sometimes by allusion and sometimes directly.

Colonial indigenous theatre speaks through many voices, and constructs multi-layered performance texts. This theatre should not be regarded as static but rather as constantly metamorphosing into new forms, always becoming part of new, contemporary theatre forms. Consequently, new voices are always emerging from this period. While the Europeans, specifically missionaries, attempted to erase popular performance by labeling it *tabbulu* (taboo) because they thought it encouraged drunkenness and promiscuity, performers like Ssekinoomu sung back to Christian music through the performance of songs and dances that were more oriented to the indigenous subject. The legacy of colonialism is most evident in the archived performances, which show traces of proselytising, oppression, and modernisation. In this section, I intend to show how indigenous performers contributed to theatre development through their 'exploration' of cultural identity.

Early recorded folk performances came from solo performers led by Ssekinoomu, a Muganda professional musician whose work blended instrumental music with social themes and political topics that juxtaposed urban and rural scenes. By projecting the contemporary experience of society, especially its social stories in relation to poverty, he presented a broad view of colonial Uganda. In 1945, Ssekinoomu made two recordings, one on social themes and the other on the first experience of the wireless receiver in the 1930s. These performances of stories which focused on colonial experiences represented the emerging climate of critical performance dialogue in Uganda. Ssekinoomu's performances echoed Florence, Sumoni and other singers of the period, in their embodied engagement with the new concern regarding identity, which is apparent in the style and themes of the narrative. In Sumoni's critical recording, *Ssesse* (Sumoni, 1940), he attempts to locate himself in a new experience of a converted Muslim. In the lyrics he sings about 'we', referring to the 'Moslems' and the 'other', as if he identifies himself as part of a segment of society that existed within the country, but which was different from the Whites or Anglicised Ugandans. Moreover, while Islam has customs comparable to those in African, for instance, its marriage customs, becoming Christians meant constructing a new identity. Hence, the performance engages with issues of living within a changing Uganda, and engaging with three cultures – Arabic, European, and Ugandan.

To illustrate how revealing these songs are for the contemporary researcher, I turn to two popular songs, '*Ekyalema Nakato*' (1945) and '*Wayalesi*' (1945) which mix characteristics of performance – story, characters, words and images to impact on the audience (listener) in an unsettling way. Collectively, these recordings develop a conversation on questions related to female sexuality, modernity, and culture. By recording '*Ekyalema Nakato*' (Nakato's Challenge) and '*Wayalesi*' (Wireless), two of the famous songs of the colonial period, Columbia Records intervened in the rendering and reception of popular performance. When we listen to the recordings we can imagine the impact of the performance on the audience. Ssekinoomu uses metaphors to narrate the events and sexual innuendo to describe the contest between Nakato and Mulinnyabigo. Our image of Ssekinoomu playing the part of Mulinnyabigo addressing Nakato and the crowd of onlookers is amusing. '*Ekyalema Nakato*' is a popular song today although artists divert from the original in favour of a dramatic license to intensify the audience's enjoyment of Kiganda Baakisimba dance. Hence, instead of performing the song in its entirety the song leader merely sings the lead line for the chorus:

Leader: *Ekyalema Nakato aa kyalema*
Chorus: *Aa kyalema Nakato e Kawanda*

Leader: Nakato's challenge aa what a challenge
Chorus: The challenge of Nakato of Kawanda (village)

'*Ekyalema Nakato*' is a multilayered text that narrated the extraordinary encounter between Mulinnyabigo, an allegedly promiscuous man, and his mistress, Nakato. While we may not know much about his live performances, the surviving recordings show that Ssekinoomu had much interest in dramatic presentation. Theatrical performances often took place in beer houses and at wedding feasts; hence Ssekinoomu and his ensemble could have performed this typical wedding song at such a feast. The opening stanza was intended to draw the crowd's attention. As happens in the traditional openings of folksongs, the singer continued his story:

Mmm mbu amazima oganza ow'ebigere olinga ali mu nkuyo
awulira enkoko zikookolima ssebo nayita olugendo
o'womukwano zuukuka tugende bukedde okole.
Yiii, olabye bw'akwatira omuggo akirako agoba ente
aa aa, olugendo olugabira wakati, nga agaba ennyam.

Mmm, they say, to fall in love with 'barefooted lover' is like playing the *nkuyo* game (game of the cone)
As soon as the cock crows at dawn, he calls out for a journey or thinks of a journey prospect:
My love, wake up and lets go, its dawn, go to work.
Yiii, see how he raises the stick at you as if he is herding cattle
aa aa, he splits the journey into two parts as if he is sharing [out] meat.

In Luganda, Ssekinoomu's reference to a 'barefooted lover' alludes to a poor man or a lover on foot; or it could refer to a promiscuous person. The pun demonstrates the performer and audience's deep appreciation for ambiguity, which was a strong characteristic of oral tradition and performance. His language appears cryptic here partly to achieve a comic effect, and because it was normal practice among the Baganda to use innuendo and metaphor when discussing topics to do with sex. It is also important to note that the word '*omuggo*' (stick) has various interpretations. In this context, the word refers to the male genitals, specifically Ssekinoomu and his crudeness, a point that is emphasised by '*bw'akwatira omuggo akirako agoba ente*' (he raises the stick at you as if he is herding cattle). Excited by the sexual metaphors, the crowds would respond with ululation. We note the interdependence between song text, music, and dramatic action, which underlines how Ssekinoomu would have manipulated the audience to applaud his performance. At the same time, the instrumentalists and the dancers would make exaggerated sexual movements intended to illustrate the singer's lyrics. In addition, there is a veiled reference to poverty echoing the belief that poor men can never court beautiful women.

Yiii, mazima bw'akulengera enkoona eyo, n'emusaliza omwoyo.
Owange ettutumu abaagala ennyo.
Ekyedde ekyeddamu kyaaki? (Ssekinoomu, 1945)

Yiii, its true, he envies you as he sees you disappear over the horizon.
My dear, people like courting popularity.
Isn't it senseless?

At this point Ssekinoomu, playing the role of the narrator, would move closer to the audience to begin his impersonation of characters. He would alternate his performance of the characters Nakato and Mulinnyabigo, with the narrator, all the time using cryptic expressions. Probably the instrumentalists would play the role of the primary audience thus drawing the secondary audience into the action on stage. This helps to draw the audience's attention to the key points of the narrative hence enhancing their enjoyment of the drama. The narrator, spurred on by the instrumentalists and audiences excited response, would extemporise and extend the narrative. Meanwhile, the audience, gathered around the performers, perhaps even joining the dancers in the performance arena to show off their individual dance skills. In this context, they would use head ties or wrappers as dance costumes.

Mmm kambabuulire
yiii bano abatamanyi kuyimba
bannange nkoleki?

Mmm let me tell you
yiii, these people who can't sing
My friends, what should do I do?

Ne b'asasiira Nakato e Kawanda
ebigambo byalema Mulinnyabigo gw'omanyi
oli mukyala w'angeriki atamanyi mukwano?
A aa kale nagula sukaali nze nali mwannyoko?

They empathised with Nakato of Kawanda
Mulinnyabigo,[4] the one you know, failed to seduce her
what kind of woman are you who doesn't know the game of love?
Aaa am I your brother to buy you sugar?

In the above dialogue, Nakato lamented why she ever accepted Mulinnyabigo's love advances. However, in response Mulinnyabigo stated that it was not his fault that Nakato is a hopeless lover (who could not pick cues of love). The parallel statements drive the audience to a state of ecstatic frenzy, dramatised with ululation and dancing.

Yiii naye omwami nakukyalira ewamwe s'akusiibula?
Yiii ye gwe ebbinika ogifumba mu ngeri ki eyo eteva ku kyooto?
Kale sukaali gw'otosaasira.

Kambalojjere amazima
abakyala mubasaasire
mubasaasire okulima
ssebo abajja batuutira, abasajja batuutira amazima
Yiii olwagala omukuule nti nze aliko omuzungu
okumanya muzungu amata tegava ku kyooto
di di di di di di diria olwo bwe batyeebule!

Yiii, my man, didn't I say farewell to you after my visit?
Yii, how long does your kettle take to boil?
You can't even show some generosity (sympathy) to the sugar.

Truly, let me narrate my truth to you
have empathy for the women
digging [sex] is hard work, be considerate to them
sir, they come when they are ripe for sex; but truthfully men are always erect.
Yiii, why do you love such a man? I have the wherewithal of a European/whiteman
to prove it, I always have an endless supply of milk
di di di di di di da diria then they dance away!

Perhaps Ssekinoomu's use of euphemistic cliché is because the dramatic dialogue mirrors new experiences in the community, specifically that of openly engaging in immoral sexual acts. Notably this section includes the favourite analogy between a wealthy man and a *muzungu*, European, '*Yiii ... nze aliko omuzungu*' (Yiii ... I have the wherewithal of a European). Here Ssekinoomu implies that the ordinary person differed from the wealthy Baganda or Europeans in wealth and manners. In addition, he uses appropriate slang terms and euphemisms, for example, '*sukaali*' (sugar) whose meaning in this context is sex or private parts, and '*ebbinika*' (kettle) that refers to male private parts. This reminds us that since this community theatre, audiences may have included children, in-laws or even the king whom the performer would not have wanted to offend.

Interwoven into his comments on Nakato's experience are comments on drunkenness. In the second part of the song, Ssekinoomu changed the theme focusing his criticism on beer. Here are some excerpts of the dialogue:

Yiii omwenge si mubi kya kunywa kizaale
aaa uu
kya kunnywa kitonde.
Kambalojjere omwenge.
Yiii wabula abagunywa be bagwoonona
bano ne badda mu nguudo
era bwavaawo n'akuba enduulu
munne akuba abantu
Ssabakulu oguteekako etteeka kutumalira bantu

Yiii there is nothing wrong with beer, it is a natural drink
aaa huu
its a drink dating back to creation.

Allow me narrate its story
Yiii its just those people who drink it who abuse it [....]
Let me warn you, there are fines imposed for both its use and abuse

The above stanza illustrates how Ssekinoomu uses identifiable conventional forms, like idioms, proverbs or even intertextual references to construct his narrative. For instance, the third line '*abagunywa be bagwonoona*' (people who drink it who abuse it), is an intertextual borrowing from a number of Luganda songs that would have been familiar to the audience.

In the following stanza, Ssekinoomu changed themes and, satirising a known personality, Keya, who served as a tax collector, he drew on the tradition of mimicry. In the following lines Ssekinoomu intended to focus the audiences attention on his mimicry of Keya:

Eya Keya mazima empale ye mbu nnamba
yiii naye mazima bwagikwoleka
amagulu n'omusono ogwo gukulema
yiii mpanvu si mpanvu, nnyimpi si nnyimpi

Keya's trousers are full length
however, I think when he puts them on....
Iiii, sincerely when he faces you may even fail to recognise the style
Iiii, its neither long but not long, short but not short

Once more, the crowd, together with the musicians, danced and made caricatures of characters presented by Ssekinoomu, mocking people who adopt European shorts in preference to Kiganda *kanzus* (tunics). The subtle shifts to more contemporary themes invigorate the audience. The dramatic quality of the text in the preceding stanza illustrates that this performance is just one example of the dramatic enactment in which a common experience is theatricalised by mimetic, verbal, and vocal expressions. Ssekinoomu uses *bisoko*, a Luganda term that means instrumental music or poetic idioms, to display his virtuosity. Although this is an archived performance of one of Ssekinoomu's performances, oral sources, for example, Sam Sserwanga and Busuulwa[5], affirm that it offers a possible 'depiction' of what travelling musician performances, for instance, Majangwa's or even Ssekinoomu were like.

Oral informers told me that the song alludes to a 1940s event in Buganda when the Queen Mother, Drusilla Namaganda, broke custom and remarried. Hence, the song portrays her as an over sexed person. Notably, contemporary performances of the songs are more explicit. For instance, in 2010 when Busuulwa performed a variation of the song at Makerere College School he intercut the original scene between Nakato's plea to Mulinnyabigo with a general comment on women's experience of public wrath with the following stanza:

Drusilla Namaganda yalya ekibe
Bali bakibabuza ssanja emmuli zabula
Bakirya mu kiro nga abaana beebase

Bamusindike agwe eri aseseme bye yabba
Bamusindike agwe eri atomere ebifunvu

Drusilla Namaganda killed (ate) a fox
They roasted it using dry banana leaves for they could not find dry reeds
They ate it at night while the children were all sleeping
People should push her away, don't care whether she stumbles and falls
Push her / let her knock against the walls

This direct comment on the Queen Mother's relationship is Busuulwa's own creation, is his own re-presentation of the event. His rendition directly names Namaganda but still uses the metaphor of the fox to refer to the undesirable sexual relationship between the two lovers. His performance, accompanied by sexually suggestive facial expressions and dramatised voice inflections illustrate the qualities of *abadongo* performers. The performer is the most important medium of artistic expression. His movements are stylised and are locally described to resemble the jerky movements of *kaamuje* (squirrel).

In the following example of '*Wayalesi*' (Wireless), recorded in 1945, Ssekinoomu focused on modernity, specifically the introduction of wireless technology to Buganda/Uganda. This song consists of eight different stanzas, each of which develops the theme of the experience of the introduction of wireless receivers to Uganda.

Waya, waya, waya, wayi wayalesi
Waya waya way' Abazungu baziyiya
Kale tubade twewuunya za tabaza mbu ez'eddoboozi limu
Sibalimba ayogera ayima Kampala nowulira eddoboozi lyoka.

Naye nze Abazungu kye mbatiirako n'eBuganda bagireeta
Sikulimba Buganda b'agisanyusa nny'okumanya nga zanyuma
Bwolaba ng'abe Mukono[6] babaterawo hmm naye baategeera
Tegereza abe Kisubi[6] babateera aa aa babawa
Mu Nakivubo wansi baagitekako mbadde nga yetugatika
Tegereza ku Lubiri[7] baagitekako nga yey'abakungu bokka
Nze ndowoza Kitaka ne Kilainingi balinga bebagireta.

Newuunya abasajja mu [ku]gaba ebbaluwa wamma gwe bakanya
Nga waliwo omusajja ow'oluberera ng'eddoboozi litta bantu
Newuunya omulala okugera engero nze simanyi kikaddekadde
Omusajja bwalikula balimuddawa nay'engero zamuyinga.

Omupiira kibuga[8] kaba gubeerako nze obukadde sibulabanga
Embaga zona zona kaba[9] zitandika nze obukadde sibulabanga
Obukadde bwe Kasubi bwajjira ku miggo bulabe ku wayalesi
Sikulimba akalala kajja n'emmindi, nay'olwo emmindi bagirinnya
Nga kali awo kitange kagiringiriza, kanno kagiyita eggi
K'aba ddaaki k'abuuza n'obusungu nti obwedda mpulira
Baana bange obwedda mpulira ddoboozi abo aboogera be baliwa

Nebamugamba nti ayogera ayima Kampala, naye lino ddoboozi lyokka
Sikulimba nako ako ka Ddamba k'agenda tekategera
Kitange omusese yajja n'omutwalo gw' enkejje bagurya
Nga ali awo anti Nakivubo agiringiriza banne bagiyita eggi
Ye nze bannange n'annyumya biki akumanya nga z'anyuma
Ba Nakalanga be Kyagwe bajja n'essami¹⁰, essami nebalitwala
Kitange Omukunja yajja n'ebirugu, ebirugu b'abirya
Musaasire owe Bukoba ey'ajja n'amenvu naye ago amenvu b'agalinnya
Ye nze bannange n'anyummya biki mbu okumanya nga z'annyuma.

Ye nze banange kye mbabulira era muleke mbabulire
Ng' abakyala ejjooje beesiwa kufa nga ne nsonda bazimwa
Ng'abaami emyaasa b'esala kufa nga n' embale beetema
Ennaku zino eziriko nsaasira abakyala ba nnyabo balabye
Si b'ebeesiba kale baly'esiba batya newankubade beesiba
Na'nasiba Mukono namutegeka newankubade beesiba
Na'nasiba kisubi namutegeka nga n'emmotoka ziyita
Yii ye nze era n'annyumya biki mbu okumanya nga beesiba
Ban'asiba batya Nakivubo wamma gw' okumusiba
Ye nze bannange n'annyumya biki okumanya nga beesiba.

Ye nz'era abakyala kye mbatiirako amagezi g'abayinga
Oba oli awo era ne bagyesiba okumanya nga beesiba
Bwolaba nga ne kavvu bamusibako so nga obulwade butta bantu
Naye nz'abakyala kye mbatiirako okuyiiya kwabayinga
Ye nze bannange na'nnyumya biki mb' okumanya nga kwabayinga.

Ye nze bannange kye mbabulira era muleke mbabulire
Bw'olaba nga ne Mawanda¹¹ bamusi… yiii muleke mbabulire
Olaba nga ne Mawanda b'amusibako muleke mbabulire
Newewuunnya yenna yenna n'atambula yii newewuunya okumusiba
Oluwo singa omumpi asibye mu mannyo, nga bajja beraga
Nkubulire omuwanvu asibye mu byenda, nga bagya beraga
Nebatwala n'omukono nebasika, abakyala tebatya
Nga bagamba nti kye kita kyasibirako muleke mbabulire
Leero luno abakyala ban'asiba batya newankubadde beesiba
Ye nze kye mbabulira era muleke mbabulire.

Ndowooza bannange kye mbabulira amagezi b'agayinga
Ye nze Abazungu kye mbebaliza, Abazungu bebale.

Wire, wire, wire wii… wireless
Wire wire wir … invented by the Bazungu
Imagine we were amazed by the streetlights that they work in unison
I swear the speaker is in Kampala you hear his voice only

I respectfully fear the Bazungu, even to Buganda they brought it
I swear to you it was very entertaining; Buganda was excited
See, they fixed the link to Mukono hmm they loved it
Imagine even Kisubi was linked up aaa aaa connected
In downtown Nakivubo they fixed one that linked us together

Imagine at Lubiri palace they fixed one for the royals alone
I think Kitaka and Clining seem to have imported it.

There was a man daily whose voice left people titillated
I am awed by another's knowledge of proverbs; I wonder whether he is middle-aged
The man when he gets old no one will challenge him for he is so knowledgeable about proverbs.
Ever since football came to town I have not seen the elderly in the crowds
Since festivities started, I have not seen elderly people in the crowds
The elderly form Kasubi came hobbling on sticks to see the Wireless
I do not lie that one old man came with a smoking pipe, but that day they stepped on it
Poor man was peeking at it; he thought it was an egg
Eventually he asked in anger that all the while I have been hearing
My children, I hear a voice but where are the people speaking from?
They told him that the person is speaking from Kampala; this is only his voice
I swear the poor man left in a confused state
The pitiless with came with a whole load of small dried fish (enkejje)
He was there peeking at it while his friends called it an egg
My friends what shall I say to show that it was exciting
The dwarfs from Kyagwe came with stocks essami (insects); they stole them
Poor man from Bukunja came with yams; yams were eaten
Sympathise with the one from Bukoba who came with sweet bananas, those sweet bananas were stepped on
My friends what should I say to show how it was so entertaining
My friends what I am telling, let me tell you.

The women beautified their skins they even shaved their fore heads
The men shaved their heads clean they nearly shaved off the skin
These days I pity women, poor things
They tightly wrap the dresses now how well will they dress then[12]
Even the one who will wrap Mukono sorts it, even if they wrap up tight
Even the one who wraps small bananas sorts them as the vehicles drive past
Iii, how can I explain this, you know, they dress well
You tell me; how they will wrap Nakivubo, wrap it tight
How will I explain to show that they dress well?
For me I hold them in high esteem; they are so clever
You wait, they will wrap it around their bodies; that is how good they are
You see, they wrapped up bundles of money yet diseases kill people
But for me I hold women in high esteem creativity overcomes them
For me my friends what will I explain to show that they are so clever
For me my friends what I tell you, let me tell you.

You see even Mawanda was ti… iii let me tell you
You see even Mawanda[13] was imprisoned, let me tell you
You wonder the way he proudly strode yiii you wonder how they handcuffed him
What if he is short and has wrapped it round the teeth, would they show off [their might]
I tell you the tallest has wrapped tight around her stomach they came to show their might
They hold the hand, pull and twist, women are fearless

They said, it is the gourd she uses to wrap tight; let me tell you
This time the women, how will they dress up even if they wrap up tight
For me I tell you so let me tell you.

I think my friends what I tell you they are too clever
For me the Bazungu for that I thank them, Abazungu, thank you.

The theme of this song W*ayalesi* (wireless) was a very topical one. In 1936, a private company, probably owned by Clining but in partnership with Chief Kitaka, had brought the wireless to Buganda. Loudspeakers had been placed in key locations in the town: in the Kabaka's palace at Mengo, Nakivubo park in the town centre, and at the Roman Catholic missionary centre at Kisubi. Not surprisingly, ordinary people were mesmerised by technology that transmitted human voices. Ssekinoomu mockingly describes the crowds as '*obukadde*' (wimpish old men), '*bunakalanga*' (gangly men), and uses diminutive words such as '*ka kitange*' (poor fellow) to suggest an invasion of the town by villagers. In addition, the audience notes his use of pejorative nouns that refer to people's places of origin, for example, '*omukunja*', someone from Bukunja country and a derogatory term for night dancers and '*omussesse*' (one from Ssesse islands, which suggests people whose diet is entirely dependent on fish). In our minds, these elicit memories of people living deep in the villages; and also suggest a consciousness of rural to urban migration and the sense of the hierarchy and superiority felt by Ssekinoomu as a member of the emerging urban community. Interspersed in the comic dialogue are culturally specific discourses on colonisation and oppression, and national identity that echo the people's resentment of imperial rule. Note Ssekinoomu's contribution to the discourse regarding the backwardness of people from the countryside. In his provocative statements in the last stanza, Ssekinoomu insinuates that the Europeans were spiteful towards the Baganda when they humiliated the King's elder brother, Prince Mawanda. Hence, the sentimental statements are intended to arouse a sense of 'nationhood' among the audience. Ssekinoomu took on the task of recording contemporary experiences by creating characters that reference people from all sections of society; not surprisingly, throughout the performance he assumes all the roles and performs all the experiences. By using the stage to entertain and satirise the Europeans' ignorance and rude behaviour he created humour. In the above song, traditional generic forms of social discourse provide the thematic focus.

Writing about these songs, Cooke comments on the use of 'allusion and metaphor in texts that can have double and even triple meanings', as evidenced in this song, is what would have made the performance allusive, hence difficult for censors to decode (Cooke, 2010). Therefore, an extended analysis of these texts will illustrate how far contemporary Ugandan theatre has borrowed from earlier forms of theatre to develop its own form of expression and style. These songs, stories and dances helped to create a cultural focus for the community hence they are still being performed. Although the characters may change their ethnic identities, and their roles may be transformed, the stories remain as important cultural symbols of indigenous popular theatre.

Censorship

The fixity of the recorded performance, which is likely to remove the dialectic of the relationship between the performer and his audience, did not prevent the composition of subversive texts. Consequently, a 'good deal of official censorship' was practised by the colonial authorities because they wanted to clamp down on indigenous practices they regarded as immoral, they were suspicious about the agitation for independence in Uganda, or they had anxieties about the emerging so-called Mau Mau rising in Kenya and the agitation for independence in Uganda (Cooke, 2010).

Music theatre was popular because it disseminated community sentiments with regard to social and political concerns. For instance, in pre-colonial times, when the royal musicians were offended by the king they composed '*Omusango gw' abalere*' (The Royal Flutists' Crime) to show their distaste of his behaviour. Here the musicians were exercising their right to reprimand the king on behalf of the community. In addition, by stating that when things go wrong they can go back to their place of origin they are asserting their cultural (clan) identity.

Anti omusango gw'abalere gwegaludde
bantwale e Bbira,
gubadde gutya?

Nze emeeme enkulungutana
Binsobedde, bantwale e Bbira gyebanzaala

Look, the case of the flutists has reached its height
Let them take me to Bbira
What has gone wrong?

My spirit is not troubled
I am perplexed let them take me to Bbira where I was born

Archived letters between Columbia Records at Hayes and Shankar Das and Sons, the recording agent in Nairobi, show that the company attempted to censor and even cancel the distribution of some Luganda recordings, claiming that they were 'unsuitable for sale' (Cooke, 2010). For instance, in 1940, '*Bamuta*' by Arajubu & Party was deemed immoral because it narrated the story of Bamuta who was found guilty of raping a prostitute. While today this might be a moral issue, it would have been regarded as a political offence by the colonial government at a time when the Christian missionaries closely identified with the colonial government. Hence, insulting Christian morals was equated with breaking colonial laws. That Shankar Das and Sons stated that they did not know that Arajubu had recorded a popular Baakisimba-Nankasa dance song that is accompanied by sexually suggestive dance movements that were socially acceptable, is not surprising since they were ignorant of its language of performance. Once again, in 1940, Columbia Records wrote to the agent requesting them to withdraw recording No. 337 (Sesse) because the Ugandan Police had noted that some of the lyrics were of a 'subversive' nature:

We regret to have to advise you that we have been informed by the police in Uganda that tier ? [the entire] subject matter of record No. 337 is such as to make it entire! [entirely] unsuitable for sale in the country. The Police have assisted us in getting a translation and we find that the subject matter recorded does not agree with the script of the words which Were [were] supposed to have been recorded. We? [We] [s]Should tee [be] glad if will cancel any orders which you have for this number[.] [A]aim [to] have the master destroyed to [ensure] ensure? [t]That no further pressings are made [.] (Vernon, 1997: 2)

The offending text recommended Islam as the religion of choice because Muslims were very clean: (Sesse 'If you have a Mahommedan as a guest you can be sure that he will get up early in the morning and be progressive. Even the water he passes he throws forward and not backward.' (Vernon, 1997: 1) Being illiterate regarding the performance aesthetics of the group, the recording company was not aware that although instrumental accompaniments are stable, dialogues/lyrics are recreated at each performance. Thus we note that in their recording of musical performances, record companies and the radio stations did not understand the theatricality of the culture outside its per-formance space; that although it alienated them from their environmental context, performers remained 'skilful theatrical entertainers who also carried news and views in their lyrics' (Cooke, 2010).

In addition to these and other songs and folk dramas, there are the important anthropological writings in Luganda published early in the twentieth century that record indigenous popular cultural and ritual performances. The most significant is Apolo Kagwa's *Empisa za Baganda* (The Customs of the Baganda, 1901).

In the above discussion, I have explored various indigenous performance forms: folk dramas and folk music of the colonial period, showing how the socio-political and historical contexts affected the performances and their reception, and how contemporary 'reading back' through recordings can help us recon-struct these performances. We also see how later playwrights like Serumaga, Kawadwa, and Mbowa's drama, and most recently, Rwangyezi's *Lawino and Ocol* (2000), drew on embodied indigenous theatre forms, and thus provide insight into performance forms and styles of both the pre-colonial and colonial periods.

NOTES

1   In 1885 the Imperial British East African Company was appointed by the British colonial government to administer British East Africa before it became the East African Protectorate. Its main aim was to develop African trade in the British area of influence.
2   People believed that if someone suffered from leprosy they would lose part of their nose.
3   All translations are the author's own.
4   Literally a name for one who climbs over fences, figuratively suggesting that he could conquer any woman.
5   This is based on the present author's interview of Sam Sserwanga and Stephen Buuulwa, pro-fessional indigenous performers, in Kampala in April 2010.
6   A village on Ntebe Road
7   Mengo palace
8   Short for *ku kibuga*
9   *Kaba* is an old Luganda word meaning 'since'. The contemporary equivalent is *kasookanga*.

10 This must be a small insect usually found around lakes (or large rivers). It is a delicacy for some people
11 King E. Mutesa's elder brother. He was big, tall and fierce.
12 There is a play on the word *kwesiba* here and he uses the meanings interchangeably i.e. *kwesiba* to wrap up tight and *kwesiba* to dress well. This specifically refers to *busuuti*, and enables the audience to recognise caricatures of women, and Mawanda presented by Ssekinoomu.
13 See note 11.

BIBLIOGRAPHY

Arujubu (1940) 'Bamuta' quoted in Paul Vernon, 'The World at 80 RPM'. Pu:feastlib:mrf:yinyue: texts:fr119worldat80.html, accessed 10/2/2010.

Breitinger, Eckhard (2004) 'Uganda'. In Martin Banham, *A History of Theatre in Africa*, Cambridge: Cambridge University Press, 247-64.

Busuulwa, Stephen (2010) *Ekyalema Nakato e Kawanda*, Unpublished.

Cooke, Peter (2010) 'Introduction Notes to Early East African Recordings', Unpublished.

Irobi, Esiaba (2007). 'What They Came With: Carnival and Persistence of African Performance Aesthetics in the Diaspora', *Journal of Black Studies*, 37: 6, 896-913.

Kagwa, Apolo Sir (1901, 1st edition) *Empisa za Baganda* (The Customs of the Baganda), London: The Sheldon Press.

Kasule, Sam (2006) 'Possession, Trance, Ritual and Popular Performance: The Transformation of Theatre in Post Idi Amin Uganda in Beatrice Nicolini', *Studies in Witchcraft, Magic, War and Peace in Africa: Nineteenth and Twentieth Centuries*. New York: The Edwin Mellen Press, 295-316.

Kawadwa, Byron (1959) St Lwanga, Unpublished.

Kawadwa, Byron (1970) Makula ga Kulabako, Unpublished.

Kawadwa, Byron (1975) *Oluyimba lwa Wankoko*, Unpublished

MacPherson, Margaret (1976) 'What happened to Majangwa?' in *Mawazo*, II: 4, 68-70.

Mbowa, Rose. (1999) 'Luganda Theatre and Its Audience', in Eckhard Breitinger (ed.) *Uganda: The Cultural Landscape*, Bayreuth: Bayreuth African Studies 39, 227-46.

Perham, Margery, (ed.) Bull, Mary (ass. ed.) (1959) *The Diaries of Lord Lugard, Volume III East Africa, January 1892 to August 1892*, London: Faber and Faber.

Roscoe, John (1911) *The Baganda: An Account of Their Native Customs and Beliefs*, London: Macmillan.

Ruganda, John (1972) *The Burdens*, Nairobi: Oxford University Press.

Rwangyezi, Stephen (2000) *Lawino and Ocol*, Unpublished.

Said, Edward (1979) *Orientalism: Western Conceptions of the Orient*. London: Vintage.

Sentongo, Nuwa. (1998) 'Historical Development of Theatre in Uganda', Unpublished conference paper.

Sekamwa, John C. (1990) *Enkuluza y'Eddiini y'Abaganda Ey'ennono* (A Baganda Traditional Religion Dictionary), Kampala: Wood Printers and Stationers.

Serumaga, Robert (1974) *Majangwa*, Nairobi: East African Publishing House.

Ssekinoomu (1945) '*Ekyalema Nakato*' MA 73, LP, London: Columbia Records.

Ssekinoomu (1945) '*Wayalesi*' MA 73, LP. London: Columbia Records.

Steadman, Ian (1990) 'Towards Popular Theatre in South Africa', *Journal of Southern African Studies*, 16: 2, 207-208.

Taylor, Diana (1998) 'A Savage Performance: Guillermo Gómez-Peña and Coco Fusco's "Couple in the Cage"', *The Drama Review*, 42: 2, 160-75.

Taylor, Diana (2004) 'Scenes of Cognition: Performance and Conquest', *Theatre Journal*, 56, 353-72.

Vernon, Paul (1997) 'Feast of East', pu:feastlib:mrf:yinyue:texts:fr145eastafrica.html (Accessed 10/2/2010)

Vernon, Paul (date unknown) 'The World at 80 RPM', Pu:feastlib:mrf:yinyue:texts: fr119worldat80.html (Accessed 10/2/2010)

The Leaf & the Soap
('Bí ewé bá pé l'ara ọṣẹ, á di ọṣẹ')[1]
A story of appropriation & resistance

CRISTINA BOSCOLO

Introduction

I am
because of memory

The period between 1850 and 1950 was characterized by rapid socio-political transformation in the area that was to be known as Yorùbáland, particularly with the consolidation and expansion of the colonial endeavour. As with many other sectors of life, this had momentous consequences for Yorùbá traditions of performance. The encounter with the colonial power led to the dislocation of Yorùbá cultural and artistic manifestations from their historical and socio-cultural frames of reference. It decentred them. Colonial paradigms silenced and marginalized them. They channelled their development and reception, predetermining the way we read back into their history even today. This becomes most evident also with the kind of performances, new to Yorùbáland, which began to appear on stage in towns like Lagos, Abẹ́òkúta and Ìbàdàn in the second half of the nineteenth century. These performances could be defined as the initial phase of a new tradition, or rather of a 'new stage' that came to enrich the wide range of Yorùbá classic performance traditions.[2] Significantly though, they have been considered most often in terms of the way they have imitated of the western format, obscuring the issue of agency on the one side, and reinforcing the centrality of western canons in the performing arts on the other.

The focus of the present paper is to consider the central decades of the period, approximately 1860 to 1920, and the development of this 'new stage', turning attention to the issue of agency and highlighting the process of appropriation and the transformations the performances went through from their inception.

This period is barely mentioned in most of the literature related to Yorùbá and Nigerian theatre history. In spite of this, I would like to argue that it is a time of particular significance for the Nigerian performing arts. First, it is exactly in this period that the trichotomic reception of the different Nigerian performance traditions and their varying degree of visibility begin to take root. Second, it is a time of ferment that contains *in vivo* all the elements that under-pinned the achievements of later Yorùbá theatrical developments: Most

90

notably, those of theatre makers like Hubert Ogunde and the travelling theatres, as well as those of the written tradition, that was so strongly to develop in the following decades.

Quite apart from setting the precedents for the performing traditions that were to follow, however, the most important reason for reconsidering this period is that the 'new stage' reveals, in my view, a neglected creative space with a highly subversive potential. In other words, this period needs to be reassessed because of its own theatrical attainments. The adoption of the 'new stage' and its slow process of adaptation to the environment offers an interesting view on the mechanisms and the complex relations of power and resistance triggered by the Yorùbá encounter with the colonial power. Far from being mere imitation, the performances of the time illustrate a significant change in the attitudes of an emerging elite. They accompany the socio-political process of Yorùbá identity formation and affirmation, while, ultimately, they show the negotiation of Yorùbá identity on stage. There is an image evoked by a Yorùbá proverb that, illustrating this process of transformation, captures its essence: *Bí ewé bá pẹ́ l'ara ọsẹ, á di ọsẹ*, that is, 'when the leaf stays with the soap, it becomes soap'. The leaf is the stage, the Yorùbá culture is the soap that by its sheer presence transforms what appeared on the Nigerian stage.

Remarkably, the transformation and appropriation of the new stage – in the imagery of the proverb, the leaf turning into soap – together with its subversive potential have been neglected. As stated above, the 'concerts' and the plays put on the 'new stage' have most often been deprecated because of their imitative character, and ultimately been considered as an entertainment form that evolved to suit the taste of the so-called 'Black Victorians'. Shifting the focus away from this perspective, the intention behind the present paper is to highlight instead the strategies of appropriation and manipulation developed by the theatre artists to assess and affirm their ethnic identity. The article intends to support a critical appraisal that evinces the process of appropriation of the 'new stage', bringing to the fore those features that step by step, or rather, performance by performance, helped to bring Yorùbá life onto the stage. They are mostly in small details, nonetheless they disclose an underrated agency that, operating within the constraints of the colonial condition, eventually transformed the look and the content of the new stage that, like the leaf of the proverb, eventually turned into soap.

The silenced stage

> I am
> because of memory.
> I exist
> in your world
> black on white
> spoken, I was ignored
> they said I belong to the night

in your world
un-heard, un-written
my existence forgot of being

As hinted at in the introduction, colonial paradigms led to the marginaliza-
tion of Yorùbá artistic performances. Busy in building an empire, the colonial
'civilizing' enterprise had no place for aesthetic considerations.[3] Basically,
missionaries and colonial agents were there to 'civilize', to teach and certainly
not to be taught. Sporadically though the colonialists' silence was broken.

On Wednesday, 22 February 1826, during his travel in Yorùbáland, Captain
Hugh Clapperton wrote in his journal:

> It is the custom during the time that the caboceers from the different towns remain
> on their visit to the king to act plays or pantomimes... The first act consisted in
> dancing and tumbling... The second act consisted in catching the boa constrictor
> ... The third act consisted of the white devil... They appeared indeed to enjoy this
> sight and the perfection of the actor's art... The spectators often appealed to us, as
> to the excellence of the performance ... and certainly the actor burlesqued the part
> to admiration. (Clapperton, 1829: 53)

The artistry and skilful exhibition described enthusiastically by Clapperton
refers most probably to a performance of the *egúngún aláré*. The popular troupes
of *egúngún* entertainers, known also as *alárìnjó* or *apídan* that possibly, already in
the sixteenth century, had become itinerant, and thus brought their performances with their astonishing transformations to towns and villages of the
different Yorùbá kingdoms.[4]

Clapperton's well known description is one of the very rare written sources
that bear witness to the rich performance tradition existing in Yorùbáland
before the colonial encounter. Most colonial written sources ignored – when
they did not deny – the existence of anything that could be called theatre or
performing arts in the colonized territories. Yorùbáland was no exception.
Accordingly, there is little or no written record of the performances that took
place during the various festivals or on other celebrative occasions that marked
the rhythm of Yorùbá social life. The Yorùbá use of music, chants, dance,
masks and poetry, was left to its eco-environment, relegated to the world of
orality and, at best frowned upon by the colonialists, especially the missionaries.
This derogatory attitude might have been determined more by preconceived
colonial ideas and indifference towards the Yorùbá performing arts, than by a
conscious critical attitude. Understandably, there was no vested interest in
asserting the aesthetic value of something that would not have buttressed the
Empire's own strong sense of superiority and, furthermore, was indissolubly
related to what was considered a 'primitive' and 'pagan' worldview.

Yet, whatever the colonial attitude,

> Life style among (most of) the indigenes continued as before. They ate the normal
> Yoruba dishes of maize, cassava, yams and Yoruba sauces. They dressed in the same
> large flowing cloak called *Agbada*, and baggy trousers (Cole, 1975: 46)

And, we may add, they continued to celebrate and perform in the various festivals, and on other occasions, even if, given the cultural bias, the local newspaper did not at first feature them.

The new stage

I am
because of memories
like the leaf sprouting timidly
cautiously buds out,
sounding space,
not even aware of existence
I started being
striving to become
out of entangled destinies

One evening in late November, 1866, an audience of merchants, churchmen, civil servants, students and artisans sat in a small house on Awolola Street listening to *the first public concert of Western music performed in Lagos*. The concert was sponsored and performed by members and friends of *The Academy*... (Leonard, 1967: 2; my emphasis)[5]

What might appear at first to be an illustration of a pleasant soirée in the bustling Lagosian life of the second half of the nineteenth century, might deservedly be considered as an historical event that, retrospectively, marks the birth of a kind of theatre new to the Yorùbá soil. Despite the importance I confer on the event, not many details have been reported about the programme of the concert held by The Academy on that night. We are told that it 'included a variety of such items as dramatic sketches, recitations, songs and glees and classical music' (Adedeji, 1971: 28). The promoters and organizers were Josiah and Samuel Crowther Junior, while Bishop Crowther himself (their father) was the patron of The Academy on that night. These are approximately the facts we have access to. What then makes this event so special?

The significance of the event opens up if we frame it against the backdrop of the history of Yorùbáland at that time, which was characterized by deep and complex societal changes. The Ọ̀yọ́ Empire[6] was spreading its cultural influence while, almost paradoxically, it was disintegrating, as it was no longer capable of controlling the empire. As a more or less direct result, new towns (such as Abéòkúta, Ìjàyè and Ìbàdàn) and new political patterns were emerging. The internal conflicts in Yorùbáland were worsened by a triple threat at the borders: the British in Lagos, the Fulani in Ìlọrin, and the Dahomeans in the west. In this climate of tension and instability, the Yorùbá attempt to manipulate foreign intrusion for the own political ends failed. Almost as a direct consequence, Lagos was occupied by the British and, in 1861 it was declared a British Colony (Soremekun, 1985).

In the meantime, Yorùbáland experienced the return of a large number of 'settlers' in a wave of migratory movement of freed slaves from Sierra Leone and, to a lesser extent, also from Brazil and Cuba, particularly after the slave

Emancipation in 1888. Known as Akus, Saros or Agudas, according to their provenance, these 'westernized Yorubas' (Smith, 1969: 141) played an essential, somewhat intermediary role in the growing colonial relationship between the British and the Yorùbá. Their personal histories, indeed their bodies, became the site on which cultural elements and traditions of different provenances met. Once back, these men and women were consciously or unconsciously, attempting to adapt and settle on a soil that was familiar and yet alien, as they no longer had deep societal bonds, because they had been uprooted from these by the events of history. That same history, on the other hand, had exposed them to mission schools and churches, and 'promised' an equal, 'progressive' society.

On that late November evening the people that met at Awolola Street embodied this new, emerging aspect of Yorùbá society. Beside the patron, Bishop Crowther, the first African bishop, the Academy intersects with the personal histories of J. P. L. Davies, president of The Academy, 'a wealthy Lagos naval merchant and an Anglicized Sierra Leonean of Nigerian descent', his wife Sarah Forbes Bonetta, who 'until her death in 1880, [was] one of the leading pianists and singers in Lagos'; and its members, who include Robert Campbell, 'West Indian journalist and printer', and Otunba Payne, 'who rose to be the registrar of the Lagos Supreme Court' (Adedeji, 1971: 28). These and many other personal histories transcended the short life of The Academy, to epitomize the social and cultural history of an emergent class, whose life-style was greatly influenced by western values, assimilated particularly through the missionary education system, which obviously emphasized western values and culture, and supported 'civilized' western forms of entertainment.

There was a keen desire on the part of the small Lagos *elite* to demonstrate an interest in and an appreciation of music and theatre in so far as these were symbols of status and culture. Moreover, most of the promoters of concerts in Lagos were people who had some experience of these musical performances overseas (Echeruo, 1962: 68)

The Academy evidenced the cultural aspirations, here manifest in their need for diversion, of that emerging elite class. It was the first of a series of cultural associations, clubs and societies for the new elite that emerged in Lagos in the second half of the century. Their names, the Philharmonic, the Lagos Esprit de Corps, the Aurora or the Literary Club suggest the kind of entertainment likely to be promoted. Both the format and content of these cultural events were based on English music-hall or vaudeville. They usually included a variety of features, such as comic and love songs, duets and solos, glees and recitations – mostly excerpts from plays or novels – and comic sketches. The musical element appears to have dominated, either in the form of classical selections or marches.

The performances, both at that time and in the following decades, were usually held in various schoolrooms and church halls, at the Government House, the Court Hall or at the Phoenix Hall. The latter, a building on Tinubu Square was particular popular, as it provided a venue of some size, and was preferred by those who did not want to perform in a church schoolroom. The stage was generally a raised wooden platform, while a screen or a curtain separated the stage from the audience. 'Suspending' and 'Chinese' lamps seem to have been the lighting devices most often used, though not without obvious problems.

The positive reception of this form of entertainment is suggested by the fact that it soon became a feature that marked all important missionary events: The opening of new churches and schools, weddings, missionary meetings, or the end of the academic year (Ajayi, 1965: 162-3). Their success must indeed have been remarkable, because the various missions started to use the theatre performances in the form of the 'concert' as a fund-raising event and thus to cater for the educational needs of the 'native subjects'. The fund-raising events were crucial, since the Lagos Colonial Government did not take much interest in education even after the 1882 Education Ordinance, and the mission-owned schools depended largely on their own budgets for survival.

It is interesting to note though that the Academy as well as the Philharmonic or the Brazilian Company, were born quite independently of any church affiliation and, I would argue, this fact needs some consideration. For, although 'the various groups and school societies interchanged talents' (Leonard, 1967: 32), these cultural enterprises offered their members something more – a common terrain, a place where they could meet outside of the missionary aegis. Simultaneously, they offered a channel through which these passionate theatre lovers could make visible their social and economic influence, since 'participation and excellence in entertainments were good ways to become known and accepted in the community' (Adedeji, 1971: 28).

It follows that social needs on the one hand, and financial ends on the other might rightly be considered driving forces behind the spread of the performances on the new 'stage'. These facets do not imply that the strictly theatrical and aesthetic aspects were of secondary importance. On the contrary, as the reviews of the time demonstrate, and the emergent press itself played an important role in setting the standards for the performances.[7] What were initially only announcements of concerts and entertainment events soon became full reviews that dealt extensively with the merits and faults of a performance. It was the *Lagos Observer* that started the practice with Cherubino, the nom de plume of a critic who was to become quite famous and exerted a strong influence on the way reviews were to be written. He gave much attention both to language and content. As to the latter, expectedly, the consciousness of the European point of reference was very present, as is evidenced in the following quotations from the *Lagos Observer*,

> Those who had experience of musical performances in Europe fully understand the reason why our in this country is always below par. In Europe artists are specially trained for their work... (2 March 1882)

> It was as a whole, a concert that would be worthy of more civilized countries... (21 June 1883)

Quite often the critic showed a very thorough and detailed knowledge of the English entertainment scene, as seen in the following response to a critique of the *Eagle* concerning the Coker's Concert,[8] featuring Macaulay, in the *Lagos Observer* dated 6 December 1983:

What does he know about Music Halls? Not much ... Let me inform the Eagle (Crow more likely) ... There are Music Halls and Music Halls as there are critics and critics; and there is as much difference between the Canterbury and Pavilion Music Halls in London or the Star and Malakoff in Liverpool as there is between the critiques of Cherubino and the Eagle – to those who know these places the comparison is plain. (quoted in Leonard, 1967: 55)

It is evident that the matrix that generated these critiques, including the socio-political environment was definitely a response to the impact of the colonial western power in Lagos. It reflects the emerging elite's choice of adherence to the symbols and lifestyle of 'a universe of freedom and equality' (Ranger, 1983: 236) that – in this phases of the relation between colonizers and colonized – had not yet revealed its true, double nature. It is this element of 'choice' that, I think, needs to be stressed, together with the awareness that, despite its importance, this is a very partial picture of the Yorùbá reality of the time. Interestingly these facets are blurred, if not obscured by looking at the new stage simply in terms of imitation. Conversely, given the power of writing, there is the inherent danger to concentrate on this data exclusively, as if it could provide an exhaustive picture of the performance traditions in Lagos and, par extension, Yorùbáland at that time. That is, sticking to the photographic imagery, this perspective proposes one of the focal points (a detail), that mistakenly risks being considered as if it were the whole picture.

Second, besides blurring the other elements of the picture (i.e. other kinds of performance), this focus on imitation furthers the centrality of western cultural canons by obscuring the issue of agency, and the element of choice mentioned above, in other words, the capacity of 'acting' of those who are reproducing the performances. In effect, there is, in the western cultural and artistic traditions, a typical premium on 'originality', a preoccupation with the 'original source'. But whereas this does not need to be the case in other cultures, it is noteworthy that being the new stage a tradition that originally came from the west, the premium on the source strengthens once again the already powerful position of western canons and, par extension, of western episteme.

Definitely, the group of 'forced' migrants that staged the Lagosian performances were availing themselves of traditions of the colonial power, yet, it is also true that this was part of a process of *appropriation*. The migrant community were using these traditions to establish themselves socially. They took possession of them, or in the sense of the Latin etymology of the verb *appropriare*, they 'made them their own', so as to gain power over them, and turn them to their own advantage. It follows that the migrants can be rightly seen as *active subjects*, as *agents*, who adopted and introduced elements of change – the new stage was one of them – in the existing Yorùbá social and cultural structure.

Busy as they were in affirming themselves, and working out their own identity within a frame of reference that promised to grant freedom and progress, at first the migrant community of repatriates (in particular the first generation) in Lagos did not care much about the interaction with the other social components of the Yorùbá society not directly involved in the colonial structures. Consequently the new stage in Lagos concerned a relatively small group of people. And if the written records tend to make it more visible than others, it should be recalled that the great majority of the Lagosian population continued to attend the events on the classical 'stage', by taking part in the various festivals, listening to the artistry of poets and storytellers, and admiring the beauty of masks in performances that continued to scan the rhythm of their social life and, indeed, were an integral part of it. Allegedly, the Lagosians might not even have attributed much importance to the various concerts and migrants' activities being performed in another language. Perhaps because 'in a culture that sees life like a river, and privileges fluidity over the discreetness of definitions',[9] there is a developed awareness of the dynamism of the facts of life, of the contact zone, so to say, where interaction takes place. From this vantage point it is the process of becoming, rather than the fixity of being that becomes relevant. Accordingly, as the Yorùbá proverb goes, they might have been well aware that *bí ewé bá pẹ́ l'ara ọṣẹ, á di ọṣẹ*, (when the leaf stays with the soap, it becomes soap). It was only a question of time, and maybe also of space, and then the leaf would have turned into soap.

The appropriated stage

I am
because of memory
like precious water vapours in the sun
I'm the word, made of fluctuant voices
echoing in the minds of lost memories.
I'm the gesture, made of supple movements
inhabiting disembodied rememberings.
like precious water vapoured in the sun
no more is. Transformed
I am

Not even one hundred kilometres away from Lagos, in Abẹ́òkúta, the dynamism and the transformative potential implicit in the relation between 'the leaf and the soap' was more visible. There, the process of appropriation of the new stage was attaining results that well illustrate the creative space inherent to appropriation itself, that is its capacity of generating new meanings.

In the Ẹ̀gbá capital there was a higher degree of interaction between the various social components, maybe because the local missionary policy was more tolerant towards Yorùbá culture or, possibly, more farsighted; or, perhaps because the migrant community was better integrated than in Lagos. On stage, this greater social interaction found expression in entertainments aimed at a wider target audience, including catering for non-English speakers. Accordingly, selected elements of Yorùbá life were put on stage, resulting in successful performances that were attended by an heterogeneous audience, including 'Mohammedans, adherents to Yoruba religion from adjacent and counter-adjacent villages, as well as local rulers, like the Alake and the Osile' (*Lagos Times*, 12 October 1881).

The Ake Church and School (CMS), through its Entertainment Society seems to have been particularly active in this sense: Yorùbá songs, popular English tunes translated into Yorùbá, as well as elements of Yorùbá life were a constant of this Society's performances. At a concert performed in 1884, for instance, they presented a recitation about 'An Ogboni Court', which at a later performance was described as depicting 'The real state of the town at present and one would fancy himself as if he really was in a true Ogboni assembly' (*Lagos Observer*, 5 February 1887).[10]

'[P]rovided (the theatrical activities) were not too provincially English to make any meaning to ordinary Nigerians' (Echeruo, 1977: 45), the participative interest of the population at large, was corroborated also by the response to the concerts organized by the Ìbàdàn Choral Society. In 1886 the Society gave its first concert for free, 'in order to create a love for the theatre'. And it was with great surprise that the organizers (CMS) discovered that the 'support of the 'masses' was so complete that [...] they had difficulties keeping enthusiasts out of the crowded halls'. The level of enthusiasm generated in the Ìbàdàn audience is shown by the fact that it did not dwindle even when, subsequently, they were charged for tickets. Actually, 'the people did not confine themselves to the normal prices asked for seats, as a good many came forward and paid [extra] sums of money' (ibid.: 75).[11]

What was happening in Abéòkúta and Ìbàdàn were the first visible signs of a process of appropriation that gradually spread to Lagos and became part of a wider discussion and reconsideration of the things 'native' (as they were called) in the press of the time. Admittedly, at first, this provoked mixed reactions, illustrated, for instance, by the reviews to the first concert performed by the newly-founded Rising Entertainment Society in 1881 at Phoenix Hall. Besides songs and recitations, the performance included 'The Rising of the Dead', a 'drama in Yoruba, possibly based on the biblical story of Lazarus' (Leonard, 1967: 70). One of the reviewers, perhaps motivated by the use of the Yorùbá language, condemned the show as a meaningless effort, and went so far as to call it 'blasphemous'. This critique, in turn, provoked an immediate rejection of the criticism, which was attributed to the critic's inability to speak Yorùbá.

These, and similar complaints, attest the persistence of prejudices, as well as the varying, coexisting attitudes that, for some time, surrounded the process of change and appropriation the new stage went through. Change was resisted, attesting the far-reaching consequences of the colonial system, and the racist implications that imbued the evolutionistic credo that informed it, with its belief in 'real' progress and civilisation obviously represented by Victorian imperialism. The *Lagos Observer*, dated 26 October 1882, offers an example of the attitude towards Yorùbá cultural expressions:

> The use of tom-tom on the stage, rude expressions in the native language, and dancing of a fantastic kind [...] engaged in by a young man who acted *jagun jagun*, or the warrior. The same practice was indulged in by the Wesleyan High School in the last entertainment ...in Yoruba language.

However, despite this initial resistance, the process of appropriation found much support. And, both the experiments aimed at integrating Yorùbá elements into the content of the performances, as well as the demand for relevant forms of entertainment continued to grow. Thus, the appropriated stage mirrored the steadily increasing cultural self awareness, itself becoming an external index of the discussions that dominated the intellectual debate of an elite that had began to recognize the value of things native. This debate is well exemplified in the famous letter signed 'Veritas' to the *Lagos Observer* (1 June 1882).

> There is an evil [...] This is the habit of disregarding and ignoring, and, in some cases, totally crying down our Native language. That a country should rise with a literature entirely foreign almost assumes, to me, the form of an impossibility [...] It only means that legends connected with our race, and some of the most brilliant exploits of our ancestors as handed down to us by tradition, must for ever be consigned to oblivion [...] What can equal for beauty and poetical embellishments the legends of Ile-Ife, that cradle of mankind as tradition relates.

Native dress, native names, native language and, in wider terms, native heritage started to become symbols of an identity of the Yorùbá ethnic group, that was now being fixed ideologically. At a teachers' conference held in 1889 the participants voted to adopt native costume in preference to European dress. Similarly there was a trend towards people using their Yorùbá names that had previously been abandoned in favour of western ones to indicate membership in the Christian faith. In 1888 the *Lagos Observer* reported 'the famed 'Adamuorisha' pageant in Lagos', a burial festival typical of Lagos. Admittedly, this had not happened often, but, according to Echeruo (1977: 69), 'when the papers did report these 'native' ceremonies... they implied awareness of their popularity and even of their beauty. The process of 'nativization' was gradually investing various sectors of the elite's daily life, and with people like Henry Venn, or James 'Holy Johnson',[12] it became outright 'nationalistic fervour', as Adedeji calls it, that found voice in strong political statements, like the following:

> We respect and reverence the country of Wilberforce and Buxton and most of our Missionaries, but we are not Englishmen. We are Africans, and we have no wish to be other than Africans. (*Lagos Times* 12 July 1882)

On the stage the process was slow and gradual. Intriguingly, even a personality like Herbert Macaulay, later to be known as the 'Father of Nigerian Nationalism', was not as impetuous on stage as he was on the political scene. Possibly, the process of identity-building just required time. There was no suitable, 'modern' frame of reference ready-to-use at the new elite's disposal, rather it had to be 'invented'.

A panoramic look at the press of the time reveals that the range and format of the typical concert performance had broadened, and included theatrical art forms like the pantomime, the cantata and the opera, showing a trend towards full-length plays. Content-wise, it evinces titles like *Red Riding Hood*, the *Flower Queen* and, a preference for plays by Molière, Gilbert and Sullivan, and an awakening interest in Shakespeare, with recitations from *Hamlet* (in 1892),

Richard II (in 1895) and a production of *The Merchant of Venice* (in 1897). Macaulay's presentation of Gilbert and Sullivan's *Trial by Jury* in 1886 included a Yorùbá song *Emi kole joko jeh*.[13] Singers like E. Johnson proposed imitations of Danmole 'the famous and popular Lagos bard and singer' (Echeruo, 1977: 68). While, one year after the production of *The Merchant*, the Abéòkúta Choral Society staged the Yorùbá version of the same play in Lagos. Further, stronger impulses to the process of appropriation of the new stage were underway, and came with the establishment of the secessionist Independent African Churches. Born to give a precise identity to their belief, the secessionist churches supported the retention and use of native elements considered compatible with the African concept of Christianity in the liturgy. And, very soon, they extended their support also to the process of nativization in the theatrical manifestations.

Towards the turn of the century the social and political situation was growing tense. The new elite were experiencing growing racial discrimination both within the church and outside it.

> These were the years of military expeditions, of multiplication and extension of European commercial firms who elbowed out the African businessmen, of extension of British administration into the interior, and of the implementation of the concept held by Europeans, of Europeans racial superiority over Africans ... (Ayandele, 1966: 205)

In other words, those Nigerians closest to the colonial structures were discovering the racism intrinsic to the colonial endeavour, and they were experiencing directly the fictitious nature of the proclaimed 'civilizing' principles.[14] In fact, civil servants like Dr. J.K. Randle, Dr. Obadiah Johnson, and Herbert Macaulay resigned their position rather than suffer further discrimination. While the divide between colonizers and colonized became more and more marked, the new elite's increasing determination to oppose discrimination and hostility eased its alliance with the old, traditional elite. This was another important historical moment. Apart from the strictly political implications, this allegiance cemented the process of 'cultural' identification that had already begun. Almost paradoxically, that part of the Nigerian society that had almost been ignored, despite its dimensions, and which had continued to exist alongside the colonial structures, started to gain some visibility also in the press. There was increased attention to and study of Yorùbá (and wider, African) culture and customs, while, for instance, *egúngún* performances were sponsored, and native dances rocked Lagos. As can be expected, this found expression also in creative and literary manifestations. It is worth noting, among others, the performance of the playlet '*Oba ati Awori Ijoye* (1900) ... an elaborately-staged, polished native drama' that was included in a large-scale programme by the Wesleyan Itesi Church (Leonard, 1967: 122); and the performance of *Gold, Silver and Copper* by the Lagos Cricket and Recreation Club. Here a Yorùbá folktale formed the basis for a presentation in Yorùbá that dealt with the theme of polygamy, which was a highly controversial subject at that time.

The main support for the theatre in this period, at least until 1912, definitely came from the secessionist Churches. The members of these churches extended their 'patriotic endeavours', as they were called in the press, to the theatre, and made efforts 'to produce an acceptable genuine native African entertainment' (Leonard, 1967: 124). The results were soon visible.

In 1903 D.A Oyedele wrote the 'first full act play' in the history of the appropriated stage: *King Elejigbo and the Princess Abeje of Kotongora* performed by the Ẹgbé Ifẹ̀ in the schoolroom of the Bethel African Church.[15] The play's success encouraged the group to present it again, one year later, at Glover Memorial Hall, where an audience of almost a thousand people watched a performance that lasted five hours.

The play was divided into three acts of three scenes each, except for the last act which had four scenes. Faithful to the performance tradition established over the past decades, and perhaps referring also to a more ancient one, it included musical items between the acts and the scenes. Apart from the dancing and the songs, other traits that reveal individual features characteristic of Yorùbá theatre are the clearly didactic aspect of the plot, as well as its involvement with the 'spiritual' world. It is worth noting not only the wholehearted support for the play by the press ('The Spirit which prompts the production of these plays should be every way encouraged.' *Lagos Standard*, 27 April 1904), but also in the very format of the criticism: For the first time the reviewer of the *Lagos Standard* presented a full-length analysis covering the plot, characterization and presentation of the play. Thus apart from the merits of the different performers, we learn that Princess Abeje (D.A. Oyedele) wore a beard, 'an undesirable thing in a woman', while King Elejigbo (J.A. Daniel) should not have swung his head, since 'native kings do not do this' (Leonard, 1967: 130).

The Ẹgbé Ifẹ̀ (later Bethel Dramatic Society) continued its activities. In 1905 it produced *The Jealous Queen Oya of Oyo and the Princess Omodosun of Mecca*, followed by *Penlepe* and *Kakanguwa Oba afi Haramu Sanra*, both written by A.A. Obadina. Remarkably, the editor of *the Lagos Standard* was asked to send to the USA reprints of *Penlepe*, so that the play (which dealt with 'the problems of the *nouveau riche* who, after purchasing an expensive new house, discovered that it was haunted') could be 'acted and published by Negro Americans' (Leonard, 1967: 137). But the Ẹgbé Ifẹ̀ was not alone. Many other secessionist churches enriched this development with their activities, for instance, the St Jude Choral Society with *Oba Arinho* (in 1905), and *Native Dialogues* and the Young Men's Choral League, who also performed the first two-play programme with *Obagbade* and *Esin Ile Ejo Oyinbo*.

Actually, the demand for local themes and content was growing apace. Significantly, the *Lagos Standard*, dated 4 May 1910, advertised

Wanted: Copyright of *good native plays* (dramatic, melo-dramatic, comic or serio-comic) not hitherto produced on the stage, for use by the *Lagos Glee Singers*. Plays to be submitted to the President O. Obasa (Breadfruit Street) or the Secretary not later than July 3, 1910 for examination by expert judges. A prize of 3 guineas will be awarded to the Author of the best play submitted. *C.B.Olumuyiwa*, Secretary, Bamgbose Street, Lagos.

The Lagos Glee Singers were perhaps the most famous secular group in the early decades of the century. And Dr. Obasa together with Dr. Randle and C.B. Olumuyiwa were among the most important names in the movement for the assertion of cultural 'nationalism' of the time.[16]

The response to the advertisement was immediate. Of the five plays submitted, two were considered particularly interesting, namely, *Asika bi Aparo* by Olympus Moore, a name already famous in the theatre circle in Abéòkúta; and *Awon Iwefa Mefa* by I.B. Akinele. The latter, 'a skit on the Oni of Ifè', was to be produced first. The performance, held at Glover Hall in 1912, was under the patronage of the White Cap Chiefs. Its review in the *Lagos Standard* (9 October 1912) mirrors the success it obtained.

> The piece was *entirely native* and though in one or two instances the dress was not quite correct [...] it conveyed the impression of *real native life*. The *dancing procession* with which the play commenced was a masterpiece and evoked roars of applause; so also did Act 3 in which O.E. Meadows, the Iwefa Kini, in his terpsichorean gyrations made the saddest mirthful...

> It is sketches like this that make us realize the *wisdom and keen sightedness* of those whom we in our so-called enlightenment look down upon as illiterate natives. What [could be] *more intelligent than the advice given by the 6 Iwefas* to frustrate the evil designs of the Oni? (my emphasis)

Between 1904 and 1920 over twenty native dramas were staged in Lagos alone, despite World War I and the success of the cinema, introduced in 1903. The performances again went beyond the patronage of the Church. Secular groups performing in Yorùbá 'mushroomed' (Adedeji, 1971: 44); among them, Egbé Ìrètì, the Sunshine Club, the Excelsior, and the Nigerian Veritarians, with plays like *Oba Olokiki Ore re Ilara* (1911), *Aso Ile Wa* (1915) *So Ore Yan* (1917) to name just a few.

To suggest the energy of the theatre life during this period, it may be enough to recall that in 1912 the colonial government decided to publish 'The Theatre and Public Performance Regulation' in the *Government Gazette*, a move that provoked sharp reactions and was interpreted as a pretext to forestall local cultural initiatives. The bill was never passed, but unfortunately, in the following decades, other events of an economic and socio-political nature, such as the conservative policy of the African Churches, the 1929 Depression, the channelling of self asserting energy into an overtly political struggle, contributed to curtail the dynamism of staged theatre life, especially in Lagos. However, the seeds for further developments were sown and the appropriated stage had set important precedents for successive expressions of Yorùbá theatre.

The entangled stage – final considerations

I am
because of memories
green, the scent of my past presence
appropriates the space

you deny me
lucent, my body foretells
the perfect ripeness
of the fruits to come
I am
(what you choose)
in your memory

'Entirely native… real native life… wisdom and keen sightedness …', the words quoted above, with which the *Lagos Standard* journalist described the performance of *Awọn Iwefa Mefa* seem to me to offer an appropriate, concluding statement for this analysis of the process of appropriation that the theatre on-stage underwent in the Yorùbá context. They reveal that the leaf did indeed become soap.

From the first concert performance to the native play, the process of change and transformation of the new stage accompanied, and indeed was one with the process through which the new, agile elite both negotiated and asserted their own identity. It follows that the process of stage appropriation in the colonial context implicitly narrates a story of resistance. It tells of the disrupting and destabilizing effects of the colonial hegemonic discourse, of the new elite's attempt to gain power, and of their need to establish continuity with a suitable Yorùbá historical past. Against this backdrop, the stage becomes a kind of 'entangled' space, where different narratives intertwine, and connect, contributing to define identities: The Yorùbá and the colonial, in their relation to one another oppositionally and in their interweaving.[17] It turns into an 'entangled' stage that narrates the elite's process of self definition and self-awareness within a net of influences and pressures of different kinds. It highlights the new elite's pragmatic selection and interpretation of certain Yorùbá cultural and historical traits against a 'modernity', or rather 'actuality', shaped to varying degrees by self assertion and also by Christianity, formal education and literacy.

More or less recent theories in the fields of postcolonial and cultural studies offer interesting critical tools for the analysis of these performances. Concepts like 'appropriation', 'colonial mimicry', or 'contact zone' throw a different light, beyond that of 'mere imitation', on the theatrical attainments of the new stage. But it is the Yorùbá concept of *àṣà*, tradition, I think, with the dynamism that contradistinguishes it, and its inherent propensity to metamorphose that best accounts for the process of transformation of the appropriated stage.

Àṣà contemplates innovation, or as beautifully described by Yaï in a most rewarding essay,

> Innovation is implied in the Yoruba idea of tradition. The verb *ṣà*, from which the noun *àṣà* is derived, means to select, to choose, discriminate, or discern. [Something cannot qualify as *àṣà* which has not been the result of deliberate choice (*ṣà*) based on discernment and awareness of historical practices and processes (*ìtàn*) by individual or collective *orí* [the principle of indivi–duality]. And since choice presides over the birth of an *àṣà* (tradition), the latter is permanently liable to metamorphosis […]. For *àṣà* is both the 'traditional' and the 'modern'. (Yaï, 1994: 114)[18]

Because of its verbal derivation (to select, to choose), the concept of *àṣà* evinces and puts a premium on agency. Similarly to 'appropriation', it highlights the important role theatre artists played in developing strategies to assess and affirm their ethnic identity. However, *àṣà* also underlines the facet of change, it supports a critical appraisal that stresses even those small details that gradually helped to bring Yorùbá life on stage. Small changes that brought about continuity with the past, supported the apprehension and expression of a Yorùbá cultural awareness. These small changes created a new tradition. To opt for the representation of the *Ògbóni Court*, or to put on stage *Aṣọ Ilé Wa* (our native dress), or any other Yorùbá play for that matter – was a clear statement; an act of self assertion whose deeply subversive meaning is evident, since it was investing the stage with a function completely different from that envisaged by the colonialists. It was an act of transgression, and of resistance and definitely one that required critical agency – the performers were making a choice, and were critically aware of what they intended to put on stage. They were progressively building their identity and selecting the elements they wanted to be part of it. They were creating a new tradition. While, slowly, almost unnoticed, as a result of their choices, little details, 'small things' Yorùbá were going on stage – they were expressions of a newly acquired cultural awareness based on Yorùbá culture and values. And slowly, almost unnoticed, the leaf was turned into soap; the marginal and invisible were being made visible.

NOTES

1 *Bí ewé bá pẹ́ l'ara ọṣẹ, á di ọṣẹ* is a Yorùbá proverb that translates: 'when the leaf stays with the soap, it becomes soap'.
2 I consider 'classic' the appropriate term for the oral traditions of performance, whose content plays such an important role also for the later, written and semi-written ones.
3 Of course this refers to aesthetic considerations of the Yorùbá artistic forms, since, in the main, 'The "cultural efforts" of the period consisted largely in collections of myth, legends and stories... carried out by a curious menagerie of collectors... [While] Even the stories collected were twisted to fit in the scheme. They were manipulated in order to corroborate western culture's own superior self- conception' (Boscolo, 2009: 6).
4 The *egúngún aláré* tradition includes itinerant performing troupes well known for their transformations. The performer is said to transform himself, when he wears the mask, and to become the power of the ancestors. Wearing the basic mask, called *ago*, he then goes through further transformations. The name *egúngún* is a clear reference to the 'religious' roots of the performance. *Egúngún* in fact defines the institution meant for ancestor worship, as well as being used par extension to designate any masquerade or masked figure. For more information on the *egúngún aláré* and characteristics of their performance, see, among others, J.A. Adedeji, 1969; Cristina Boscolo, 2009; Kacke Götrick, 1984.
5 Lynn Leonard's unpublished M.A (1967) study on the period offers an unparalleled rich source of materials that really deserves to be mentioned.
6 Led by the *aláàfin* (the highest authority), the Ọ̀yọ́ Empire was one of the most powerful Yorùbá kingdoms, which in turn were related to each other by varying degrees of allegiance.
7 The first Nigerian newspaper was the missionary fortnightly *Ìwé Ìròhìn* (1859–67) published in Abẹ́òkúta by Rev. Henry Townsend. At first it was written entirely in Yorùbá and then, a year later, it became bilingual (Yorùbá and English). More ambitious attempts were to follow in Lagos. In 1863 Robert Campbell, an Afro-West Indian, founded *The Anglo-African*, the only local paper until 1880. Rapid economic growth in Lagos in the 1880s saw a concomitant

growth in the Lagos press. Among the most successful newspapers were the *Lagos Times* (1880), owned by R.B. Blaize and edited by A.M. Thomas, the *Lagos Observer* (1882), edited by I.B. Benjamin, and the *Eagle* and *Lagos Critic* (1883), edited by O.E. Macaulay. As to their characteristics, Echeruo observes: 'the Lagos newspaper was [...] essentially a kind of local gazette. First it provided the community with a record of community life [...]. Secondly, it served as the organ for the dissemination of official news [...]. Thirdly, the newspaper served as a trade journal [...] in a number of cases, [it ...] even served as an employment clearing house [... and] as a kind of popular educator.' (Echeruo, 1977: 5).

8 R.A.Coker, a foremost musician, started his activities in Abẹ̀òkúta and then moved to Lagos as music teacher at the CMS female institute. In 1882, after his return from England, he organized a series of concerts that must have represented a rather special occasion, if only because of their dimensions.

9 Olabiyi Yaï, personal communication, 1997, reported in Boscolo, 2009: 190.

10 The Ògbóni, often referred to as a secret society related to the cult of the earth, was a kind of town council yielding considerable power in diverse spheres of social life. Although its authority has become notably reduced, it still exists today, and it is divided into two different factions: the 'Aboriginal' and the 'Reformed' societies.

11 In the mid-1880s, ticket prices ranged from 2 shillings for unreserved and back sets to 3 or 4 shillings for reserved ones. As a point of reference, the salary of a catechist was around Lst 30. Free admission was very unusual (Leonard, 1967).

12 Just a few remarks to hint at their personalities: 'Reverend Henry Venn, Prebendary of St Paul's London, and for thirty years, 1842 to 1872, the Secretary of the Church Missionary Society. Single-handed and deliberately, he urged Africans to be prepared to assume the leadership of their country...' (Ayandele, 1966: 180). As to James Johnson, '"Holy Johnson", as he was nicknamed in Lagos [...] was a rebel from Sierra Leone and he fought all his life to see that the African of ability got his due respect and that the Church which held out so much promise to the African was made "not an exotic but a plant indigenous to the soil". He came to advocate a reform of the liturgy that suited local conditions' (Ajayi, 1965: 235).

13 I have left the orthography of this, and following Yorùbá titles, as quoted in the bibiographical references and newspapers of the time.

14 The racist policy of the British government was most explicit during Egerton's governorship. It's enough to think that by 1900 there was only one black person, Henry Carr, who held a position similar in rank to that of a white civil servant. Nonetheless, in 1907 Egerton was forced to send a circular to all officials in Southern Nigeria asking them to treat their African subordinates in a humane manner!

15 Here follows the story according to the review of the play by 'Janus' in the *Lagos Standard* (27 April 1904). 'The Elejigbo of Ejigbo while in council with his courtiers was greatly enamoured with the singular beauty and graceful demeanour of Abeje, a princess royal of Kotongora who was touring with her friends and now a visitor at the court of the Elejigbo. The King resolved to have her for a wife and therefore sent messengers to the court at Kotongora asking the Emir for the hand of his daughter in marriage. Omens were consulted by both parties individually and the responses in either case were unfavourable – death and dire disaster being predicted. Despite this warning of the gods and winsome admonitions of his Ifa priest to desist, King Elejigbo persisted to carry out his heart's desire. On the other hand the difficulty, which had existed between the two kings owing to differences in religious views they entertained, was bridged over by the Elejigbo when he professed Islamism. The Emir of Kotongora became unnerved and from courtesy and the expressed desire of his daughter approved of the contract. The dowry having been paid, the princess, accompanied by her maids and the courtiers of King Elejigbo, was sent away with all due ceremony to her future home. While the party was yet a long way off news approached the Elejigbo of the approach of his longed-for bride. He immediately turned out his courtiers and seated himself with pomp and splendour on his throne awaiting their arrival. At the sight of the woman the King was seized with a fit of fever-love. He began to motion and beckon to her to take a seat by his side, whereupon the girl entered into an artful song demanding conditions which would make her accede to the King's request. Although these terms portended evil to the King, yet he was unable to fathom the situation in his hysterics of love. He yielded to them all, nay, even to his own death. The issue of this

transaction was a bloody war between the two countries, which cost the loss of many precious lives. Eventually his son Prince Arowobusoye was nominated and installed in the room of his father. The morals I leave to you readers to deduce.' Also reported in Leonard, 1967: 128.

16 Obasa, together with Randle, was one of the founders of the People's Union (1909), a political organization dedicated to the cultural emancipation of Nigerian peoples that had nothing to do with religion (see Ayandele, 1966).

17 For the understanding of 'entangled space' I draw on the use of the concept 'entangled history' in cultural and historical studies as defined by E.H. Gould (2007): 'Entangled histories ... examine interconnected societies. Rather than insisting on the comparability of their subjects or the need for equal treatment, entangled histories are concerned with 'mutual influencing,' 'reciprocal or asymmetric perceptions,' and the intertwined 'processes of constituting one another."

18 *Ìtàn* is usually translated as 'history', 'story'; its implications are most enlighteningly outlined in this same article.

BIBLIOGRAPHICAL REFERENCES

Adedeji, Joel A. (1969) *The Aláriǹjó Theatre: The Study of a Yorùbá Theatrical Art from its Earliest Beginning to the Present-Time.* Unpublished doctoral dissertation, University of Ìbàdàn.

Adedeji, Joel A. (1971) 'The Church and the Emergence of the Nigerian Theatre, 1866-1914,' *Journal of the Historical Society of Nigeria*, 6.1, 25-45.

Ajayi, J. F. A. (1965) *Christian Missions in Nigeria, 1841-1891: The Making of a New Elite*, London: Longman.

Ashley, Kathleen and Veronique Plesch (2002) 'The Cultural Processes of "Appropriation"' in *Journal of Medieval and Modern Studies*, 32: 1 (winter): 1-14.

Ayandele, E. A. (1966) *The Missionary Impact on Modern Nigeria 1842-1914*, Ibadan History Series, Ìbàdàn: Longman.

Boscolo, Cristina (2001) 'Strategies Neglected. The Yoruba Play Revisited', *Matatu, No Condition is Permanent*, 329-58.

Boscolo, Cristina (2009) *Odún Discourses, Strategies, and Power in the Yorùbá Play of Transformation.* Amsterdam & New York: Rodopi.

Clapperton, Hugh (1829) *Journal of a Second Expedition into the Interior of Africa*, London: John Murray.

Cole, Patrick (1975) *Modern and Traditional Elites in the Politics of Lagos*, African Studies Series, Cambridge: Cambridge University Press.

Echeruo, Michael J. C. (1962) 'Concert and Theatre in late Nineteenth Century Lagos', *Nigeria Magazine*, 30, 74: 68-74.

Echeruo, Michael J. C. (1977) *Victorian Lagos. Aspects of Nineteenth Century Lagos Life*, London: Macmillan.

Gould, E.H. (2007) 'Entangled Histories, Entangled Worlds: The English-speaking Atlantic as Spanish Periphery' in *The American Historical Review*, 112, 3, accessed 14/02/10 at http://www.historycooperative.org/journals/ ahr/112.3/ gould.html

Götrick, Kacke (1984) *Apidan Theatre and Modern Drama*, Stockholm: Almqvist & Wiskell.

Leonard, Lynn (1967) *The Growth of Entertainments of Non-African Origin in Lagos from 1866 -1920 (with special emphasis on concert, drama and the cinema).* Unpublished M. A., University of Ìbàdàn.

Ranger, Terence (1983) 'The Invention of Tradition in Colonial Africa'. In *The Invention of Tradition*, ed. Eric Hobsbawm and Terence Ranger, Cambridge: Cambridge University Press, 211-62.

Smith, Robert (1969) *Kingdoms of the Yoruba*, London: James Currey.

Soremekun, Fola (1985) 'The British Penetration and Conquest'. In *Nigerian History and Culture*, ed. Richard Olaniyan, Ibadan: Longman, 135-58.

Yaï, Olabiyi Babalola (1994) 'In Praise of Metonymy: The Concepts of "Tradition" and "Creativity" in the Transmission of Yorùbá Artistry over Time and Space'. In *The Yoruba Artist*, ed. Rowland Abiodun et al., Washington and London: Smithsonian Institution, 107-18.

The Representation of Khoisan Characters in Early Dutch-Afrikaans Dramas in South Africa

MARISA KEURIS

This article is an exploratory study of how Khoisan (so-called 'Hottentot' and 'Boesman') characters, as well as some of the other indigenous peoples of South Africa are portrayed in a few early Dutch-Afrikaans dramas; in particular Boniface's *De Temperantisten*, A. G. Bain's *Kaatje Kekkelbek*, some of Melt Brink's plays, and S. J. du Toit's *Magrita Prinslo*. In order to get a sense of the period (1832-1920) an introductory section focuses on the historical and cultural contexts in which Dutch-Afrikaans drama and theatre developed in this country. These contexts had a direct impact on this development and give some form of understanding as to why Dutch-Afrikaans theatre and English theatre in South Africa developed so differently from each other. The role played by the emergence of the Afrikaans language (as well as Afrikaner Nationalism) within these contexts is also briefly discussed. The main focus of the article is finally on the portrayal of Khoisan characters as found in the four above-mentioned authors' work.

The development of South African drama and theatre (1832–1925)

English theatre versus Dutch-Afrikaans theatre

From the start of settler history in South Africa a division existed between the Dutch and British communities in South Africa because of the events that characterised their respective settlements in this country. The establishment of a Dutch trade station in 1652 at the Cape led to the gradual growth of a mainly Dutch community in the country, although various other groups, including German, French, and Malay people came to the Cape during the seventeenth and eighteenth centuries. According to Van Jaarsveld:

> Holland maintained her position in South Africa for 150 years as long as she remained supreme on the sea. Thereafter, however, England's strong sea power enabled her to take over the Cape in 1795 and again in 1806. It was in the 150 years of the Dutch rule that the Afrikaner community (*volk*) was conceived. (1961: 9)

The development of Dutch theatre in South Africa (later Dutch-Afrikaans theatre and eventually Afrikaans theatre) can be clearly demarcated from the development of English theatre in South Africa. Afrikaans literary historiographers (cf. Antonissen, S. A. & Dekker, 1958), as well as theatre historians (c.f. Binge, 1969; Bosman, 1951 & Bosman, 1980), show in detail that the early eighteenth and nineteenth century Dutch-Afrikaans theatre developed within its own tradition (Dutch-European), while English theatre in South Africa developed separately, with strong links to its British origin (see Fletcher, 1994).

> This separate development of Dutch and English theatre in South Africa – almost from the first days of British settlement – can mainly be attributed to the fact that the communities within these two language groups rarely mixed socially and, in fact, in time even developed a certain animosity towards each other. J. du P. Scholtz quotes W. W. Bird (*State of the Cape Hope in 1820*) who remarked that even in the 1820s little social intermingling between these two groups took place. Commenting directly on the theatre scene, Bird says: 'Company, dancing, and the theatre, are to the taste of all; but the habits of the Dutch and English are not as yet sufficiently amalgamated to allow them to associate and mix in the same free manner as is usual between individuals of a common stock'. (J. du P. Scholtz, 1939: 164)

Different newspapers for the two groups, namely *The South African Commercial Advertiser* (started in January 1824) and *De Zuid-Afrikaan* (first published on 9 April 1830), only deepened the divide between them. Whilst *The South African Commercial Advertiser* defended the British interests in the Cape colony, and became an organ for the philanthropic movement, mainly pursued by British missionaries, like Dr Philips; *De Zuid-Afrikaan*, on the other hand was a mouthpiece for the Dutch conservative community in the Cape, and later sympathised with the colonists who participated in the Great Trek, as well as with the colonists settling in the Boer Republics in the North.

Language divided these two European groups in the Cape, and the broader cultural contexts in which they operated also exacerbated these differences. J. du P. Scholtz quotes John Howison (*European colonies*, 333) who maintains that even in 1834

> The Dutch and English residents of Cape Town have little social intercourse. The Dutch complain of the *hauteur* of the English, and their love of ceremony and unpliant disposition, and excessive attachment to their own customs. The English, on the other hand, coming from a distant country, have few feelings, views or interests in common with those persons who have been born and reared in the colony, and received little pleasure from their society. Dislike on the one side, and indifference on the other, throw the two parties asunder, and it is not likely that a mutual accommodation will ever take place between them; and the more so as many individuals of both nations speak no language but their own. (J. du P. Scholtz, 1939: 82-3)

In the ensuing years British occupation was strengthened at the Cape and a direct policy of Anglicisation was followed, especially under governorship of Lord Charles Somerset, which was successful in some sections of the Dutch community, mainly in Cape Town; but further troubled relationships between these two groups, especially within the Dutch communities in the interior who resisted this policy. A correspondent in *De Zuid-Afrikaan* wrote in 1851 still of 'a certain unpleasant, indefinable anti-Dutch, anti-English feeling' pervading in the country (ibid.: 99).

The birth of Afrikaans and the growth of Afrikaner Nationalism

The historical divide between the two mainly European groups in South Africa (Afrikaans/Dutch and English speakers) grew deeper during the twentieth century, after the Anglo-Boer war (1889-1902) and the rise of Afrikaner Nationalism.[1] Attempts by the English-speaking ruling class to Anglicise government departments and schools, led to even deeper resentment against the British for most Afrikaners. These actions by the British rulers were one of the main contributing factors which led to the birth of the *Eerste Taalbeweging* ('First Language Movement') in 1875 and a commitment within Afrikaner communities to protect and develop their young language, Afrikaans. It is important to note that from the very beginning the Afrikaans language issue was linked to the broader issue of Afrikaner Nationalism. According to Nienaber and Nienaber (1970:24) this movement received momentum with the occurrence of particular political events in the Transvaal, notably the annexation of this republic by the British under Lord Shepstone, which succeeded in bringing the Afrikaners together in solidarity against the British imperialist actions.

It is also worth noting that the relationship between Afrikaans and Dutch in these early years of the development of Afrikaans was not without its own internal tensions and ambiguities. Although the large group of Dutch-Afrikaans speaking Afrikaners during this period was proud of the fact that their language had developed mainly from Dutch, and they cherished this link with nineteenth century European civilization, a community of Dutch speakers in the country (mainly based in Pretoria) opposed the efforts of the Dutch-Afrikaans group to strive for the official establishment of this new language (Nienaber and Nienaber, 1970: 41). The struggle to develop, establish and obtain official status for Afrikaans in South Africa was thus not only one that was characterised by the fact that the early speakers of Afrikaans had to fend off the onslaught of Anglicisation from the British occupiers and Settlers during the nineteenth and early twentieth century, it was also ironically marked by the fact that they had to defend their position against a sector of the Dutch community. The situation was only resolved when Afrikaans received official status in 1925.

The precursors to Afrikaans theatre were the Dutch theatre companies active in the Cape colony, especially the association *Door Yver bloeit de kunst (1865-1887);* and the Rhetoric Guilds, *Aurora,* and later the *Afrikaans-Hollandse Toneelvereniging* (1907) in Pretoria, in the Transvaal. Although it is clear from Bosman's (1980) detailed and comprehensive work on the history of South African theatre that Afrikaans theatre developed from the Dutch companies active in the Cape and later in Transvaal, Binge (1969: iv) makes the interesting point that it was not only original Dutch work which was performed by these companies. According to him 60% of the 204 Dutch plays performed at the Cape were translations from German (79), French (59) and only 23 were original Dutch work. One should thus rather state that the influence on Afrikaans theatre was more broadly European than the more generally perceived notion of an only Dutch influence.

The portrayal of the Khoisan in early Dutch-Afrikaans theatre

Apart from a few short articles (see: Van Vuuren, 1999) very little work has been done in South Africa which focuses on a study of how the Khoisan were depicted in early Dutch-Afrikaans drama. Although many plays were produced in this period, I will limit myself in this discussion to the works of Boniface's *De Temperantisten*, A. G. Bain's *Kaatje Kekkelbek*, general remarks on some of Melt Brink's plays, as well as S. J. du Toit's *Magrita Prinslo*. The reason for this choice is that Boniface and Bain are seen as forerunners to the development of Afrikaans drama and theatre in South Africa. Although Boniface's play was never performed, it was the first published play in South Africa which included so-called 'Hottentots-Afrikaans' dialogue, while Bain's short piece was performed and presented with its main character a Khoi girl speaking a mixture of early Afrikaans-Dutch and English. Although most of Melt Brink's plays are written in Dutch-Afrikaans he is commonly described as the 'father' of Afrikaans drama in South Africa and is thus also an important figure to include in this discussion. I conclude this short study by focusing on S. J. du Toit's *Magrita Prinslo* – the first *Afrikaans* play to be published.

Khoisan studies as a research field has its own history and development: from the first descriptions found of the Khoisan in early travel writing in Southern Africa (see Barrow, 1802 & 1806; and Lichtenstein, 1928 [1812]); through the various anthropological studies made of them (Schapera, 1965), to in-depth research done in this field, for example the *Research in Khoisan Studies* series (Szalay, 1995). For a contemporary review of their place in Southern African (post-colonial) history one can also consult studies with a broadly historical perspective (Shula Marks in *The Journal of African History* or David Johnson in *Eighteenth-Century Studies*).

As Margaret Lenta foregrounds in her article, *Speaking of the slave: Britain and the Cape, 1751-1838*, the central question to be asked when one decides to focus on the portrayal of Khoisan characters in literature (1999: 104), is still the one formulated by Spivak, namely 'Can the subaltern speak?' This question also permeates my discussion of these texts. Although we find Xhoisan characters present (speaking and acting) in these texts one must still speculate as to what degree these depictions and portrayals are 'real', in the sense of being the people's own voices, or whether they are simply the creations of these playwrights based on generally perceived or believed stereotypes of these characters during that period. This question is also at the heart of the debate surrounding the Khoi girl in *Kaatje Kekkelbek*.

Two forerunners to Dutch-Afrikaans theatre in South Africa: Boniface's *De Temperantisten* (1832)

I begin with Charles Etienne Boniface's play *De nieuwe ridderorde of De Temperantisten* (1832) (The new order of knighthood or The Temperance Society).[2] This lengthy play (more than 100 pages) was never performed, only read. However, it is considered to be important within the history of Afrikaans (and South African) theatre, because it is the first published and oldest original play in South Africa. The play adheres so closely to the events of the day as they occurred in Cape Town during this period, namely the establishment of the new 'Temperance Society', that according to Binge (1969:1) one could follow these events by reading the *Commercial Advertiser* of 17 December 1831, and of 1 and 8 February 1932. According to Fletcher, Boniface's play was 'too libellous to be performed'; it 'was written at a time when Cape Town was full of temperance societies … and all of them concerned with reforming the allegedly hard-drinking Cape citizens and their slaves' (1994: 50–51). Boniface vehemently opposed the Temperance Societies and wrote *De Temperantisten* (as it is commonly known) 'to prove that the greatest sinners were the societies themselves and their converts' (Fletcher, 1994: 51).

Although the play was never performed, it was very popular at the time and printed copies of the 'script sold out almost as soon as they were printed' (ibid.). The reason why Boniface's play is considered to be important today does not lie so much in its professed popularity, but insofar as it is the earliest example of so-called 'Hottentots-Afrikaans' as spoken by Khoisan characters in the play. In the 1954 edition of Boniface's play, edited by F. C. L. Bosman, Bosman not only gives a long introduction (56 pages), as well as numerous footnotes and explanatory notes on the text, but also includes a long section written by a well-known Afrikaans linguist of that time, Prof. J. L. M. Franken entitled, 'Die Afrikaans van Boniface' ('The Afrikaans of Boniface').

De Temperantisten is a satirical piece in which Boniface ridicules the idea of a temperance society for the Cape as proposed by various clergy (inter alia Dr Philips) during 1831 and 1832. The idea of such a society was generally unpopular (according to Bosman in his introduction to Boniface's play the whole of the Dutch community and most of the English-speaking colonists were opposed to it), which explains why Boniface's play was so popular. It is, however, clear that the problem of the abuse of alcohol (especially in the Khoisan community) was also generally accepted as a substantial societal problem of that period.

The play is presented in four acts, but is only loosely structured with little action or intrigue, since it is mainly one of the meetings of this society that is depicted in the play (Boniface, 1954: 43). Khoisan representatives from Bethelsdorp (mockingly renamed as *Bedelsdorp* [p. 101], i.e. beggar's town) have been invited to become part of this society. They are a group of six, described as '*Hottentotten onlangs tot de Orde ingelyfd*'/ Hottentots recently incorporated to the Order. In accordance with the convention of satirical pieces, and consistent with how the other characters in the play are named (e.g. Dr Philip is *Domine Humbug Philipumpkin*), these six characters also have descriptive and silly names: Klaas Galgevogel, Hans Droogekeel, Piet Dronkelap, Dampje Waterschuw, Manus Kalfachter and his wife, Grietje Drilbouten. Although apparently funny, many of these names indicate a negative association in reference to alcohol: *Droogekeel* means Dry throat; *Dronkelap* is Boozer; and *Waterschuw* means Afraid of water.

The name of the only female in the group, *Grietje Drilbouten* (Grietje 'Shaking buttocks') recalls an even more controversial issue, namely how the female Khoisan anatomy has been depicted and discussed in scientific circles of that period.[3] In the play one of the society members, D. Tremens (*Delerium Tremens*, Hoofd Medicus der Orde), in answering to the question as to whether something special will happen that evening, states that they will accept some *'Natuurmensen'* (persons of nature) that evening into the society. He immediately adds the following rider: 'waarvan het ras zich van onze door eene belangryke eigenaardigheid zoo zeer onderscheid'/ of which this race distinguishes itself from our race through an important peculiarity (Boniface, 1954: 152). Bosman adds a footnote to this rider and speculates that this is in all probability a reference to the 'posterioria' of the Khoisan woman which Le Vaillant also mentions in his writing.

When Grietje and Kalfachter arrive in Cape Town it is clear that they do not know the society or have any idea what it is all about. When asking directions from a bystander, Quizz (an anti-temperantist), Grietje apologises for the fact that they are 'een bietjie *stukkend'*/ a little drunk (ibid.: 102). On eventually finding the society, Grietje manages to sneak into the meeting room, as women were not invited to be part of the society, and starts drinking from what she assumes are bottles of water on the table. They are in fact bottles of gin and Boniface implies thus that the members are in fact deceiving everybody. When Grietje realises this she hides under a table and proceeds to drink as much as she can. When Kalfachter finds her eventually, the truth of the situation is revealed and they decide to return home without the Khoisan group becoming part of this society.

As the Khoisan group was originally invited to become part of the society, it suggests that this society was not exclusively white in its membership; however it is clear from various remarks made by the white members that they saw the Khoisan in a paternalistic light, as 'natuurmense'/ persons of nature, and as being from 'de lagere klassen'/ lower classes (ibid.: 26). Their ignorance regarding European social customs are mocked: for example, Grietje, on seeing the 'water' bottles proceeds to drink directly from the bottle, declining the invitation to rather use a glass, to the amusement of the member offering the glass (ibid.: 175). Most of the actions and conversation by the Koisan characters is, in fact, clearly used in the play for comic affect.

When Kalfachter realises that only he is bound by the society rules ('Jy kan jou lekker dronke zuipe, en ik moet dat met nugtere ooge aanzien!'/ You can enjoy getting drunk, but I must keep sober! (1954: 189), they decide that the whole society is nonsensical and he decides to return home.

Although the Khoisan characters do play an important role in this drama and do get various and lengthy turns to speak, the substance of these conversations revolves around the question of alcohol (mis)use both personally and within their community. It is clear that they are a marginalised group of people – at best seen through a paternalistic lens and at worst dismissed as being of little worth. The broader issues of why this should be the situation is not discussed or even referred to in any of these conversations.

Critics agree that Boniface's *De Temperantisten*, particularly in its portrayal of the Khoisan and the use of 'Hottentots-Afrikaans', influenced the next play under consideration.

Andrew Geddes Bain: *Kaatje Kekkelbek* (1838)

Kaatjie Kekkelbek or Life among the Hottentots, 1835[4] is the second most fre-quently mentioned play in early Afrikaans theatre historiography. It is mainly a monologue given by Kaatjie, a Koisan woman, interspersed with songs and little bits of prose and is presented in a mixture of English and 'Hotnot-Afrikaans' (Dekker, 1958: 8). There is interest in this work from both English and Afrikaans literary historians; most Afrikaans and English commentators[5] refer to the fact that the piece is written in a mixture of Afrikaans-Dutch and English, and was the 'the first theatrical piece to use Afrikaans on stage' as spoken by a Khoi girl (Fletcher, 1994: 65-6).[6] They note too that Kaatje is also 'the first indigenous woman character in South African theatre' (Gray, 1990: 76).

On a first reading of this piece one might be inclined to assume that Kaatje is an authentic representative of the Khoisan community of the Kat River Settlement, but on reflection it is clear that this is not the case. Through the figure and 'voice' of Kaatje the Khoisan people is portrayed as cunning, lazy and dependent on alcohol. Lenta argues that 'Though the poem puts words into the mouth of a black woman, there is not even an attempt to claim that Bain's purpose is mimetic. Kaatje is required for purposes of political and comic effect to convict herself of drunkness, promiscuity and theft' (1999: 116).

Damian Shaw distinguishes between two divergent approaches to Kaatje, namely between those who see her 'as a spokeswoman for the rights of the 'Hottentots'', according to him this would include Stephen Gray and Pieter Conradie; and critics like Michael Chapman and Margaret Lenta, who hold the opposite view, namely that she simply fulfils a political and comic function in the piece (Shaw, 2009: 5). By focusing on the historical context of the play, Shaw convincingly argues that *Kaatje Kekkelbek* is not a representative of the prevailing Khoisan viewpoint, but is, in fact, the opposite: 'a vessel to voice settler dissatisfaction' with the Kat River Settlement (ibid.: 7).[7] By portraying Kaatje negatively, as a liar and a thief, she does not provide a 'voice' for the Khoisan settlement, but she is ironically appropriated as a 'voice' for the settlers.

Shaw, like other commentators, establishes a link between Boniface's *De Temperantisten* and Bain's *Kaatje Kekkelbek,* arguing that in both works the

Khoisan are portrayed in a negative light – with a specific focus on their alleged alcohol problem. There is, however, also another link, which these commentators have missed. Most of them refer to the suggested association between the person of Kaatje Kekkelbek and that of Saartje Baartman, namely that when Kaatje presents her posterior to the audience at the end of the piece the image conjures reference to Saartje Baartman's humiliating exhibition of her body to Europeans in the nineteenth century. Nobody, however, seems to have noticed that this association is already implied in the character of Grietje in *De Temperantisten*. This reference is both in her designated name, Grietje Drilbouten (Grietje 'Shaking buttocks'), and in the more overt words of D. Tremens, where explicit reference is made to the 'posterioria' of Khoisan women. Not only should the play by Boniface be seen as a forerunner to Bain's piece, but the character of Grietje should also be seen as a precursor to the person of Kaatje.

Melt Brink: The 'father' of Afrikaans drama and theatre

Brink, who was deeply involved with the golden age of *Aurora* (period II: 1866-87),[8] wrote many plays mainly of a humorous nature. They were often short, and were very popular for many years. His many works (see list in bibliography) today seem naïve and often didactic; for example including 'lessons' on how to be a good wife in *Die Egskeiding* (The divorce, 1920f), or mother in *Berouw kom meestal te laat*, (Regret usually comes too late, 1920e); the perils of betting in *De Weddenschap* (The wager, 1905); or ridiculing the idea of woman suffrage in *O, die muise of stemreg* (Oh, the mice or the vote, 1930). Afrikaans literary historians (Dekker, 1958; Anthonissen, s.a.) acknowledge his contribution to the establishment of early Afrikaans theatre, but are in general also quite critical of the quality of his work. What is interesting from a contemporary perspective is not so much the dramatic/theatrical aspects or value of his work, but broader issues, namely the language aspect (what his use of Dutch-Afrikaans demonstrates in terms of the development of this young language), as well as how indigenous people are portrayed in his plays.

The portrayal of Khoisan characters in some of Melt Brink's plays

The portrayal of Khoisan and black characters in general are superficial and often stereotypical, and are limited in most of his plays to that of a servant. That this relationship can, however, be nuanced may be deducted from the range of forms of address found in these plays. The four common ones are: 'bediende' (*servant*), 'kneg' (also *servant*, but often with an underlying secondary meaning of *slave*)[9], 'meid' (*'(coloured) maidservant, servant-girl')*.[10] The latter is today seen as a racist form of address, but in Brink's time it was used without this racist connotation as a common form of address. One also finds the male counterpart, namely 'jong(e)' (*'boy, (coloured) servant'*). The word 'kaffer' (*kaf(f)ir or native*) is also found in his plays.[11] These forms of address are found both in the character lists of the plays, and when these characters are talked to or about by the white characters.

It is noticeable that even where plays have been changed in later editions, the changes only occur on the language level, not in terms of how the various race groups addressed each other. Compare, for example, *Groot-vader zijn pijp* (1911, second edition) [1905] (Grandfather's pipe) with *Grootvader se pyp* (1927, fourth edition) [1905], where the policeman and messenger of the court is called, Heintje Pakhem. When he addresses the white men in the play, he uses the designation *baas (Master)* in both editions: (Fourth scene: '*Baas Jan, ik moet jou arresteer! In naam van Zijne Majesteit! Jij het baas Klaas beleedigd!*' / Master Jan, I must arrest you! In the name of Our Majesty! You have insulted master Klaas (p. 11, second edition, 1911), versus: '*Baas Jan, ek moet jou arresteer! In naam van Sy Majesteit! Jy het baas Klaas beledig!*' (p. 13, 1927 edition) Although the later edition shows clearly how the language has changed (from Dutch to Afrikaans) in the period 1911 to 1927, there was no corresponding change regarding designated modes of address between these groups in sixteen years: Heintje still addresses the white men as 'baas' (master). Brink also uses the designation *Hottentot* or *Hotnots* in his plays, for example in *Die mislukte trouwpartij* (The unlucky wedding party, 1920b: 17).

Although Khoisan characters usually only play minor roles in Brink's plays, in *Een Progressief* (A progressive, 1900) two Khoisan characters, Daantjie Tamboer and Sampie Druiloor, play important roles in the drama. Various references are also made to the existence of a large community of Khoisan people in the vicinity who also participate in the dramatic events. The play is about an English-speaking visitor, Klaas Klauterberg (a so-called 'Progressive') who tries to get the local Khoisan people (who are referred to through-out the play as either 'Hottentotte' or 'Hotnots') to vote for him by giving them large quantities of liquor. The 'Afrikaanders' in the play ridicule both what he says, and his plan. Although Klaas makes all sorts of promises to the Khoisan, it is clear that he is an opportunist and not at all interested in their welfare; he simply wants to use their vote to get into parliament. His plan backfires when the Khoisan insist that Klaas gives them more alcohol and threatens to break their promise of voting for him if he does not comply with their demands. In the end, fearing for his life, Klaas flees the town on his horse.

Although Daantjie and Sampie have substantial parts in the drama, and speak directly to Klaas, stating their demands clearly, it is obvious that they are mainly portrayed from the perspective of the 'Afrikaanders' and that this is not a flattering portrayal.

A remark such as 'Een Hotnot denk moes nooit verder dan zijn neus lang is'/ A Hottentot does not think further than the length of his nose (1906: 13), made by Gert, one of the Afrikaner farmers, is not disputed by any one. The 'progressive', in fact, not only seems to agree with this statement, but replies cynically: 'Oh, they won't require thinking. I shall denkt ver hulle' (I will think for them). The progressive, Klaas wants to get the 'Coloured vote' by buying it with free liquor (not a 'bribe' according to him), because he is also aware of the general view that the Koisan like alcohol a lot.[12] When he does start to dispense free wine, the situation quickly gets out of control with people clamoring for more and more wine. It is clear from the rest of his conversation with Dirk that

Klaas is aware that the Khoisan can become easily dependent on alcohol. In response to Dirk's remark that they will have to work to earn money to buy liquor, Klaas agrees and adds that it is quite easy to exploit them:

> Well, when they come by the farmers, then they have only to say kijk as jul nou een maand lang goed werk (look if you work well for one month), then I give you a full bottle sampanje, … You can get cheap Sampanje for seven and sixpence een bottle; di Hotnot werk hem morsdood daarvoor (the Hottentot will work very hard for it), than you get him to work ver jou cheap. Anders moet jij hem van £2 tot £3 per maand betaal (Otherwise you have to pay him £2 to £3 per month). Wat zeg jul daarvan (what do you say about this), isn't that an excellent plan? En een goeie uitvinding van mij? (And a good invention of mine?) (1906:18)[13]

Although we thus find in many of Melt Brink's plays the *presence* of Khoisan characters, most of them are servants of the white Afrikaners or colonists, and their portrayals rarely deviate from the stereotypical depiction of a subservient underclass to the colonists. As was the case in Boniface's *De Temperantisten* and Bain's *Kaatje Kekkelbek,* Brink also foregrounds the misuse of alcohol by the Khoisan. The underlying broader socio-historical issues linked to this problem, are, however, not confronted in these plays.[14]

S. J. du Toit's *Magrita Prinslo, of Lijfde getrou tot in di dood* (*Love true unto death*, 1897)

According to Binge (1969: 25) *Magrita Prinslo* was the first printed Afrikaans play and the best known performance of an Afrikaans play before 1900. It was performed in the Paarl City Hall on 27 and 28 January 1897 at the Second Language Festival. It is an historical play about the Great Trek of Commandant Potgieter and Commandant Retief from the Cape Colony to Natal, climaxing with the dramatic murder of Retief by Dingaan.[15]

Against the broader canvas of dramatic historical events, this is the story of Magrita Prinslo's faithful and steadfast love for her fiancée, Pieter Botha, who had to stay behind in the Cape colony. Koos Potgieter, the son of Commandant Potgieter, falls in love with Magrita, and tries desperately to win her love during the trek to Natal. In this short play a relatively large cast of characters (20) are used – probably to convey the historical context. It is noticeable that within this group of European Afrikaner characters two indigenous characters are listed: 'Danster, Hotnotsjong fan Klaas Prinsloo' and 'Swartland. Kaffer dolos-gôier, jong van Komm. Potgieter.'

Although both of these two characters are servants (Danster is in service to Klaas Prinslo, Magrita's father, while Swartland is the servant of Commandant Potgieter), they are not marginalised in this play but play important roles in this drama. Swartland, described as an African 'dolos-gôier', a bone-thrower or soothsayer, occupies a dramatic position on an historical, as well as personal level in this play. He throws his *dolosse* ('knuckle-bones') and predicts Retief's disastrous end – an act of dramatic prescience framed within the broader historical event of Retief's planned visit to Dingaan's *kraal* (Act 5, scene 10). But Swartland also receives a more personal request, namely one from the love-sick Koos Potgieter, to throw his *dolosse* to see if Koos will eventually succeed in his quest to win Magrita's love (Act 2, scene 5). When Swartland informs Koos that the *dolosse* keep on telling him that Magrita will stay steadfast in her love for Pieter, Koos implores him to concoct a *paljas* ('a love potion') to help him win her heart.

When Swartland seems at first to be reluctant to react positively to the request of Koos, Danster, who is a more opportunistic figure, quickly intervenes and indicates to Koos that Swartland will make this *paljas*. Danster is the original *trickster* figure and always on the look-out for an opportunity to get something, usually more alcohol and tobacco for himself. He is more cunning than Swartland and tries to manipulate Swartland's visionary powers for his own good.

Conclusion

One finds then that in all four of the authors' work discussed there is much evidence of Khoisan presence and participation in the lives of white colonists and settlers.

In Boniface's *De Temperantisten* a large party of six 'Hottentots' play a significant role in the dramatic events. Boniface uses their arrival in the Cape and participation within the 'temperance society' as a dramatic intervention to expose the false and ridiculous nature of this society. Bain's work, *Kaatje Kekkelbek*, although only one character, the Khoi girl-woman, has a significant and prevailing influence on South African literature.[16] In most of Brink's work we find Khoisan and black characters, but they are almost always placed on the periphery and usually portrayed in the subservient role of servant or slave. He rarely depicts in these master versus servant relationships any overt abuse of the servants or slaves, although some form of verbal abuse is introduced at times to provide comic relief in these farces. The relationships are often portrayed in a benevolent paternalistic manner, for example the words uttered by Sarie, the 'huisbediende' (servant in the house) in *Die National scout of die verloren ceoon*: 'Ons het almal hier so lekker geleef. Oubaas, Ounooi en al julle kinders is so goed vir ons'/ We have all lived so happily here together the [old] master and [old] missus and all your children have been so good to us (1958: 47). In S. J. du Toit's *Magrita Prinslo* Swartland and Danster play quite important parts in this drama. One can describe them as being both outsider and insider figures in the community of the white trekkers. They accompany the white trekkers to Natal and are clearly placed in the subservient role of servants ('jonge') to these trekkers, thus they are on the 'outside' of the white community. However, they are also fully informed of everything that is taking place and discuss their perceptions of these trekkers with each other, which means that they have inside information on all developments regarding this community. Their destinies are closely linked to those of the white trekkers and they are thus also in danger when the Zulus attack, because they were seen as part of, or 'inside', the white community.

It is also clear from most of the work discussed previously that the Khoisan (and black) characters were generally depicted in subservient roles, and often also used as comic relief in these plays – especially in Brink's short farcical plays. The comical element is often immediately apparent when the character is introduced; their names are on the whole meant to be funny and descriptive of their role for the audiences of these plays. That this practice is not perhaps as innocent as one may have presumed at first (seeing as that many of these plays are supposed to be farces or humorous works), is clear from Van Zyl's article on the matter of name giving to the Khoisan and slaves (2002: 5), especially in the nineteenth-century. According to Van Zyl this form of humour is an indication of

> ... 'n ironiese afstand en van 'n meerderwaardige houding wat tot uiting kom in 'n vorm van verbale magsuitoefening deur lede van die dominante kultuur, 'n poging om die *ander* se identiteit te bepaal in aanpassing by die eie kultuur en perspektiewe. (2002: 5)

> ... an ironic distance and of a superior attitude which comes to the fore in the form of a verbal power exercise by the members of the dominant culture, an effort to determine the *other's* identity in accordance with the own culture and perspectives. (author's translation)

Although the portrayal of Khoisan characters differ in the examples discussed: some only occupy a minor position, merely executing orders given by the master or mistress; others fill important dramatic roles and participate actively in the unfolding of the dramatic events. Although the latter often occupy 'speaking' roles, it is not really possible to state that these characters (e. g. Grietje, Kalfachter, Swartland, Danster) are the 'voices' of their communities. As Damian Shaw and Margaret Lenta argue regarding the portrayal of *Kaatje Kekkelbek,* these portrayals focus only on the stereotypical, negative characteristics ascribed by the settlers and colonists to the Khoisan and other indigenous people, and do not address the broader socio-historical issues of *why* this may be the case. It is thus still clearly not the authentic voice of the Khoisan that we are hearing.

Although the stated focus in the article was only on a small selection of plays by a limited number of playwrights during the period which marked the birth of Afrikaans theatre from early Dutch-Afrikaans drama and theatre (1832-1920), it is clear that one could undertake a much broader and more in-depth study of this topic during this period, as well as in the ensuing years. Such a study would entail a further exploration of the Khoisan presence in later Afrikaans drama and theatre – the period after 1925 when Afrikaans theatre received great impetus from its language being officially recognized, as well as Afrikaner Nationalism being actively promoted through culture.

NOTES

1 See F.A. van Jaarsveld's *The Awakening of Afrikaner Nationalism 1868-1881* for a detailed overview of all the factors which led to the rise and development of Afrikaner Nationalism. He links this development directly with 'a reaction to the British Imperialism in South Africa', adding that 'this factor appeared with the annexation of Basutoland in 1868' (1961: 214).

2 Boniface was the first editor of *De Zuid-Afrikaan* (Dekker, 1958: 7). It is perhaps also of interest to know that he was for a long period in a relationship with a Khoisan woman and fathered three children with her. According to Bosman (1954: 17-18), this was the main reason why he was later ostracised from mainstream Cape society.

3 This echoes the whole Saartje Baartman controversy.

4 The play is sometimes ascribed to A. G. Bain and George Rex – however, according to J. du P. Scholtz it should just be ascribed to A. G. Bain. Although Bain and Rex are mentioned by Gray, one finds in the Afrikaans article by J. du P. Scholtz on the authorship of *Kaatje Kekkelbek* a strong and detailed argument why only A. G. Bain should be accepted as the author of this piece.

5 In Afrikaans see for example, Helize van Vuuren (1999: 6): 'Die taalgebruik in "Kaatje Kekkelbek"… is 'n mengelmoes van Afrikaans-Hollands en Engels' (the language in "Kaatijie Kekkelbek" is a mix of Afrikaans-Dutch and English); and in English see Damian Shaw's comment that '*Kaatje Kekkelbek, or Life among the Hottentots* was first performed, apparently 'with unbounded applause' at the Graham's Town Amateur Theatre on 5 November 1838, advertised as a 'Characteristic Comic Song'. It was written in a patois of English and Kitchen Dutch ("kombuistaal" or Proto-Afrikaans)' (2009: 5).

6 Fletcher also mentions that although Kaatje's role is female, at this time she would have been played by a male actor: '*Kaatje Kekkelbek* spoke to the people about their own situation, in their own language, and had to be repeated. It would be interesting to know who played the part of that first performance? It could have been Frederick Rex himself, but more probably Louis Meurant … Whoever it was, he (no woman could have appeared on the Grahamstown stage at this time) had the honour of delivering the first Afrikaans words in a play, on a stage; a step forward which would not be followed up for many years.' (1994: 66)

7 *Kaatje Kekkelbek* starts with Kaatje saying, 'My name is Kaatje Kekkelbek/ I come from Katrivier'. According to Shaw (2009: 6), 'The Kat River Settlement was set up as a "reserve" in 1829 (after the expulsion by the British of the amaXhosa chief Maqoma) where Khoikhoi or "Hottentot" people were entitled to own their own land and to possess firearms'. This scheme (and especially the issue of firearms) was controversial and according to Shaw not popular with Dutch or British colonists.

8 The second half of 19th century was influenced by the *Aurora* (Rhetorical Guilds): a typical Dutch phenomenon dating from the Middle Ages (15th century), made up of poetry, recitations and dramatic art, i.e. a type of arts society. The first one (*Thespis*) was established in Paarl by Rev. G. W. A. van der Lingen, on 23 June 1858, a great supporter and upholder of the Dutch language and culture. There was a great influx of Dutch immigrants between 1856 and 1859. The golden age of these Rhetorical Guilds at the Cape was, however, during the second period, *Aurora II*, from 1866 to 1887, with Melt Brink as chair (1842-1925) (Bosman, 1980: 453).

9 Sometimes the word is used in a neutral sense and only refers to workers, for example: *'Jonas Spoelkom: kneg bij Schenkin'* in *Die mislukte trouwpartij* (1920b) (The unsuccessful party to a marriage); *'Kees Spoeler: kneg by Tandman'* in *By die Tandedokter* (1921a) (At the dentist). In other plays the master verbally abuses his servant e.g. *'Hans Domper: kneg van Klaas'* in *De kwaaie huishoudster* (1923) (The bad-tempered housekeeper).

10 Such designations are found in *Gestrafte nuwsgierigheid* (1920d) (Punished inquisitiveness): 'Mina: huismeid and Kaatjie: kokmeid'. In HAT (2000) the word *meid* is defined as 'a (racist) outdated designation for a female Coloured or black servant; a word which is currently not used much, but which is seen as an offensive word and which should be avoided'.

11 In *De diamante of Verborgen liefde* (1917) (The diamonds or Hidden love): the designation *'kaffers'*

is used four times (a racist designation today, but commonly used by colonists in that period to refer to black people).

12 In the words of one of the characters: 'Een Hotnot is gekker naar wijn als en vlieg naar Bossies stroop'/ A Hottentot is more crazy about wine than a fly over "Bossie" syrup (1906: 18).

13 The practice described by Klaas was, of course, common – and one probably practised by many settlers and colonists (see Marks, 1972:78).

14 See for example Shula Mark's article entitled 'Khoisan resistance to the Dutch in the Seventeenth and Eighteenth centuries'. He sums up the Khoisan's relationship with the white colonists in this period as follows: 'Yet the majority of the Khoisan were converted into the menials of the white man, depressed socially, politically and economically. Though in more settled areas they remained the transport riders, guides, messengers, and even in the interior some were able to retain considerable independence as skilled ivory hunters, their position on the farms in the remoter districts may well have been considerably worse than that of the slaves of the west'. (1972: 78)

15 *Magrita Prinslo* is a typical example of what Binge (1969: ii) refers to in a general remark on early Afrikaans drama, namely that 'Die Afrikaanse toneel is deels omdat hy so laat begin, 'n toneel van die terugblik, dit wil sê 'n toneel met voorliefde vir die behandeling van die volksgeskiedenis'/ Afrikaans drama is partly, because it started so late, a drama of retrospection, i.e. drama with a predilection for the treatment of national history. A copy of the play (originally printed in *Di Patriot*) can be found in Bosman (1942).

16 Not only is this work still discussed by contemporary critics (e.g. Shaw), but the piece itself has been an inspiration for Guy Butler to write a play, titled: *Cape Charade or Kaatje Kekkelbek* which was first performed in Grahamstown (where the original *Kaatje Kekkelbek* was also first performed) on Settlers Day, 4 September 1967.

REFERENCES

Primary sources

Bain, Andrew G. (1971) *Kaatje Kekkelbek*, In Nienaber, G. S. (ed.) *Afrikaans in die vroeër jare*. Johannesburg, Voortrekkerpers Beperk, pp. 67-70.

Boniface, Charles E. (1954) [1832] *De nieuwe ridderorde of De Temperantisten*, Uitgegee met Inleiding en Verklarende Aantekeninge deur F. C. L. Bosman. Johannesburg: Voortrekkerpers Beperk.

Bosman, F.C.L. (1942) *Di bedriegers, Magrita Prinslo*, Johannesburg: Voortrekkerpers Beperk.

Brink, Melt J. (1921) *Diamantkoors of einde goed, alles goed*, Pretoria: J. H. de Bussy.

—— (1917) *De diamant of verborgen liefde*, Pretoria: J. H. de Bussy.

—— (1917a) *Zo zijn er meer of weggeschop met de kous op de kop*, Pretoria: J. H. de Bussy.

—— (1958) [1916] *Die National scout of die verloren ceoon*, Kaapstad: Nasionale Boekhandel Beperk.

—— (1920) [1916] *Die slimme boertjie of die vergiftigde wors*. 2ⁿᵈ Ed. Pretoria: J. H. de Bussy.

—— (1920a) [1916] *Die ware liefde?*, 2ⁿᵈ Ed. Pretoria: J. H. de Bussy.

—— (1920b) [1914] *Die mislukte trouwpartij*, 2ⁿᵈ Ed. Pretoria: J. H. de Bussy.

—— (1930) [1908] *O, die muise! of die stemreg vir vroue*, 5ᵗʰ Ed. Pretoria: J. H. de Bussy.

—— (1920c) [1908] *O, die muise! of die stemreg vir vrouwe*, 4ᵗʰ Ed. Pretoria: J. H. de Bussy.

—— (1920d) [1907] *Gestrafte nuwsgierigheid*, 3ʳᵈ Ed. Pretoria: J. H. de Bussy.

—— (1907) *De haat verstomt waar liefde komt*, Kaapstad: Hollandsch–Afrikaansche Uitgevers Maatschappij.

—— (1920e) [1905] *Berouw kom meestal te laat*, 3ʳᵈ Ed. Pretoria: J. H. de Bussy.

—— (1921a) [1905] *By die tandedokter*, 4ᵗʰ Ed. Pretoria: J. H. de Bussy.

—— (1920f) [1905] *Die egskeiding*, 3ʳᵈ Ed. Pretoria: J. H. de Bussy.

—— (1927) [1905] *Grootvader se pyp*, 4ᵗʰ Ed. Pretoria: J. H. de Bussy.

—— (1911) [1905] *Groot-vader zijn pijp*, 2ⁿᵈ Ed. Pretoria: J. H. de Bussy.

—— (1923) [1905] *Die kwaaie huishoudster*, 3ʳᵈ Ed. Pretoria: J. H. de Bussy.

—— (1906) *Een progressief*, Kaapstad: Hollandsch–Afrikaansche Uitgevers Maatschappij.

Butler, Guy. (1968) *Cape Charade or Kaatje Kekkelbek*, Cape Town: A. A. Balkema.

—— (1905) *De weddenschap*, Kaapstad: Hollandsch–Afrikaansche Uitgevers Maatschappij.

Secondary sources

Antonissen, Rob. (s. a.) *Die Afrikaanse Letterkunde van Aanvang tot Hede*, 3rd Ed. Kaapstad: Nasou Beperk.

Barrow, J. (1802 & 1806) *Travels into the Interior of Southern Africa*, 2 Vols., London: Cadell & Davies.

Binge, L. W. B. (1969) *Ontwikkeling van die Afrikaanse Toneel (1832 tot 1950)*, Pretoria: J. L. van Schaik Beperk.

Bosman, D. B. (1928) *Oor die ontstaan van Afrikaans*, 2nd Ed., Amsterdam: Swets & Zeitlinger.

Bosman, F. C. L. (1951) *Hollandse en Engelse Toneel in Suid- Afrika: 1800 tot vandag*, Pretoria: J. H. de Bussy.

—— (1980) *Drama en Toneel in Suid-Afrika Deel II: 1856 – 1912*, Pretoria: J. L. van Schaik.

—— (1954) *Inleiding*. In Bosman, F. C. L. (ed.) *Boniface, C. E. De nieuwe ridderorde of De Temperatisten*, Johannesburg: Voortrekkerpers Beperk, 7-56.

Chapman, M. (1996) *Southern African Literatures*, London: Longman.

Conradie, Elizabeth. *Hollandse skrywers uit Suid-Afrika: 'n Kultuur-historiese studie Deel I (1652-1875)*, Pretoria: J. H. De Bussy, 1934.

Dekker, G. (1958) *Afrikaanse Literatuurgeskiedenis*, Kaapstad: Nasou Beperk.

Fletcher, Jill. (1994) *The story of South African Theatre 1780-1930*, Cape Town: Vlaeberg.

Gray, S. (1990) 'Women in South African theatre', *South African Theatre Journal*, 4:1, 75-87.

HAT (Verklarende Handwoordeboek van die Afrikaanse Taal, 4th Ed) (2000), Midrand: Perskor Uitgewers.

Johnson, D. (2007) 'Representing the Cape 'Hottentots,' from the French Enlightenment to Post-Apartheid South Africa', *Eighteenth Century Studies*, 40: 4, 525-52.

Lenta, M. (1999) 'Speaking for the slave: Britain and the Cape, 1751-1838', *Literator*, 20: 1, 103-117.

Lichtenstein, H. (1928) [1812] *Travels in Southern Africa in the years 1803, 1804, 1805 and 1806*, Translated by Anne Plumtre, Cape Town: Van Riebeeck Society.

Marks, S. (1972) 'Khoisan resistance to the Dutch in the Seventeenth and Eighteenth Centuries', *The Journal of African History*, 13: 1, 55-80.

Nienaber, G. S. & P. J. (1970) *Die opkoms van Afrikaans as kultuurtaal*, Pretoria: JL van Schaik.

Nienaber, G. S. (1971) *Afrikaans in die vroe?r jare*, Johannesburg: Voortrekkerpers Beperk.

Schapera, I (1965) [1930] *The Khoisan peoples of South Africa. Bushmen and Hottentots*, 5th Ed., London: Routledge & Kegan Paul Ltd.

Scholtz, J. du P. (1939) *Die Afrikaner en sy taal*, Kaapstad: Nasionale Pers Beperk.

—— (1964) 'Outeurskap en ontstaanstyd van "Kaatje Kekkelbek",' *Standpunte*, 17: 5, 12-17.

Szalay, M. (1995) *The San and the colonization of the Cape 1770-1879. Conflict, Incorporation, Acculturation*, Köln: Rudiger Köppe Verlag. (Research in Khoisan Studies, Band 11).

Shaw, D. (2009) 'Two "Hottentots", some Scots and a West Indian slave: the origins of Kaatje Kekkelbek', *English Studies in Africa*, 52: 2, 4-14.

Van Jaarsveld, F. A. (1961) *The Awakening of Afrikaner Nationalism 1868-1881*, Cape Town: Human & Rousseau.

Van Vuuren, H. (1999) 'Saartje, Kaatje en Lena:' n Krities-historiese ondersoek van 'n vroue-karakter in die Suid-Afrikaanse letterkunde', *Stilet*, 11: 2, 1-13.

Van Zyl, D. (2002) 'Base en klase: perspektiewe op en deur die ander in enkele 19de-eeuse Nederlandse en Afrikaanse tekste, met 'n fokus op naamgewing, aanspreekvorme en die land-skap', *Stilet* 14: 1, 167-84.

Images of Africa
in Early Twentieth-Century
British Theatre

STEVE NICHOLSON

Africa! Land of mystery!
Africa! Wonderful – weird!
Many stories are told,
We will now one unfold
Of those whom its flames have seared.

So promises the title page of *Leopard Men*, an action-packed melodrama set in Northern Nigeria and first presented at the Crown Theatre in Eccles, Lancashire, in September 1924. It focuses on a group of Europeans struggling to survive the hell that is West Africa, as they seek to impose and maintain British rule and systems of commerce on the local population:

Four white men in a station
Six looked on as a crowd,
In the hottest hole in creation
Where the 'skeeters move in a cloud…
Where even the natives swelter
And stink with their oily skins
And under their palm-thatched shelter
Laugh at the white man's sins
Knowing that sooner or later
The Coast will claim its price
The law of our one Creator
Death, the reward of vice.

The main interest, however, centres on a native woman's obsessive desire for Jimmy, a dissolute white trader who, having previously seduced her, has now brought his wife over from England. The abandoned Fatuma Fulani is so distraught ('brown woman got heart same – like white woman') that she determines to take bloody revenge by adopting the garb and weapons of a local cult whose members disguise themselves in leopard skins and attack their enemies ('*She instantly grips his throat with claws fixed to her hands*'). All ends happily. Jimmy gets his just desserts and dies in hysterical agony ('Look! Look! That claw! It's getting nearer – nearer – take it away!'); Fulani is killed by a good African ('I go to hell – but you come with me!'); and Jimmy's wife accepts the

122

love of a good European ('I have always loved you – dear – big – soul-mate') and a new role at the station ('You cannot realize the restraining influences that your mere presence has created – not only with the few white men here, but even the natives would give their all for you').[1]

Leopard Men was one of a number of plays staged in Britain between 1924 and 1929, in which imagined Africas were made present not just as backdrops but as major features of the drama. The theatre was not alone in manifesting such interest. The display of Africa in fictional films and documentary travelogues went back to the late nineteenth century, and the tradition of showing off the Empire through living exhibitions of its peoples and cultures also had a considerable history. In 1924, the largest such exhibition so far was held at Wembley, with palaces and pavilions spread over more than 200 acres. It was designed 'To bring home to the heart of the Empire what the Empire is', and included an 'African town' with separate buildings representing East Africa, South Africa, Gold Coast, Nigeria and Sierra Leone. 'Never in our history has there been anything like the Exhibition, either for size or value, reported *The Times* (Anon, 1924). A visit to Africa by the Prince of Wales the following year doubtless generated further public interest. Commercial theatre was bound to look for ways to capitalise.

This article will concentrate on examples of the stage plays – all of them now written out of theatre history – discussing not only the texts but, where possible, productions and critical reception. Tone, attitude and approach varied – though images and stereotypes derived from Conrad's *Heart of Darkness* frequently seeped onto the stage. Any doubts about the basic project of colonisation, or how Europe underdeveloped Africa, were generally suppressed, though the European characters – as in *Leopard Men* – were likely to include decadent drifters or failures as well as heroes. All the plays appear to have been written by European playwrights, most of whom had probably never visited the countries or continent they wrote about. African landscapes were confidently painted onto backdrops, music, dance and ceremonies were represented, and pidgin-English and pseudo-African languages were sometimes employed. More often than not, the primary focus was on the destructive effects of Africa on the European settler – the war between the civilisers and a strange and hostile continent which was not to be easily subdued. Occasionally, African performers were cast in minor roles – adding a touch of extra glamour and perhaps legitimacy to a production: 'All the natives are real ones, not stage ones', as the caption to one publicity photograph proudly declared.[2] But the main parts – and often the minor ones – were played by Caucasian actors, coloured up to represent 'natives'.

Many dramas were unsophisticated even by the standards of the time. *Ungungwanga*, staged in the Drill Hall in Hampstead in March 1926, opens with a chorus of warriors brandishing their spears and shields as they dance around a cooking pot to the beat of what the script describes as a tom-tom. A coronation is taking place, and a repeated (and untranslated) chant of 'Ungungwanga, Ungungwanga, wanga gu! Gagu, wanga gu' builds up 'to a frenzy', only for the new king to shatter the authenticity by launching into a solo about the pleasures of cannibalism, sung 'to the tune of "Dashing Away with the Smoothing Iron"':

> We're black in Ungungwanga,
> In darkest Ungungwanga,
> We're cannibals and heathen
> In Ungungwanga land...
> We eat the cassowary,
> The hippo and canary,
> The monkey, tough and hairy,
> In darkest Africa;
> But what we'd really rather take,
> Is white man – either grilled or steak

Yet beneath the absurdity, *Ungungwanga* alludes to a serious issue. In taking office, the new King distances himself from the ways of his predecessor:

> Mbote, the King, was a fool, though it is I, his son, who say it. He put down the ancient customs of our people; he changed our laws; he swore away our ancient liberty to the Great White Chief. But I, his son, am no fool, and I hereby decree that the ancient customs of our people shall be re-established.

His followers laud this declaration of intent: 'Oh mighty King, thou hast well spoken! Too long have we suffered the anger of the gods for our departure from the ways of our fathers'. However, the only form into which the play casts this reassertion of traditional values is that of eating any Europeans who stray within their compass. Thus the missionaries, being 'lean and full of gristle', are temporarily consigned to 'the fattening pens', and the axe falls on a German trader – an equally safe butt for jingoistic British laughter: 'it ees monstrous – it ees outrageous! I vill write to my beloved Jermany to gomplain'.[3]

Mavana – a play chosen for production at London's Savoy Theatre in 1927 to raise funds for Queen Charlotte's Hospital National Mother-Saving Campaign – features amongst its African characters the 'Head of a band of professional poisoners', and a comically fat schoolteacher who, having been educated by Europeans, ineptly imitates their dress, speech and attitudes. The plot centres on a beautiful young native woman who is forced to marry the chief against her will, and whose lover is punished with death for trying to help her escape to a village where European law will protect them ('There is no killing where the white man is'). The play contrasts the oppression and silencing of women in African society with the freedom and equality they evidently enjoy in Europe:

> You talk as they say the white woman talks to the white man. 'No I won't do this but I shall do that.' 'No, I shan't go there but I shall stay here.'... It is not the blood of my people that talks like this.

The action of *Mavana*, takes place in a village in the central African forest and, like *Ungungwanga*, the script opens with several pages of what purports to be African music, dance and ritual enactment:

> *Heard off, a native drum beating up for a dance. Presently voices, and the patter of feet; then Batubabina, Ma-we! Batu bi-i-i-i-i-nal and the sound of dancing and clapping of hands in time to the beats of the drum and a chant sung by men and women...*

.... A number of natives are dancing in two lines, facing each other, the women on the right, the men on the left... Back curtain shows open and undulating country.[4]

The middle acts of John Galsworthy's *The Forest*, which opened at St Martin's Theatre in London in March 1924, and which was twice broadcast on the radio at the start of the following decade, also took place in the jungles of Central Africa (Galsworthy, 1924). In many respects, however, this was a very different and much more politically committed play, with a very different agenda. Set at the end of the nineteenth century, *The Forest* demonstrates how the European exploration of Africa is cynically exploited by London financiers motivated by greed and self-interest. An established novelist and dramatist – and a friend of Joseph Conrad – Galsworthy already had a high reputation for creating human dramas centred on social issues, and for a highly moral and quasi-socialist outlook. 'Mr John Galsworthy turns from one facet of our social system to another, and on every occasion shows himself a liberal humanitarian', announced the *Daily Herald* at the start of its review. Here, 'he fights a round against Empire-building', demonstrating 'that it is founded on shady finance, and built with the sufferings and lives of black men and white' (March 1924). Or as another review put it: 'The Empire-maker does not care about the means by which his end is achieved; the financier wants his shares in Associated South Africans to rise' (*Daily News*, March 1924).[5]

Galsworthy's central conceit is to parallel the 'dog eat dog' brutality of the central African forest, with life in the commercial city of London, and to find few differences between the worlds of nature in the raw and European 'civilization'. Both are equally red in tooth and (especially) claw. His attack is aimed primarily at the unscrupulous financiers for whom compassion has no place and who, in their pursuit of wealth and self-aggrandisement, trample and destroy whatever gets in their way. 'Galsworthy has forsaken his obstinate impartiality in *The Forest*', reported the *Westminster Gazette*; 'There can be only one side in this play and Galsworthy takes it'. Of course, some reviewers found a different side: 'The moral here is a trite one and enforced by rather shoddy illustrations', claimed one review, which accused the playwright of dealing in caricatures:

> There is a wicked financier named Bastaple, and a brutally idealistic financier (genus Cecil Rhodes) named Beton. Bastaple wants to manipulate the share market and to pile up yet more money. Beton wants to secure the whole of the African continent for the white race and is willing to go to any lengths for this.

This was all too much. 'We know, of course, that the pioneers of the Empire have not been always, or even usually, the Sunday School heroes they are so often represented to have been. But, on the other hand, neither have they been mean and shallow scoundrels'.

Whatever its message, *The Forest* still depended for its impact largely on exotic settings. 'I have never seen the still, brooding horror of the wilds so realistically conveyed', commented one reviewer. While the venue hardly seemed to lend itself to representing the heart of the African continent: 'On the tiny St Martin's stage natives must jostle, and the forest itself has to be fitted in', the design was praised for so successfully capturing 'the unquenchable fertility

THE END OF THE EXPEDITION: STROOD (LESLIE BANKS), A SAVAGE, HERRICK (JOHN HOWELL), AND AMINA (HERMIONE BADDELEY).

1. *Production of* The Forest *by John Galsworthy, staged at St Martin's Theatre, March 1924. Production photograph published in* Illustrated London News, *15 March 1924, p. 459.*
(© *Illustrated London News /* Mary Evans Picture Library)

of the all-submerging forest with a few canvases of powerful arboreal impressions'. For *The Times*, 'It would be misleading to call the forest the background of the drama; it is, rather, a protagonist'. More important than any message, was the opportunity for exciting action which Africa provided: 'It may be a very partisan statement of a case, but, separating the purpose from the story, you have a very powerful and thrilling melodrama'. The *Manchester Guardian* described the narrative as 'full-blooded enough to satisfy the public of the sixpenny magazine and the poster-flaunting kinema', and the *Saturday Review* agreed that 'The forest scenes are as tempestuously eventful as any film-fed lover of battle, murder, and sudden death could desire'. Under the headline 'Blood-Curdling Action in Africa', one reviewer described with a sort of appalled relish 'the culminating horror of the explorer being killed by a half-caste Arab girl whom he had flogged'. The moment seems almost to have emulated the effect of a scene in a grand guignol: 'As Hermione Baddeley, the only actress in the cast, jumped on Strood's back like a wild cat and stabbed him there was a gurgle of horror in the theatre'. Baddeley herself attracted mixed responses, with one critic noting 'a wonderful suggestion of primitive savagery about this brown-skinned girl', and describing her performance as 'uncanny in its realism'. Yet perhaps some doubts about the representation of Africans were not far below the surface – even if they were expressed in terms of accuracy rather than principle: 'if she will forgive me for saying so, she ought to

2. *Production of* The White Assegai *by Allan King, staged at the Playhouse, January 1930. Production photograph published in* The Sketch, *29 January 1930.*
(© *Illustrated London News* / Mary Evans Picture Library)

remember the great example of the actor who, being obliged to play Othello, blacked himself all over. Her African tint left – shall we say? – a distinct tidemark – about the shoulders'.[6]

Swamped it may have become, but Galsworthy's political perspective was an unusual one. Rather more typical was *The White Assegai*, a particularly implausible drama written by Allan King and staged by Sir Barry Jackson for the Birmingham Repertory Theatre in 1929. The central character in King's play is Hardress McKenzie, the Native Commissioner for the M'Soi territory, and a Sunday school hero if ever there was one. McKenzie is so worshipped by the people over whom he rules, that when his wife persuades him to abandon his office for a life in Ascot, where the golf is better, the natives are so distraught that one stabs him in the leg with a poisoned assegai, and the others refuse to provide an antidote for the 'creeping death' inflicted unless he reverses his decision. If McKenzie goes, we gather, a civil war will surely follow – and one which the 'bad' natives – that is, the ones who refuse to pay their taxes to the British crown – may win. But as a man of honour, McKenzie cannot give in to blackmail, and prefers to die rather than bargain for the antidote. 'The deep crooning note of the mourning natives' is heard lamenting his death as the curtain falls. Or, as a more jaundiced review put it: 'Whereupon a horde of Zulus, five to be exact, raised their spears and uttered paeans'. Fortunately for everyone except the bad natives, McKenzie's cousin – an equally good egg – is ready to take on the burden of looking after the shop, until McKenzie's own son is old enough to accede to the solemn role of father to the natives; doubtless to be followed in turn by his son, and so on for ever more.

The White Assegai shows us very clearly that the real reason the British remain in Africa is for the good of the native peoples, and that the sacrifice their own comforts – and even lives – in order to fulfill the responsibilities and duty of care. 'Lord, they are *your* children', the local chief reminds McKenzie, and the Commissioner himself has no doubt: 'I hold the balance true amongst the missionaries, the traders, the would-be exploiters of all kinds. I stand for the natives. It's my work'. In fact, it is his foolish and misguided wife who creates the crisis by selfishly placing her own comfort and wishes above the national duty.

King's play also features a disturbing sub-plot, in which it is again the irresponsibility of the European woman, and her failure to understand the nature of Africa and the ways in which its people must be treated, which provokes problems. Mrs. Giles, the wife of the British station-master, is newly arrived in Africa. 'Blond and blousy and most indecently voluptuous', she refuses to acknowledge that African men are unable to control their basic physical instincts – especially when they see a white woman. She makes the mistake of allowing her house servant see her in a dressing-gown, and he – inevitably – cannot resist the temptation:

> Mrs Giles: (*with an attempt at authority*) Charlie, go at once.
> Charlie: (*advancing slowly towards her – softly*) Charlie stay here.
> (*He halts and surveys her admiringly*).
> Mrs Giles: (*Clutching her gown to her bosom, hysterically*) Charlie, do as I tell you!
>   (*backing into a doorway, left*) Go away!

Following what we presume to be an attempted rape off-stage, her husband kills the servant, and McKenzie – always fair – feels obliged to punish the station master for this murder by relocating him in another part of the colonial Empire. But it is the woman's naivety which the play invites us to criticise: 'They don't teach you that – that things are different here. They don't teach women they've got to keep themselves up in a black country'.[7]

The assumptions which lie behind King's play may shock us – or may seem unsurprising – but at least some of them did not go unquestioned. *The Times* spoke of the play's 'laborious comicality' and its 'pompously heroical ending', while W.A. Darlington in the *Daily Telegraph* 'found myself not believing a word of it'. Other reviews disparaged the writing – as having 'a jolly, Fourth Form flavour' – the playing – 'Several gentlemen, Mr William Heilbronn at their head, painted large portions of themselves black and acted with enthusiasm' – and the narrative – 'I doubt whether even the author of "The Rape of the

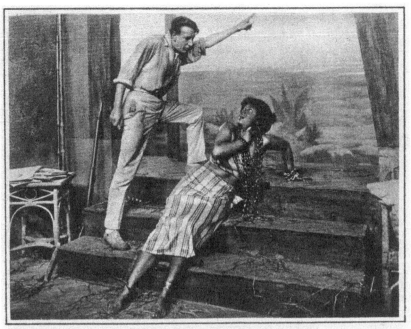

"NOW GET BACK TO THE BUSH!"—WESTON (MR. FRANKLIN DYALL) PUNISHES THE HALF-BREED WOMAN POISONER, TONDELEYO (MISS MARY CLARE), IN "WHITE CARGO," AT THE PLAYHOUSE. Weston catches Tondeleyo in the act of poisoning her English husband, Langford, and makes her drink her own dose. In the photograph Weston has the phial in his right hand.—[*Photograph by Stage Photo Co.*]

3. *Production of* White Cargo *by Leon Gordon, staged at the Playhouse, 1924. Production photograph published in* Illustrated London News, *7 June 1924, p. 1056.*
(© *Illustrated London News* / Mary Evans Picture Library)

Lock" saw that so small a thing as an insufficiency of petticoats on the part of a stationmaster's wife in M'Bongoland would lead to a native rising and the overthrow of thirty years of British rule'. Even in 1929, the crude message and somewhat disingenuous politics of King's play did not have everyone nodding their heads in agreement. 'Considered as a collection of notes for the guidance of he-men proposing to run the more distant parts of Empire, and incidentally curb the "blackamoors"... the play is probably better than I think it is'.[8]

In 1925, Galsworthy published an article under the title *Is England Done?* He proposed that 'emigration to the Dominions' should be increased, but only 'with a frank recognition of the fact that the Dominions will not accept spoiled material'. He therefore proposed that no-one over the age of 18 should be sent, since 'the English adult, in the main, is spoiled for this adventure' (Galsworthy, 1925). It was certainly spoiled men who were at the centre of the play which became the dominant stage fictionalisation of Africa during the twenties – Leon Gordon's *White Cargo* – 'a wonderful picture of the life and environment of those who build up the Empire and the Empire's trade in corners of the earth where the white man is scarce and the white woman unknown'.[9] The introduction to the published text compared

Gordon favourably with Kipling and Conrad, placing him 'in the front rank of fearless searchers for realism' for this study of 'a strange and singular nook of the world' (Gordon,1925: 7).

Subtitled 'A Play of the Primitive', *White Cargo* premiered in New York in November 1923 before opening in London at the Playhouse in May 1924. Over the next few years, the production transferred to the Fortune, Princes, Strand and Regent theatres, receiving over 800 performances, while three separate companies simultaneously toured outside the capital. As well several American productions, the play was reportedly produced in France, Italy, Germany, Austria, Holland, Belgium, Australia, Scandinavia and Czechoslovakia. In 1929 it was filmed in England, and released in both silent and talking versions, and in 1942, a partially updated Hollywood version was released by MGM, starring Hedy Lamarr and Walter Pidgeon. Gordon – who went on to work quite extensively in cinema – wrote the screenplay for both versions. The original play was also revived in Britain in both the 1930s and 1940s. This, then, was an Africa that many people witnessed.

During *The White Assegai*, a Medical Officer declares: 'It's a terrible thing living in a black man's country'.[10] *White Cargo* sets out to convey the reality of this. Gordon's background was as an actor and a journalist, and he had at least travelled in Africa – though he also based this play closely (too closely, since he was successfully sued for not crediting the original author) on a novel called *Hell's Playground*, published in 1915 (Simonton, 1915). The action is set in the living quarters of a group of white men responsible for running a rubber plantation, 'somewhere in the dreary expanse of the west coast'. A quotation on the title page of the published pays tribute to their real-life counterparts:

> When you're riding in your motor,
> Do you ever stop to ponder,
> Where we get the rubber for your tires? (Gordon, 1925: 12)

But Gordon set his drama firmly within a political as well as a commercial context, describing it in the programme and alongside the published text as 'an attempt to portray the struggle for development in a country which steadily defies the encroaching civilization'. In this play, it is by no means clear who is winning the struggle, for we are in a world 'which breeds inevitable rot – a rot which penetrates not only the vegetation and inanimate objects, but the minds and hearts of the white men who attempt to conquer it' (Gordon, 1925: 6). The opening stage direction tells us that the dried-up creek and stagnant river which form the backdrop makes an audience feel 'the oppressing lack of vitality; its hopelessness'. Gordon evokes the stultifying and yet threatening atmosphere not only visually but also through sound: 'Throughout the entire action of the play the continual buzzing of combined armies of insects can be heard' (Gordon, 1925: 15–16). Once again, reviewers insisted that this setting was far more than scenery or mere backdrop: 'Mr Gordon has so devised the protagonist of his play that though it be never visible, yet is ever present, the miasma haunting the day, the poison infecting the night'; indeed, the character embodying the heart of this play's darkness is in fact 'the rot of West Africa upon white men, body, mind and spirit' (Gordon, 1925: 11).

White Cargo opens with the arrival from England of Langdon, a new recruit to the station, smartly-dressed and full of youthful idealism and high morals which he is determined to maintain. What the narrative then enacts is his 'unfortunate ... lapse from the white man's tropical code'.[11] Langford immediately encounters the cynicism and knowing voices of those who know from experience the reality of this sapping environment:

> We all come out with great ideas of what we are going to do, but in the end we do just the same as the other fellow. It's just a matter of time until the damp-rot sets in... I'll tell you how it will start... First you'll stop shaving regularly... Then you won't bother to keep your clothes clean... And as the monotony grows your temper gets shorter. You'll take it out on the niggers physically and on the few white men you'll meet mentally.

Above all, the code Langford aims to follow is that of sexual abstinence – anything else is unthinkable. But here, too, the cynics warn him: 'You'll stagnate and you'll deteriorate and in the end you'll mammy-palaver' (Gordon, 1925: 40-41).

'Mammy-palaver', taking a native woman as a lover (or, in Langford's case, as a wife) symbolises the ultimate collapse of morality and decency. Yet here, we gather, it is commonplace. In play after play, inter-racial sexual attraction and coupling is represented as the final taboo. It means the death of racial purity and the irreversible pollution of the white race. In approving *The White Assegai* for public performance, the Lord Chamberlain's Office (which had responsibility for the censorship of all new stage plays) had been worried by the suggestion that just such an encounter was taking place in the assault on Mrs Giles by the native servant. In the end, they decided against intervening on the grounds that it was a rape rather than consensual: 'it is not disgusting as it would be if the woman were willing'.[12] In *White Cargo*, most of the Europeans on the plantation have already given up: 'Black bread is better than no bread at all', sneers one of the characters; 'We all come to Mammy-palaver sooner or later'. The church opposes it: 'Do you call taking one of these savage women something?' demands a missionary, 'What fellowship of mind – what companionship is there in such a union?' But it is fighting a losing battle. 'Beggars can't be choosers' (Gordon, 1925: 28-9). Langdon is horrified at the suggestion that he, too, will succumb:

> Witzel: You'll be dragging in a woman after a month or two. They always do.
> Langford: I didn't know there were any women out here.
> Witzel: No white ones.
> Langford: But you don't think that –
> Witzel: My God, don't tell me you're so green that you've never heard of mammy-palaver.
> Langford: Why, of course I've heard of it as one hears of plagues and other unpleasant things. Damn it all, you're not suggesting that I might...
> Witzel: I'm not suggesting that you might. I'm prophesying that you will...
> Langford: No!... I'm white and I'm going to stay white. (Gordon, 1925: 39-41).

One of the ironies inhabiting this and other dramas is that while the narrative ostensibly expresses shock and outrage at the very idea of sexual attraction across race, the expectation is often that the audience will be attracted by 'the other', even as they condemn. Much of the publicity for *White Cargo* centred on the seduction of Langford by Tondeleyo – a caricature who might not unreasonably be described as a 'tart of darkness'. The cover of the programme featured a drawing of them kneeling in a passionate embrace, and *The Play Pictorial* carried similar photographic images. Certainly, the stage directions for Tondeleyo's first appearance seem calculated to entice not only Langford but the audience:

> Suddenly in the doorway Tondeleyo appears. Langford... turns and sees the figure of the native girl silhouette itself against the soft light of the open door. She is a girl of about twenty. The exquisite lines of her sensuous young figure are displayed by the manner in which she has draped her body in a soft, many-coloured cloth; the predominating colour contrasts pleasingly with her coffee-coloured skin. Her bare feet have been stained with vermillion and on one ankle a beaten copper anklet is worn. Unlike the average native woman, her arms are innocent of bangles, but the most arresting note of all is her features, which are small and regular after the fashion of the Hindoo girl, with the exception of the lips, which are over full... She smiles, displaying a row of small white teeth... Her eyes move slowly up and down, weighing him... She leans languidly against the open door and speaks slowly and in perfect though stilted English...(Gordon, 1925: 55).

This is the cliché of the femme fatale, the irresistible seductress who knows how to manipulate men and get what she wants. Inevitably, what she wants is wealth and possessions. Langdon, determined not to enact Witzel's prophesy, insists on marrying her. He immediately discovers what she is after, and her attractions quickly pall:

> Langford: Don't you ever think of anything but jewellery?
> Tondeleyo: Tondeleyo want more.
> Langford: (*Hopelessly*) Tondeleyo always wants more. She is also the sexually voracious female. (*She runs her hands caressingly through his hair and over his shoulders*)
> Langford: Please don't do that. I can't stand it in this heat. (*She tries to kiss him*) I can't stand being mauled twenty-four hours a day. (Gordon, 1925: pp. 94–5)

And she is unable to comprehend the European concept of marriage:

> Doctor: Not only your body, but your mind and your thoughts belong to him. And while he lives, no other man may ever mean anything to you... Now you can never go. No white man will ever protect you. It is a white law, and if ever you – become – well, how shall I say – promiscuous ...
> Tondoleyo: Eh?
> Doctor: Give yourself to another man. The white man's vengeance will reach out and get you no matter where you are. (Gordon, 1925: 97–8)

Tondeleyo eventually attempts to poison Langdon in order to get rid of him, but is intercepted by Witzel, who forces her to drink the poison herself. She exits 'jabbering incoherently', and Langdon, realising that Africa is not for him, returns to England a wiser man (Gordon, 1925: 113). The play ends with the arrival of his successor, and a sense that the cycle is starting all over again.

Reviews (and photographs) of Galsworthy's *The Forest* show that rather than being fully blacked up, the actress in the original production resembled an 'Arab girl'. As the Lord Chamberlain's Examiner wrote in relation to another play in 1929, 'The pursuit of a white woman by an Arab is unpleasant, but ... an Arab is not a nigger'.[13] In *White Cargo* it is similarly significant that Tondeleyo – like Mavana in the play of that name – is of mixed race parentage. This apparently makes them physically attractive to white Europeans, but also allows them to be credited with qualities of intellect and perception which could not have been allowed to a black African. In the case of Mavana, it makes her more able and willing to see beyond and challenge the female oppression practiced in the African society in which she grows up in. In the case of Tondeleyo, the European inheritance is viewed less positively:

> Witzel: Tondeleyo is the only really good looking nigger I've ever seen. Of course she is more than half white, but her blood and her instincts are all nigger.
> Roberts: The only concession she made to her French father are her features and her brain. She's a bad example to the natives and a menace to the whites. Tondeleyo is the worst kind of... harlot... Her shrewdness and her white blood make it all the more damnable. What the others do through ignorance she does from sheer wantonness.
> Witzel: But she is damned good looking (Gordon, 1925: 30).

What also comes across from several reviews is that representing an African (or half-African) may have licensed the (white) female performer to adopt a greater freedom in terms of costume and performance than was generally the case in 'respectable' theatres. Unusually for a play they had approved, the Censorship inspected the production and took exception the skimpiness of her costume and the physicality of her acting. They instructed the management that they must 'increase the lady Tondeleyo's clothing, both at the waist and the hip', and insisted 'that in the love making scene the lady be less demonstrative and does not paw her victim to the extent that she does at present.'[14] Even so, when the production arrived at its third West End venue in the second year of its run, Tondeleyo was described as being 'played with much skill and little clothing', and when it was revived nearly ten years later, the *Daily Telegraph* suggested that although it now seemed 'crudely written', one of the play's strengths was that 'it gives its leading lady a chance to paint herself brown practically all over, and go to the limit in wickedness'. As the *Sunday Times* put it, '"Mammy-Palaver" is sinuously and seductively represented by Olga Lindo'.[15]

The 'problem' of mixing races is at the centre of the last of the plays I want to discuss here, *Bongola*. Indeed, it is referred to in the play's title, for we are informed that the word – a nickname for the main character – means 'mule'. To some of the characters, it is axiomatic that just as mules are infertile, and so incapable of passing on their mixed genes, so the human 'Bongola' should not do so.

Bongola – a three act play credited to Lilian Cornelius and Owen Payne – opened at the Q Theatre in West London in April 1926. Regrettably, there seems to be no documentation of its performance history, and no reviews or evidence of how it was staged or received. All that remains is the script as passed for performance by the Lord Chamberlain, and the reports and notes which document his Office's responses. The narrative centres on the relationship between a white English woman and a mixed race South African, and this was bound to raise qualms with the Censor. 'It is an unpleasant play that will meet with criticisms from some quarters', noted the Examiner. But the Office decided that in fact it could be approved as 'a well-written object lesson of the harm of mixing white and black'. Indeed, they suggested that 'this sort of play may have its uses' as effective propaganda, since 'anything that helps towards discouraging marriage between black and white races is to the good of the human race generally'.[16]

The first act, set in comfortable Surrey, contrasts the theoretical idealism and liberal beliefs of Carol and her family with the cynicism of two white South African visitors, for whom the black population are 'Kaffirs, with no more intelligence than a baboon'. They treat the 'cranky notions' of equality voiced by Carol's father with utter contempt:

> Grant: 'Brotherhood of man!' Lot he knows about it! Let him come out to South Africa, that'll soon knock any notions of 'Brotherhood of man' out of his head. I tell you it makes me sick, all this talk by the people who don't know... I know what you're going to say. Educate them. And a mighty power of good that does. A lot of cranks have tried it, they come along swimmingly up to a point, and there they stick. They never get past it. They've got no staying power. I've lived among them, and I know... they never grow beyond children all their lives.[17]

They are equally dismissive of the vision and ambition expressed by Danvil (Carol's husband, and the 'Bongola' of the title) to educate what he calls 'my poor black people' to the level of the whites. His aim is that the Africans should 'evolve their own civilization from within, and not from without', since European civilization itself is 'an alien thing which cannot fit them'. To the whites such as Grant, this represents a threat, and Danvil himself embodies an illegitimate position:

> Grant: I've got nothing against him, but he's not pure breed – black blood in him one side or the other – and black and whites don't mix, I tell you, so I have nothing to do with him... He gets some ideas into his head about the *uplift of the black race* (*He puts great scorn into his voice*) Educate my black brother till he's my equal – ach – turns it all into some damn fool mission, and stirs up all sorts of mischief that he won't know how to stamp out.

The middle act shifts to South Africa, where Carol finds herself isolated by both the white and black communities. Determined to understand the world in which she now finds herself, she attends a traditional healing ceremony taking place in 'the Kaffir Compound' which is being conducted to cure her husband's sick aunt. It proves a traumatic experience for her, and again, the production relishes the opportunity to present such an event to the touristic gaze of the audience:

Kaatje Okkers, a black woman, lies on the bed. She is evidently in a fever and moans heavily from time to time... At her head squats a kaffir woman, fanning her with a branch to keep off the flies. Four other kaffirs squat around, their eyes instantly fixed on the fifth, who is a witch doctor. He has a weirdly shaped head-dress of dingy fur. Round his waist, suspended by a leather thong, are numerous wild cats' tails. Round his neck a similar thong carries teeth, pieces of metal, small horns, etc. He wears many copper bracelets on both arms and legs. He is throwing bones to divine the cause of the sufferer's sickness.

The scene moves into a lengthy ritual involving dance, percussion, chants and screams:

The kaffir woman, her body now rigid, now violently shuddering, at intervals emits the long trailing shriek. The witch-doctor begins, now to bound on all fours, now the slow, bent, stamping march, now seeming to pluck something from the sick woman's body, and hold it up with a yell.

Carol is horrified to witness such primitive practices, and her husband is equally disgusted by such superstitious rituals, dismissing the witch doctor as a charlatan, and pointing out that such practices are against the law. But Carol's father is so overcome by the atmosphere that he has a heart attack and dies. Carol becomes hysterical, and includes her husband in her accusations: 'These black people! These black people! They're his black people! They've killed my daddy!' She shrinks from him, 'Don't touch me! Don't come near me!' and tells him that she can never see him again because 'I should only see the black in your face'.

In the final act, Carol seems adamant that there can be no going back and no reconciliation. Her husband pleads with her to think of their coming child, but this makes matters worse and provokes her more: 'If she is black I dread – I dread in my soul that I shall hate her, as I hate Africa'. In her despair, she tells him that 'if I could I would tear it out of my body, and give it back to this Africa that I hate'. The continent itself has now become the savage and unconquerable enemy of the European:

I feel as though Africa is alive, a dark woman of mystery, brooding over her own dark people, and hurting those whites who do not come under her sway. I hate her and I am afraid of her... if I stay here she will hurt me again. She will make my baby black. I will not stay here. I will go home to my peaceful, safe England... perhaps, then, God will let me have my own baby, and not – not a black one.

Carol now aligns herself with Grant's insistence that 'any fusion of the races is unthinkable' and that the duty of the European is 'to preserve the white civilization'. But when Grant's companion insists that 'Africa belongs to the whites', Danvil confronts him in a powerful and rhetorical declaration, which is surely intended to sway the audience:

The country once belonged to us – by what right do you make it yours? We outnumber you by seven to one, yet you deny us any but the lowest and meanest work in your service. The poorest white man has a vote, and the right to represent his peers, and take a hand in the government of his country. Every free man would fight for that. When you deny it to us, do you not virtually make us slaves? You walk arrogantly and push us from your path. All men are equal in the sight of the God who made us both, your preachers say. Empty talk! Why then do you spit on our colour and refuse our just rights? I warn you! Because of what you do to us we shall become a nation in the great future, a nation of colour. Our race consciousness has awakened. We demand the right to live and work as your social and political equals in this country which belongs to us. Only so may the day dawn in this dark world when the colour of a man's skin shall be no bar to the outlook of his soul.

In the final moments of the play, Carol has to decide whether to stay with her husband and work with him to create a new Africa, or to return to the safety of England. Excruciating though the curtain image may be, and problematic though some of the play's more liberal assumptions remain, she gives herself to his vision:

> (*Carol… looks at Theo, at the house and round at Africa. Slowly she comes down one step, then looks back at the house, and again at Theo. Slowly she comes down the remaining steps, and crosses to him.*)
> Theo: Carol! (*He sinks to his knees, takes one hand, and hides his face against her. She places her other hand on his head, and looks down at him*).

In effect, she has moved from a naïve innocence in which she had not begun to grasp the immensity of what she was embarking on, through profound crisis and disturbance, to a newly mature and realistic confirmation and re-statement of values. Though the Lord Chamberlain's Office – with its confidence that audiences would see the play as a straightforward warning against the compatibility of white and black – either entirely missed this shift, or assumed that the audience would not make it with her.

It is not particularly surprising that there should have been a strand in British theatre which took for inspiration the exoticism, horrors, thrills, and cultural differences embodied in the struggle to control and exploit an Empire. There was no shortage of dramas featuring mysterious Chinese villains with mystical powers, secretive religious cults in India, or Arab Sheiks kidnapping white women in deserts. Such plays generally traded in self-perpetuating stereotypes and clichés, and few of the authors had had any direct contact with the culture they presented for the titillation and horror of their audiences. Yet in excavating this small area of British theatre history of the inter-war period, we should not assume that plays were necessarily one-dimensional, or that audiences always took them at face value. Some texts did allow conflicting positions to argue with each other, and reviews suggest that even where an intended message might seem unequivocal, it may not have been swallowed whole.

An article such as this one can only begin the process of exploring how Africa and Africans were presented on the British stage in the early decades of the twentieth century, as the Empire began to come apart. It is impossible to gauge how far the images, narratives and ideological assumptions embedded in the texts and the stagings may have helped shape the opinions and beliefs of those who saw them, and how far they simply reinforced – or, occasionally, challenged – attitudes which already existed. But when the playwright and the production got it right, they were certainly good box office.

NOTES

1 All quotations taken from the unpublished manuscript of *Leopard Men* in the British Library archive of Lord Chamberlain's Plays, 1900-1968.
2 The photograph was publicising the production of *Blue Peter*, a West African play by Temple Thurston, staged at the Princes Theatre and the Royalty Theatre in London in the autumn of 1924. See production file for *Blue Peter* in the Victoria and Albert Museum Theatre and Performance Archives.
3 All quotations taken from the unpublished manuscript of *Ungungwanga* in the British Library archive of Lord Chamberlain's Plays, 1900-1968.
4 All quotations taken from the unpublished manuscript of *Mavana* in the British Library archive of Lord Chamberlain's Plays, 1900-1968.
5 All quotations from reviews sourced from the Production File for *The Forest* in the Victoria and Albert Museum Theatre and Performance Archives.
6 Ibid.
7 All quotations taken from the unpublished manuscript of *The White Assegai* in the British Library archive of Lord Chamberlain's Plays, 1900-1968.
8 All quotations from reviews sourced from the Production File for *The White Assegai* in the Victoria and Albert Museum Theatre and Performance Archives.
9 All quotations from reviews sourced from the Production File for *White Cargo* in the Victoria and Albert Museum Theatre and Performance Archives.
10 See unpublished manuscript of *The White Assegai*.
11 See Production File for *White Cargo*.
12 See British Library Archive of Lord Chamberlain's Correspondence Files 1900-1968: *White Cargo*.
13 See British Library Archive of Lord Chamberlain's Correspondence Files 1900-1968: *Sinister House*.
14 See British Library Archive of Lord Chamberlain's Correspondence Files 1900-1968: *White Cargo*.
15 See Production File for *White Cargo*.
16 See British Library Archive of Lord Chamberlain's Correspondence Files 1900-1968: *Bongola*.
17 All quotations taken from the unpublished manuscript of *Bongola* in the British Library archive of Lord Chamberlain's Plays, 1900–1968.

BIBLIOGRAPHY

Anon, (1924) report of The Empire exhibition *The Times*, 23 April 1924, xiv.

Author unknown. (date?) *Leopard Men*. Unpublished manuscript: British Library archive of Lord Chamberlain's Plays, 1900-1968.

Author unknown. (date?) *Mavana*. Unpublished manuscript: British Library archive of Lord Chamberlain's Plays, 1900-1968.

Author unknown. (date?) *Ungungwanga*. Unpublished manuscript: British Library archive of Lord Chamberlain's Plays, 1900-1968.

Cornelius, Lilian & Owen Payne (1926) *Bongola*. Unpublished manuscript: British Library archive of Lord Chamberlain's Plays, 1900-1968.

Galsworthy, John (1924) *The Forest*. London: Duckworth and Co.

Galsworthy, John (1925) *Is England Done* [an article reprinted from *The Sunday Times*]. Hove: Privately printed for H.V. Marrot.

Gordon, Leon (1925) *White Cargo*. Boston: The Four Seas Company.

King, Howard (1929) *The White Assegai*. Unpublished: Production file in the Victoria and Albert Museum Theatre and Performance Archives.

Simonton, Ida Vera (1915) *Hell's Playground*. London: Gay and Hancock.

Thurston, Temple (1924) *Blue Peter*. Unpublished: Production file in the Victoria and Albert Museum Theatre and Performance Archives.

The First African Play

Fabula: Yawreoch Commedia & its influence on the
development of theatre in Ethiopia

JANE PLASTOW

-This article discusses both the newly translated playscript of *Fabula: Yawreoch Commedia* (Fable: The Comedy of Animals) and the influence of this first Ethiopian drama on the subsequent development of national theatre. *Fabula* is probably the first original African play ever written and produced. We are therefore particularly delighted to be able to offer in this volume a first translation from the original Amharic by Belayneh Abune, a drama scholar, and currently Dean of the Faculty of Arts at Addis Ababa University.

There has been considerable debate amongst authorities on Ethiopian culture about the dates of performance and publication of *Fabula*.[1] As far as I am able to ascertain this is because no one has read the script for many years. Indeed when I first started searching for it many people interested in the area seemed unsure as to whether a full text still existed. Eventually, however, Belayneh Abune tracked down a text of the second edition in the library of the Institute of Ethiopian Studies at Addis Ababa University, and from this made his translation from Amharic into English. It is particularly helpful that it is this second edition which has been translated since in his *Background* section of his Introduction the playwright gives much useful information about motivation, publication and performance. Contrary to some previous speculation the writer explains that the original publication of 1912 was not a playscript; rather it was a collection of eight animal fables written by Tekle Hawariat and designed as moral teachings for the young emperor, Lij Iyasu.[2] (We have not on this occasion translated the eight stories which are included in the second edition publication.) In his *Background* the playwright makes it quite clear that he wrote the playscript as a direct response to his disdain for the prevailing Ethiopian understanding of what constituted theatre, and that the script is an adaptation of the fables previously written in story form. The translated playscript claims to have been first published in 1921.[3] It also becomes clear that although Empress Zauditu[4] ordered the destruction of printed copies of the play because she had been told by courtiers who had seen the play that it disparaged the crown she did not actually see the original production at the Teras Hotel for herself. Haile Selassie (previously Ras Tafari) obviously had no problem with the play since he allowed a second production after Zauditu's death in 1930. All this

138

information has radically modified my own previous understanding of the circumstances of production of the first African play,[5] and demonstrates instructively how fantasies can quickly be woven by scholars regarding dates, influences and events when they are working from second hand sources.[6]

Tekle Hawariat and *Fabula: Yawreoch Commedia*

Tekle Hawariat was born around 1884 and as a boy distinguished himself at the historic battle of Adwa in 1896, where Italian forces were defeated by the Ethiopian army.[7] His reward was to be offered by Emperor Menelik the most unusual opportunity of travel to Russia; apparently through close links between the Ethiopian and Russian Orthodox churches.[8] Here he rose to become a colonel in the Russian Imperial Army, but he fell under the influence of liberal members of the Russian aristocracy who were beginning to question the most oppressive aspects of feudalism. He acquired an admiration for European culture, agriculture and education during the course of extensive travels.[9] This urbane, cosmopolitan man returned home in 1912 to an Ethiopia which was at that time peculiarly riven by intrigue at the highest levels.

The great expansionist Emperor, Menelik II,[10] was old and increasingly incapacitated by a series of strokes. His grandson, Lij Iyasu, was the heir designate, but was scandalising the country with his self-indulgent behaviour. As Tekle Hawariat explains in his *Background* to the play, 'Lij Iyasu ... was merrymaking, misbehaving and roaming around town'. Matters were further complicated in that the Empress Taitu was doing all in her power to win the throne for her preferred candidate, Zauditu, Menelik's acknowledged but illegitimate daughter by another woman. Menelik died in 1913 and Iyasu was proclaimed emperor though his official coronation was postponed, ostensibly due to his youth. Over the next three years he faced a number of armed challenges to his power, and involved himself with extensive slave raids in the non-Christian south of the Empire. Harold Marcus describes Iyasu as follows:

> From the very beginning of his de facto reign, Lij Iyasu showed that he was not the stuff from which great monarchs were made. He was bright, but also impulsive, cruel, lascivious, prone to depressions and egocentricities, and politically inept. (Marcus, 1995: 251)

A final reason for resistance to Iyasu becoming emperor was the suspicion that he had Muslim sympathies. This would have been impossible for the Amhara ruling class to accept, since Christian Ethiopia widely believed that their Emperor was a semi-divine inheritor of the crown of King Solomon and the leader of God's chosen people.[11] In 1916 Iyasu was deposed. Zauditu became empress, while Ras Tafari (who later took the crown name Haile Selassie) was appointed regent and heir to the throne.

Tekle Hawariat, as is apparent in his introductory writing, was horrified by Lij Iyasu's behaviour. He attempted to influence the young ruler through writing a series of allegorical stories, which according to Reidulf Molvaer (1997: 51), were particularly influenced by the fables of La Fontaine and the Russian, Ivan Krylov, and which were published in 1913. When these made no impact Tekle Hawariat made no further attempt at education through writing until after Lij Iyasu was deposed in 1916. As the *Background* makes clear, it was Tekle Hawariat's appalled reaction to the musical show he was taken to after Ras Tafari had become regent that led him to adapt these stories into a play, in an attempt to show Ethiopians what was meant by theatre as he had seen it in Europe; hence the *Introduction* to the first edition which attempts to educate his readers about Western forms and uses of theatre. Tekle Hawariat writes as one shocked that Empress Zauditu could have seen his play as an attack on her, but he does not choose to clarify the intended subject of his satire, and it seems likely that many of his observers had rightly perceived the play as a thinly disguised attack not only on Lij Iyasu, but more generally on court corruption and abuse of responsibility by the monarchy. Zauditu's orders that all copies of Tekle Hawariat's book be confiscated seem to have led to an effective halt to any theatrical developments at court throughout the rest of her life. Tekle Hawariat continued to write; the first Ethiopian constitution (at the request of Haile Selassie), agricultural theses and a two-volume unpublished autobiography, but he never again attempted a play, though he was happy to revive the piece when Haile Selassie assumed the throne, and to republish both stories and plays in the 1940s.

How *Fabula* shaped the future of Ethiopian theatre

The influence of Amharic poetry and language

Although the furore caused by *Fabula* might make it seem that this production was a somewhat abortive start to a new dramatic tradition, I am going to argue that Tekle Hawariat was sowing the seeds for the growth of the particular hybrid that grew into Ethiopian drama.

It is important to recognise in discussions of official Ethiopian art that what is almost always being referred to is only Amhara culture. Ethiopia contains some 85 language groups, but until the overthrow of the Marxist government of the Derg[12] in 1991 by the northern Christian Tigre people, the empire had been ruled for the vast majority of its long history by the Amhara, a group who make up around a quarter of the national population. Preferment was historically dependent on assuming Amhara identity; on speaking Amharic, the *Lesane Negus* (language of the king), and on becoming an Orthodox Christian. The Amhara ruling class were the equals of any European colonist in failing to recognise any possible worth in the cultures of the conquered or in minority groups. In the case of theatre history there are no records of a drama tradition evolving in any language apart from Amharic, other than in Eritrea which was part of Ethiopia from 1952 to 1991 and has theatre traditions in both Tigrinya and Tigre.[13]

In his *Introduction* Tekle Hawariat explains that he is seeking to bring Western drama to Ethiopia with the intention of establishing a theatre tradition; something he sees as having been previously lacking in Ethiopia, but desirable both as a sign of increasing civilisation and as a means of conveying moral messages. From the tone of his introductory writing, Tekle Hawariat obviously thought Ethiopia had much it could usefully learn from European culture – he mentions in his *Background* to the play that he speaks and dresses 'as a European' and his lecture on European theatre that makes up the first *Introduction* definitely has a didactic tone. However he does not seek to simply imitate European form. Rather he merges indigenous and imported ideas and forms to create the hybrid which gradually develops to become immensely popular amongst the urban Amhara, and later an important tool of political debate.[14]

Fabula is written according to the rules of one of Ethiopia's oldest and most common poetic forms. *Yewel Bet* would be recognised throughout Amhara speaking areas, being a metrical pattern of six stressed syllables in each line. The play's construction also fits exactly with what Thomas Kane describes as the usual mode for Amharic poetry.

> Amharic poetry is mostly rhymed, usually in couplets on the pattern aa, bb, cc, ad infinitum. However this scheme is by no means rigid and a rhyme may be repeated more than twice in succession. (Kane, 1975: 24)

It is no surprise that Tekle Hawariat chose a poetic form as his mode of introducing drama to Ethiopia. He was familiar with Shakespeare and Molière's use of poetic metre, and within Ethiopian Christian cultures poetry was highly regarded. The poetic tradition (*qene*) is intimately linked to the church. In the old capital of Gondar in the eighteenth century the *qenebeit* (poetry house) had nearly 300 teachers, and acolytes known as *debtera*, linked to the church, attended courses for up to ten years in the creation of improvisatory poetry according to a series of strict rules about a range of poetic forms. Poetic ability was therefore highly regarded and something the Ethiopian court would have been very familiar with, helping to make the new form accessible.

Readers of *Fabula* will be immediately struck by the strong religious imagery. The people are portrayed as sheep who should be protected by those in charge of them, just as Christianity repeatedly uses the image of Christ as the shepherd of humanity. One might think that Tekle Hawariat was urging Iyasu/Zauditu to take on the role of the shepherd – as they undoubtedly should have done as God's semi-divine representatives on earth, since as he says in his *Background* that he is seeking to use his writing to influence the wrong-doing of Lij Iyasu; to: 'try my best to straighten up the behaviour of this young boy'. However, I have come across a phrase of Iyasu's which struck a note with a number of commentators. He apparently referred to the advisory council that sought to keep him in order as 'my grandfather's fattened sheep' (Bahru Zewde, 2001: 123). It seems highly likely that Tekle Hawariat would have been aware of this description. In the context of the play this would place Iyasu not as the Shepherd but more in the role of the predatory Wolf seeking a tasty meal. The other major religious symbol, is of course the delightfully wicked Snake who relishes his historic role as tempter and confuser, and seeks to assault not just the sheep but even the all-important shepherd.

In the years following the reintroduction of drama to the Ethiopian elite the use of both poetic form and strong biblical influence dominated from the 1930s through to the late-1950s. Haile Selassie employed schoolteacher playwrights Malaku Baggosaw and Yoftahe Negussie in the 1930s to produce a series of pageant plays such as *Talaku Dagna* (The Great Judge), which in 1934 emphasised historical parallels between King Solomon and Haile Selassie. And later the court theatre was dominated for some time by the plays of the highest non-royal in the land. *Ras Bitwodded* (Prince Beloved) Makonnen Endalkatchew was Ethiopia's prime minister from 1955 to 1961 and simultaneously wrote a series of religiously dominated history plays. One of my favourites is *Salisawi Dawit* (David the Third) where the king's devout son dies in sorrow at his parent's love of secular music, leaving the suitably chastened parents to learn their lesson: 'They came to hate music, regarding it as the principal cause of the untimely death of their beloved son.' Only when a tranche of young playwrights brought new ideas of realism and socialism back to Ethiopia from travels in the West in the late 1950s would this elite poetic and religious drama wither away.[15]

A further reason for Tekle Hawariat utilising poetic form is the age old Ethiopian tradition of *semena worq* (wax and gold). *Semena worq* is a technique whereby poets are taught to wrap a hidden internal meaning – the gold – inside an ostensible, different, outer message – the wax.[16] At one level *Fabula* can be seen as a simple moral fable about the need for the strong to guard the weak, and for us all to avoid temptation and danger from the forces of evil. But we see from Tekle Hawariat's introductory material that he was also seeking to give a diplomatically veiled lesson to poor rulers, and from Zauditu's extreme reaction in banning the play it would appear that the court read strong political messages into Tekle Hawariat's comedy.

Semena worq was highly valued in Amhara culture, and links in with Amharic ideas that it is somewhat crude to speak openly, and that circuitous veiled language is the proper way to conduct conversation. In a society often dominated by intrigue and where political manoeuvring at court was the norm, the ability to manipulate language was highly admired and as Molvaer explains, Amharic is an excellent vehicle for verbal gymnastics:

> Amharic is eminently suited to express more than one meaning in the same word or phrase ... Minstrels and scholars have used it to express delicate views at royal and noble courts ... later, political awakening and a new social consciousness made authors seek ways of expressing protest and dissent and still getting their books printed, especially from the 1950s onwards. The same old techniques of *double entendre* served their purposes well. (Molvaer, 1980, preface)

Tekle Hawariat's *Fabula* is only the first of dozens of plays which throughout the twentieth century used allegory, metaphor and symbolism to convey hidden, radical political messages to their audiences.

Molvaer claims that Tekle Hawariat's animal satires drew on the fables of La Fontaine and the work of the Russian fabulist Ivan Krylov. Tekle Hawariat acknowledges the influence of European fables but also refers to his study of presumably local 'oral' fables. This seems to be an area of real cultural crossover. In Ethiopia, as in so much of Africa, there is a long oral tradition of anthropomorphic animal stories, always with a moral aspect to them. Moreover the idea that certain animals represented typical human characters would have been immediately recognisable to Tekle Hawariat's audience. Indeed there is a rich vein of Ethiopian art that pictures anthropomorphic animals for either satiric or didactic purposes. The idea of characters as representing types rather than psychologised and individuated beings was widespread in Ethiopian story-telling, whether religious or secular. Although I know of no other plays which utilised animal characters, for many years to come Ethiopian theatre would be dominated by the idea of the actors as primarily representing either a human type or embodying an idea. Indeed when later in the 1940s the first attempts were made to write plays about ordinary individuals and their lives the elite audience was resistant, preferring allegorical or historical plays. Drama taking the life of ordinary individuals as a valid subject for theatrical examination would only begin to gain popularity in the 1960s as audiences expanded; those educated in the university or citizens came to see the theatre as a place for the discussion of the radical ideas generally censored in the tightly state-controlled media.[17]

I have already touched on the issue of language, but in the continuing cross-continental debate as to the languages African writers should write in, and in view of how Ethiopian theatre would develop, it is crucial that *Fabula*, unlike most early scripts across Africa, was written in an indigenous language; Amharic. Realistically it could have not been otherwise. Amharic was the *lingua franca* of the Ethiopian empire, and most members of the court, and many inhabitants of Addis Ababa, would have used it as their mother tongue. Ethiopia had never been colonised and it had a well developed written form so the idea of using a foreign language for theatre, unlike almost everywhere else in Africa, would never have arisen. The schools from which the first actors were drawn did have foreign staff who did promote the use of theatre in English and French. Ethiopia's first purpose-built theatre was at the French-medium Menelik School in 1934.[18] However, it seems they also promoted drama in Amharic. The Ethiopian playwrights who emerged just after Haile Selassie came to the throne were schoolmasters from the Menelik School. They taught Amharic as a subject in school and became the favoured court playwrights in the early 1930s. Consequently Ethiopian drama was from its inception associated with the Amharic language. This has been hugely advantageous to the strength of Amharic theatre in that it never needed to go through the struggles experienced by so many other African playwrights regarding how to express their culture in an alien tongue, or agonising over which language should be used; though of course the languages of three quarters of the empire's peoples have been continually culturally marginalised by this dramatic tradition.

The idea of drama may have come from Europe, but because they were always in charge of the language of production, the Amhara were able to use it from the very beginning to express themselves and their culture in a relatively unmediated fashion. I would argue that this is a key reason why drama grew to be so strong and popular in Ethiopia; particularly when it emerged in the 1960s from court control to become a voice for the urban populace. Apart from the exclusion of other Ethiopian language groups from participation in the development of drama, the only other significant downside to a theatre culture amongst the strongest in Africa – there are five large state-supported theatres in the capital of Addis Ababa – is that the outside world knows so little of this theatrical tradition. Ethiopia's foremost playwright, Tsegaye Gebre-Medhin wrote three plays in English; Mengistu Lemma, the leading comic playwright, translated two of his own plays in the 1960s and there have been a couple of other attempts by lesser playwrights. Until this translation of *Fabula*, however, there has been no similar undertaking for any of Ethiopia's many important plays and playwrights.[19] I think this is largely because Ethiopian culture has tended to be a world very much unto itself, but also due to the fact that few Ethiopian theatre personnel have travelled much abroad or have the level of multilingualism required to translate Amharic into a major international language. The situation is not unique. Tanzania also has some notable playwrights, but nearly all cultural production is in Kiswahili and almost nothing has been translated.

Elite theatre and popular performance

It is highly significant to the future development of Ethiopian drama that Tekle Hawariat rejected the designation of the performance of indigenous music and dance (to which he was taken by the Addis Ababa mayor) as theatre. Instead he asserted that only a dialogue-dominated form derived from European tradition could be honoured with the name. The result was the simultaneous development of two strands of performance in Ethiopia's theatre spaces. For the elite there evolved a play tradition, at first limited to the few modern schools, the nobility and court, but gradually widening to bring in the slowly growing educated classes of Addis Ababa. In the years after the second world war and the Italian occupation of Ethiopia, when Haile Selassie returned from exile in England,[20] this drama often shared a theatre space, but on different afternoons of the week, with populist commercial *kinet*[21] performances. These combined music, song, dance, comedy and slapstick skits in variety shows often lasting up to four hours for the entertainment of the urban masses. The bifurcation of performance traditions has continued right up to the present day so that the state theatres of Addis Ababa: the National Theatre, the City Hall Theatre, the Hager Fikir and the Ras all maintain two companies, one performing drama and one presenting *kinet*. Moreover, unlike much of the rest of Africa where dramatists have sought to find theatrical means of reconciling popular indigenous dance and music forms with Western imported notions of drama, in Ethiopia and Eritrea there has been little or no recognition that there can be any marriage between the two performance traditions.

In large part this has derived, I think, from a particularly strong class consciousness in Amhara society which has affected every area of life. Traditionally there is a group or caste of Amhara performers known as *azmaris*. Whilst they were recognised at every level in society for their musical and poetic skills and every noble family would maintain an *azmari* as praise-singer, socially they were outcasts; when not employed in noble households often forced to live on the edge of settlements alongside other marginalised craftspeople such as metal workers and butchers. *Azmaris* are a fascinating and under-researched group, whose organisation extended to having a private argot or language, known as *yeazmari quenqua*. Their low status seems to have derived from both the fact that they performed manual labour (only farming and military activities were seen as respectable manual occupations in traditional Amhara society) and because they were creators; the crafting of things whether cultural or physical being seen as deeply suspect, possibly because it challenged the status of the Abrahamic God as the only legitimate maker. The position of the *azmari* is vividly reflected in a 1966 play by Ethiopia's most famous playwright, Tsegaye Gebre-Medhin. His play, *Azmari*, includes this passage from the heroine's brother who hates his family's caste position:

> Lulu: Condemned you shall remain in the eyes of all who are clean and respectable. What are you, who decent people turn their backs on? What are you, blinking from the gutters of society, clowning for the benefits of society, and insulted by society itself? What are you? Who are you? What's your name? (*Azmari* Act II Scene I)

It was the *azmaris* who popularised *kinet* as a modern commercialised version of their age-old vocation, but such a lower class performance tradition could not be, I suspect, seen by a Westernised member of the nobility like Tekle Hawariat as having anything in common with the sophistication of the drama that he sought to introduce to Ethiopian elite life.

Indeed Tekle Hawariat was already being radical and challenging orthodoxy by writing at all, let alone becoming involved in such a frivolous pastime as creative writing. Traditionally the act of writing had been seen as manual labour and therefore unbecoming to the aristocracy who, as result, could often read but seldom wrote. Con- sequently, although Ethiopia has a written script dating back to the eighth century BC[22] and the Amharic vernacular form dates back to the 1500s, traditionally only clergy and clerks put pen to paper. Tekle Hawariat seems to have been breaking ground in making writing an acceptable pursuit for a gentleman, something that Haile Selassie was later to encourage as an acceptable manifestation of elite modernity to such a degree that by the 1950s there was quite a fashion for playwriting amongst the Amhara nobility.

However, while it was one thing to have aristocratic playwrights, it would have been quite another to have expected the upper classes to act, and only the upper classes or the clergy were able to read playscripts. This question of literacy is another reason for the division between the later development of *kinet* as separate from the drama. *Azmaris* could not read and write. Theirs was an oral tradition, and even when the *kinet* companies later started to include sketches and short plays as part of their variety performances the producer usually told the cast the scenario of the drama and left the performers to improvise around his outline.[23] Improvisation was no part of Tekle Hawariat's vision for the theatre. As we see from the script of *Fabula*, this was a carefully constructed piece using recognised poetic form and requiring literate actors. We have no knowledge of who performed *Fabula* and Tekle Hawariat says nothing about the process of putting it on except that for his second production after Zauditu's death 'I staged the play after doing some rehearsal'. What we do know is that the next group of playwrights, the schoolteachers and then the aristocrats, press ganged school boys from the elite Menelik School into service as actors. Their evident reluctance was recorded by a schoolboy who later turned professional actor who told his interviewer, 'The students were doing the performances in fear of their teachers. Even though there were voluntary students, some of them were forced'(Abebe Kebede, 1983:7). Since there is no mention of anyone else acting it seems highly likely that Tekle Hawariat too used schoolboys. It would certainly only have been boys. While *azmaris* included both men and women, no woman appeared on the Ethiopian stage until 1954, and even then the first actresses were lower-class women commonly assumed to be prostitutes. I think this is one of the most striking differences in the evolution of drama in Ethiopia from what went on in many other African nations. When one charts early dramatic history in countries as diverse as Nigeria, Kenya, Southern Rhodesia and Eritrea one sees the early days as being marked by coteries of young educated people coming together either at universities or in voluntary associations and making theatre as a mutual assertion of their modernity, and often as an expression of their wish to bring together cultural and political engagement through the arts. However, these movements happened decades later, notably in the 1960s. In feudal Ethiopia in the early twentieth century, Tekle Hawariat's peers would not all have been able to read, few would have had any understanding of his concepts of what constituted drama, and above all they would have been grossly insulted to be expected to act.

Tekle Hawariat was certainly his own director, and first of a line of playwright/directors who controlled the theatres right up until the 1980s. Actors, whether schoolboys or *azmaris,* were socially hugely inferior to the elite playwrights. Until around the 1980s when actor training began at Addis Ababa University actors in Ethiopia were seen purely as tools for expressing the playwright/director's ideas and language. In years to come to be a writer/director was consequently seen as being of high status, and as a professional stage emerged could be highly lucrative, with playwrights taking up to 50 per cent of box office receipts, while actors, employed by the theatre houses, both imperial and municipally endowed, worked for a pittance, sometimes failed to receive any wages and were often forced to look to other work to supplement incomes. Tekle Hawariat's elitist attitude to the introduction of drama to Ethiopia laid the foundations for an exploitative and hierarchical relationship between playwrights and performers that was to endure, albeit in modified form, right up to the present day.

Ethiopian theatre and politics

My final connection between *Fabula* and the theatre that was to follow concerns politics and playwrights. Tekle Hawariat launched an only thinly concealed attack on the court and Ethiopian rulers, and while immediate action was taken by demanding the copies of the playscript no punishment was handed out to the playwright. On the contrary, 1918 saw the Tekle Hawariat appointed governor of Jijiga and moving on to various other government posts. It is probable that his allegiance to the regent, Ras Tafari, may have offered a measure of protection. Ras Tafari was a young man and wanted to be seen as a moderniser and reformer. He had also known Tekle Hawariat in his childhood, so there were a number of reasons why he may have offered support. But it is also a fact that leading playwrights have often subsequently got away with work that has been widely seen as subversive, at least until the final overthrow of the monarchy in 1974, within a culture where censorship and rigid control of media and publishing was the rule.

When Ras Tafari came to the throne in 1930 as Haile Selassie he immediately started promoting theatre (there was a revival of *Fabula* as early as 1930), building and endowing a series of theatres in Addis Ababa, even importing equipment and for a short while personnel from Europe in 1955 when he rushed through the building of the Haile Selassie I Theatre (now the National Theatre), with a seating capacity of 1,400 for the occasion of his Silver Jubilee. Up until the 1960s most of this theatre was strongly in support of the crown. However, after their return from training in the US, Britain and France, key modern Ethiopian playwrights such as Tsegaye Gebre-Medhin, Tesfaye Gessesse and Mengistu Lemma, who had travelled abroad with the emperor's blessing, a raft of new plays started being performed that were heavily critical of autocracy and the feudal state. Since the emperor personally read all scripts submitted for performance in the capital's theatres he knew all about these plays; indeed he often attended premieres, but while he expressed coded displeasure by snubbing playwrights, sometimes cutting runs short and on at least one occasion arranging for the removal of all the chairs from an auditorium the day before a show began, he never imprisoned the playwrights and continued to support a level of drama production unequalled at the time in any other African nation. It seems evident that Haile Selassie was a genuine lover of theatre, and indeed of Amharic literary culture in general, to such an extent that he actively sought to use drama as one of a panoply of means to promote the status and prestige of the crown. Even when that tool was turned against him he was reluctant to stifle an art form that would gradually turn from being the preserve of the elite to a major means of promoting ideas of radical change and ultimately revolution amongst the mass of citizenry in Addis Ababa, who in the 1960s and 1970s would flock to the theatres to witness plays making unprecedented attacks on the *status quo* and discussing unheard of concepts such as socialism, Marxism and the establishment of democracy. The veneration given to Ethiopian playwrights by the emperor, and later by the urban populace, would make Ethiopian theatre a key site of political debate and calls for state transformation that seems to have all begun with the first theatrical experiment by Tekle Hawariat and his *Fabula: Yawreoch Commedia*.

NOTES

1   Authorities have varied in their opinions as to when the play was performed. Kane argues that: 'This play was written in 1911-1912 and staged much later in 1920-21' (Kane, 1975: 7). Debebe Seifu contends that it probably took place: 'At the end of the first decade of this century' (Seifu, 1986: 92), while Molvaer thinks it was written during Empress Zauditu's reign which began in 1916 (Molvaer, 1997: 52). None of these people had Tekle Hawariat's original script. The problem is also compounded because the Ethiopian calendar uses the Gregorian rather than the Julian date calculations used by most of the rest of the world. This means that Ethiopian New Year falls in September and their year count is always seven or eight years behind the rest of the world.

2   Lij Iyasu (1895-1935) was the designated emperor of Ethiopia from 1913-1916. He was nominated by his grandfather, the great Emperor Menelik, from a number of possible candidates, after Menelik began to be incapacitated in 1908 by the series of strokes that finally led to his death in 1913. However, Iyasu was never crowned, hence the common usage of the term *Lij* (child) before his name. This was both because of infighting over the succession at court and because Iyasu proved an unreliable, capricious and self-indulgent ruler. He was deposed in 1916, excommunicated and kept as a privileged prisoner for much of the rest of his life.

3   The play text says the first edition of the stories was published in *Hamle* in 1904, which translates as July 1912. The first edition of the play is dated *Pagume* 1913. *Pagume* is the 13th month of the Ethiopian calendar and translates as September 1921.

4   Empress Zauditu (1876-1930) was the granddaughter of Emperor Menelik II. She assumed the throne after Iyasu was deposed in 1916 and ruled, with Ras Tafari as regent, until her death in 1930.

5   My earlier writing on *Fabula* in *African Theatre and Poltics* (1996) was based on my interpretations of the writings of such as Kane and Seifu, but this new access to Tekle Hawariat's own writing has significantly changed my understanding of the circumstances of the play's production.

6   It is quite entertaining to see what various people have written and to speculate on their original sources, not all of which are always apparent. Ricci (*Literature dell Ethiopia*, 1969) is rumoured to have had a copy of the play in his possession, while Molvaer (*Black Lions*, 1997) says he bases his information on extracts from Tekle Hawariat's unpublished autobiography and discussions with people who knew the playwright, including his son. Others extrapolate theories without giving any particular authority, and no one has been able to quote directly from Tekle Hawariat's publications before now.

7   The Battle of Adwa is one of many proud moments in Ethiopian history. The Italians were seeking to invade Ethiopia with a view to expanding their Eritrean colony. In a unique event in European colonial history an African army defeated the Italian army which was forced to agree the present border between Ethiopia and Eritrea as binding.

8   The highlands of Ethiopia and the ruling classes were Christianised in the fourth century AD, and a strong link was maintained between church and state throughout the imperial period. The Russian Orthodox Church and the Ethiopian Orthodox Church have a number of similarities and both were imperial states. Russia was therefore seen as a favoured nation for travel by Ethiopians in the early twentieth century.

9   Tekle Hawariat travelled in Italy, Germany, France and England as well as in Russia.

10   Menelik II (1844-1913) is one of the most famous Ethiopian Emperors. He hugely expanded his empire through a series of conquests to the south and was greatly interested in modernisation and foreign ideas.

11   All Emperors claimed descent from the Jewish King Solomon and a liaison he supposedly tricked the Ethiopian Queen of Sheba (Makeda in the Amhara version) into. Historically

Ethiopian Christians and Jews *(falasha)* believe that the subsequent taking of the Ark of the Covenant from Israel by Solomon's Ethiopian illegitimate son, Menelik, back to his homeland led to Ethiopians becoming God's chosen people.

12 The Derg (Committee) was the name popularly given to the military government set up by those who conducted the coup against Haile Selassie on 1974. Its political flavour was initially uncertain, but it became increasingly hardline Marxist once Mengistu Haile Mariam seized control. He was overthrown by northern Tigre liberation fighters in 1991.

13 For further information on Eritrean theatre see Jane Plastow, 'East Africa: Ethiopia and Eritrea', in *A History of Theatre in Africa*, Martin Banham ed., pp. 192-205, Cambridge: Cambridge University Press, 2004.

14 Theatre has been seen as playing a particularly important role in politicising the people, firstly in relation to the radical changes in society that took place when Haile Selassie was overthrown by a military coup in 1974, and later in relation to spreading Marxist ideas and by both sides fighting in the Eritrea-Ethiopia war of 1961-1991. See Plastow 1996.

15 For further information on Ethiopian theatre history of this period see Plastow 1996: Chapter 2.

16 The allusion is to the local method of gold artefact production whereby the molten gold was poured into a wax mould which could later, when the gold hardened, be removed.

17 See Plastow 1996, Chapter 3.

18 Ladislas Farago described this theatre as follows:

> The Menelik school [...] possesses the only theatre in Abyssinia, a big zinc shed; the pupils performed a folk piece in English for my benefit. We sat quite alone in the auditorium and could only follow the play with difficulty, because the stage of this unusual theatre is not lit. Though the building is wired for electric light, there is no money for fuel to work the dynamo. (Ladislas Farago, *Abyssinia on the Eve*, London: Putnam, 1935, p. 170)

19 The Ethiopian plays published in English to date are:
By Tsegaye Gebre-Medhin, *Tewodros*, *Ethiopian Observer*, 1966.
Oda Oak Oracle, London: Oxford University Press, 1965.
Azmari, *Ethiopian Observer*, 1966.
Collision of Altars, London: Rex Collings, 1977.
By Mengistu Lemma, *Marriage by Abduction*, *Ethiopian Observer*, 1962.
Marriage of Unequals, *Ethiopian Observer*, 1963.
By Abe Gubegna, *The Savage Girl*, 1964.

20 Ethiopia was occupied by Mussolini's Italian army from 1935 to 1941.

21 *Kinet* is the name given to popular performance usually rooted in indigenous music and dance traditions.

22 Amharic derives from the ancient Ethiopian language of Ge'ez which is still the liturgical language of the Ethiopian Orthodox Church and which spawned a family of modern languages in the region; Amharic, Tigre and Tigrinya, much as Latin is the root of European romance languages. Early inscriptions in a form of proto-Ge'ez have been found dating back as far as the eighth century BC.

23 The most famous 'playwright' for the popular theatre was probably Iyoel Yohannes who reputedly produced some 70 scripts for the Hager Fikir Theatre's *kinet* troupe. Since these were not seen as literature they appear to have been lost.

BIBLIOGRAPHY

Farago, Ladislas (1935) *Abyssinia on the Eve*. London: Putnam.

Gebre-Medhin, Tsegaye (1966) 'Azmari'. *The Ethiopian Observer.*

Gerard, Alfred (1971) *Four African Language Literatures: Xhosa, Sotho, Zulu, Amharic*. Berkeley: University of California Press.

Kane, Thomas L. (1975) *Ethiopian Literature in Amharic*. Wiesbaden: Harrassowitz.

Kebede, Abebe (1983) *Actors in the History of Ethiopian Theatre*, unpublished.

Marcus, Harold (1995) *The Life and Times of Menelik II: Ethiopia 1844-1913*. Lawrenceville, NJ & Asmara: Red Sea Press.

Molvaer, Reidulf K, (1980) *Tradition and Change in Ethiopia. Social and Cultural Life as Reflected in Amharic Fictional Literature. 1930-1974.* Leiden: Brill.

Molvaer, Reidulf K (1997) *Black Lions: The Creative Lives of Modern Ethiopian Literary Giants and Pioneers.* Lawrenceville, NJ and Asmara: Red Sea Press.

Plastow, Jane (1996) *African Theatre and Politics: the evolution of theatre in Ethiopia, Tanzania and Zimbabwe. A comparative study.* Amsterdam. Rodopi.

Plastow, Jane (2004) 'East Africa: Ethiopia and Eritrea'. In *A History of Theatre in Africa,* Martin Banham (ed.), Cambridge: Cambridge University Press, pp. 192-205.

Ricci, Lanfranco (1969) *Letterature dell'Etiopia.* Milan: F. Vallardi.

Seifu, Debebe. (1986) 'A Note on Post Revolution Ethiopian Theatre', 9th International Conference of Ethiopian Studies, Moscow.

Zewde, Bahru (2001) *A History of Modern Ethiopia* (2nd ed.). Oxford: James Currey.

Translator's Note
Tekle Hawariat's *Fabula: Yawreoch Commedia* 'The Comedy of Animals'

BELAYNEH ABUNE

Back in 1986, when Professor Jane Plastow was teaching in the Theatre Arts Department of Addis Ababa University, we were colleagues and as such enjoyed many discussions. One of our conversations concerned the translation of Ethiopian plays from Amharic to English. Although there have been a number of plays written and staged in the public theatres every year, only about five plays have been in English. Three were written originally in English, namely *Oda Oak Oracle* and *Tewodros* (the latter also written in Amharic) by Tsegaye Gebre Medhin, and a play by Abe Gubegna entitled *The Savage Girl*. The other two plays were in Amharic and later translated by Mengistu Lemma, the writer himself. These were *Marriage by Abduction* and *The Marriage of Unequals*.

Even the plays mentioned above are little known to the outside world. This fact disturbed Jane in those days and she kept nagging me and Manyazewal Endeshaw (another colleague of ours) to attempt to translate plays, especially the comedies of Fissha, a teacher in the department and a gifted writer who really knows how to make his plays rich with traditional wisdom and folklores. One of his plays which Jane had seen and which was very popular at the time was *Simegn Sintayehu*, named after the female central character. Jane told Manyazewal and me that if we got the play translated she would contact the publishers and have it published. We took this opportunity and set a schedule to translate the play. We thought it would not be difficult and we would finish within a month. However, we were not able to translate even one page after we had worked for two weeks. The problem was that the play had been so textured with the traditional idiomatic expressions and the culture of the rural people of Ethiopia that it was difficult for us to come up with equivalent expressions, let alone translate it directly. That was the end of the idea.

So when Jane Plastow contacted me about translating Ethiopia's first written play, *Fabula*, I remembered my last experience and hesitated. But before I gave her my answer I looked at the play afresh. To my relief, I found that it was not as difficult as Fissha's play had been. I thought for a while about why they were different. My answer is that Fissha had been born and grew up in the rural areas before he joined the university. Therefore he was very close to the traditional

151

life and colloquial language of the rural people. On the other hand Tekle Hawariat went to Europe as a young man and lived there for many years before he wrote this play. So I found his language easier to translate than Fissha's.

I followed a direct translation style so as to give the audience the original meaning and flavour of the play. I have faced some problems with some of the old Amharic language which is not in use any more. In such instances I tried to get these archaic meanings from old people who were speaking the language almost 90 years ago.

Finally, I thank Professor Jane Plastow for giving me this opportunity to translate the first play of Ethiopia and Africa.

Fabula: Yawreoch Commedia
'The Comedy of Animals' (2nd edition)

TEKLE HAWARIAT

Introduction to the first edition by the author
(entitled *The Comedy of Animals – Satire*)

Anyone who has visited Europe knows what theatre is. Theatre is a place of a game. But we should be careful of those who do not know its secret and who simply consider it as a joke, time wasting, and flattery. On the contrary, its main purpose is to make people conscious of their actions and turn them away from indulging in unseemly behaviours. It creates laughter or sadness when turning people away from conflict to affection, from wickedness to goodness, from being a scoundrel to being benevolent, from being an idler to a person of integrity, and it does so by exposing the malicious and wrong deeds of people.

Theatre, therefore, has three genres: Tragedy, Drama and Comedy. Tragedy portrays serious danger and grief. Drama concentrates on the violence and turmoil that occurs among family members. Comedy shows the incongruity of a situation and makes us laugh, witnessing a character being disgraced or falling down as a result of his mistakes.

At present, we do not boast of having an organised body that could establish any of the genres or theatre ideas. However, just to make a start on this noble idea, we have now written a Comedy through the personification of animals. If this is found proper and suitable to our country's present situation and is also entertaining, we will attempt the other forms (genres), as our strength allows us. The very fact that our ideas were accepted by other people will encourage others, who have the natural talent and knowledge proper to the art to come forward. Time will call them for itself.

We, therefore, have taken the initiative and have written, 'The Comedy of Animals', to set an example for establishing a theatre. We hope that our country's fellowmen would accept our gesture with good will.

September 1913, Addis Ababa

153

Introduction to the second edition by the author

Background to the play

I feel obliged to explain to the readers the reason that motivated me to write this short play entitled *Fabula* (Fable).

Ras Bitwoded Tessema Nadew's[1] (the guardian of Lij Iyasu) death led Lij Iyasu[2] to a state of frolicking like a horse which has got rid of its reins. He was then probably fifteen. There were flatterers all around him. I had been called suddenly to come to Addis Ababa from Hirna. However, not knowing the exact date and place which had been decided for me to meet him, I remained idle for some time. Lij Iyasu, on the other hand, was merrymaking, misbehaving and roaming around town. No one tried to bring him to his senses. I could not but burn with anger and shame observing his situation. Immediately, I started arguing with myself. Is this the way a crown prince, the sole candidate chosen to become the King of Kings of Ethiopia, replacing Emperor Menelik, should be brought up? Is it proper for me to remain silent having seen such misbehaviour? But what can I really do? Why do I not try my best to straighten up the behaviour of this young boy? This sounds a good idea … but who would give me the chance to get close to him? I dress and act as a European. I know that I am looked upon as a stranger.

Having kept myself in such a depressed mood for a while, a new idea suddenly struck me. Children often enjoy and lose themselves completely in a game. But if one relies on it, it surely devastates the person's life in the end. So, I had better write a composition that has a significant issue in it relevant to Lij Eyasu. The fact that I have been brought up in Europe could help me to do this. What else did I do as a young boy when I first started clinging to my education? Was I not studying *fibula* (fables) orally?

Therefore, I would let myself prepare the composition and present it to him. This might give me a chance to be close to him. The closer I got, the better position I would be in to explain to him the right ideas … So it would be easy to turn his mind to education. And education is always a means to move in the right direction … If not possible … Well it is worth trying.

Immediately, I put my ideas into practice. I remembered the fables of the European writers that I had been studying for years and wrote an imitation of them. I read what I had written to Ato Tessema Eshete,[3] having waited for the right time to do so. He was a courtier to Lij Iyasu at the time. He immediately led me to him and I got the chance to read my composition. After that I became Lij Iyasu's courtier. However, mine was a completely different role from that of others. I had planned from the start that my relation to him must be only on important matters. I tried to serve him that way without involving myself in improper activities, like frolicking, merry-making and joking. But, unfortunately, I came too late to be of any service to him or to be his true courtier. In other words, he was up to his neck in trivial business. The flood that swallowed him was so powerful that I was not able to bring him to his senses. However I struggled, it was beyond my power. Well, I tried hard for a while before I lost hope completely and then I had to resign from my post.

After Lij Eyasu had been deposed from his post, Prince Ras Tafari, the regent and crown prince of Ethiopia gave me permission to get my book printed. Then one day, in between, I received an invitation letter from Ato Hiruy, the Mayor of Addis Ababa. It said, 'Tonight we are going to present a theatre performance at Ras Hotel and we kindly request your permission to come and see our show.'

There had never been a play in our country before. Therefore, I went eagerly and in a hurry to see how they had managed to stage the performance. What I saw was a band of singers and dancers (men and women) singing and dancing accompanied by a drum, *masinko* and *kraar*.[4] I had been saddened observing the upbringing of Lij Eyasu. Now I got more sad watching how Ethiopians had been led to the road of modernity. I immediately realized the need to straighten up such leadership. I wished there and then to write an exemplary play. But I knew that I could not do it quickly because I was engaged fully with my work. Suddenly, an idea occurred to me. The idea was that it could be easily directed and presented if I used the animals in my earlier composition of *Fabula* (fables), as characters and gave them dialogue to speak to each other. I did that within a short time and was able to show it in the presence of the crown prince, Ras Tafari at Teras Hotel. That helped the printed books to be sold. Many people were looking for them and within one day about 300 books were sold.

The news soon reached Queen Zauditu. The people who broke the news were many and among them some interpreted my play negatively and said that it had been written to attack her. The queen thought this to be true and became very upset. She further wrote a letter to the crown prince about her bad feelings. I was summoned to the crown prince and he told me about her views. He further ordered me to hand over all the printed books to Lij Makonnen Endalkachew.[5] He told Endalkachew to collect the books that had been sold. From the 3000 books, I was able to hide 300 books and I handed over all the rest.

After the death of the queen,[6] the books that had been detained were released to me and with permission I staged the play after doing some rehearsal. Therefore, *Fabula* was not only my first composition but also the source of the first theatre in our country.

When I returned to my country after 20 years of exile, because of the Italian invasion, many people asked me to publish the play. From the 3000 books printed earlier, I found only one. I felt the need to make a second edition to answer their request.

It is true that many young writers have been able to write and present plays to the public after this pioneering play of mine. More writers could come to the scene. I had been able to reflect the idea in my introduction to the play that as more writers appear the more Ethiopia will leap to civilization. This would give us satisfaction. Lastly, we urge the readers to know the books written earlier. You should not refrain from reading books often.

NOTES

1   Ras (Lord) Tessema Nadew was regent to Iyasu from 1909 till his death in 1913. The regency was in place because Emperor Menelik was incapacitated and Iyasu was a minor.

2   Lij Iyasu (1895–1935) was the designated emperor of Ethiopia from 1913-1916. He was nominated by his grandfather, the great Emperor Menelik, from a number of possible candidates, after Menelik began to be incapacitated in 1908 by the series of strokes that finally led to his death in 1913. However, Iyasu was never crowned, hence the common usage of the term *Lij* (child) before his name. This was both because of infighting over the succession at court and because Iyasu proved an unreliable, capricious and self- indulgent ruler. He was deposed in 1916, excommunicated and kept as a privileged prisoner for much of the rest of his life.

3   Tessema Eshete (1876–1964) was the son of an *azmari* (popular singer and/or musician), a group popularly despised in Amhara society of the time. However, when his father died he was brought up in Emperor Menelik's orphanage from where he was selected to be the Emperor's first chauffeur and was sent to Germany to learn about cars from 1908–1910. Whilst in Germany he also recorded the first records by an Ethiopian. On his return he was favoured by Lij Iyasu and promoted to become minster of posts and telegraphs. I presume Tekle Hawariat would have consulted Tessema Eshete about his writing because both were artists with exposure to European and Ethiopian arts and because Tessema was in Iyasu's confidence.

4   The *masinko* is a popular stringed instrument played with a bow. The *kraar* is a five or six string bowl-shaped lyre.

5   Makonnen Endalkachew was one of Haile Selassie's most trusted noblemen. He rose to become the first Ethiopian prime minister with the highest title the Emperor could bestow – *Ras Bitwodded* (Prince Beloved). He also came to follow in Tekle Hawariat's footsteps in that he wrote a number of highly religious plays.

6   Zauditu died in 1930.

'The Comedy of Animals'
Act I

Scene 1

(*The sheep, inside their fenced enclosure, wake up from their sleep and start addressing each other*)

1st sheep   Biaa … Miaa …
    Nature has made such unperverted law
    Between the animals, the wild and us
    To share day and night often in the raw
    The sun, stars, the earth and the sky
    Alternate in timely fashion, counting their hours.
2nd sheep   Never know disorder governed by one law
    Never label one as an ally or foe
    Never been envious, biased or fickle
    Devoid of emotion whatever they feel
    Far from problems, never show any fear
    Being watchful master to all creatures.
3rd sheep   Patience they have, it is so amazing
    Just live in harmony, their pledge standing.
4th sheep   Praise is what God most deserves

We beg you please, keep us from evils.

5ᵗʰ sheep   We passed the whole night being fearful, wary
Now it is day light, go out, don't worry.

6ᵗʰ sheep   Well … Come, let us eat our food
Listen all of you, the young and the old
Be in the group; don't isolate yourself when you go the field
We only crave for water or green grass
But we are not idle, when it comes to us
If we are not careful, that is the end of us.

7ᵗʰ sheep   Since olden times, we have been born as feeble creatures
We lack courage to defend ourselves
So, we mostly run away from strangers.

8ᵗʰ sheep   Oh, my heart is throbbing! What brings this day?
I hear rustling, though I cannot say,
Is it a beast or a human being?
Time to run away, don't stumble along.
Biaa … Miaa … Let us run … Run fast
Biaa … Miaaa ... Don`t talk, stay quiet.

(A young sheep (lamb) left alone)

The lamb   Mae … Mae … Meee … Meee…
Caught off guard by sleep, where I have slept alone
Nowhere my father or my mother … Apart from me, no one.
Well then…where can I go to find my mother?
I roaming in the wood, she surely is losing her dearest,
I am in the dark, which way to look for her?
She too worries too much, wherever she is now.
I am thirsty for water, not fed well of her breast.
If I follow this road, I might get water
What comes first is, to slake my thirst.
Well … Crossing this hill takes me to the river
I then look for my mother, drinking the water.
If I don't get it, it is the will of God
His sole decision, mother finds me instead.
What a relief! Here is the water, I thank you my lord
Let me kneel down, drink as much of the water as I can.

Scene 2

(A wolf speaks to the lamb, both staring at each other)

Wolf   Well …Well …Well !
I am wearing myself out, to get clean water.
So you are the one that makes it dirtier
How dare you? You think of such an arrogant act,
You are mocking me; I will punish you for that.

Lamb   Oh no ! Honorable lord, God is my witness
I have seen you coming, from down here
And downstream here is where I am, from your position

How then can I turn the water dirty and unclean?

Wolf Ohh ! ohh! He dares to deny it! That makes it worse.

Anyone can see how arrogant you are!

Remember, you also insulted me this time last year

Lamb How could I do such a misdeed?

It is less than a year since I have seen the world.

I still suckle the breast of my mother.

For God's sake my lord, you'd better stay calm.

Wolf If it is not you then it is your brother.

I am just fed up with your behaviour.

Lamb I am the only son, have no brother,

I am just a small lad, I never act badly sir.

Please do forgive me; you see I am just a child.

With false accusation, I won't be offended,

You blamed me enough, I won't make such mistake.

You judge me with truth, which is all I ask.

Wolf You said you are an only son, without a brother.

Well, I have been harassed and you know who by.

Your many relatives and their cruel herdsmen

Setting free their dogs, I was chased by everyone.

And when I met you here, just by the will of God

Do not bore me saying, for justice I stand.

Truth or falsehood… what do I benefit

When left with hunger every day… every night?

Why should you be worried, when you are taken care of?

God has made you lucky, since you have become yourself

He has given you the grass and the leaves, to be your daily food.

But I think you are hurt, that you have been forced

To bend your neck down grazing around.

But you are safe from any accident.

As a strong shield, you have men on your side.

You don't need to work hard to get your daily food.

It is just my fate that I was born being cursed.

Ignorant of heaven, ill-treated on earth.

When God made me a wolf, from my birth

He has done me injustice, limiting my food choice.

Always looking for meat, I can't eat leaf or have grass,

I live worried, day in and day out.

Do not know a home life where I sleep when I want.

I pass my day hunting, wandering everywhere.

But I don't get your lot, you are always alert,

You live comfortably; you don't need to bother,

Justice is only made towards the needy.

Falsehood or truth, does everyone get happy?

If one gets hungry, and has become a judge

Solving first his needs, makes him a person of knowledge.

When one gets settled, justice will be re-examined
Taking all his time, the case will be re-opened.
Now my good friend, if you seek justice
I will give my soul, to stand for truth.
I swear by my life, not to pass false verdict.
Let God strike me, if I am not impartial.
I am just fed up with such fruitless talk.
When I think of my lunch, it is you that I look at.
I only cool off when I get my food.
We then come to justice, truth or falsehood,
All of them if we could.
This is my verdict, whether you like it or you hate it,
I am dying of hunger, shut up and lie quiet.

Lamb   Biaa … miaaa … Woe is me ! Woe is me!
I never get my fill or enjoy life really,
Yet being a small child I have been subjected
To a hungry wolf, that I be his breakfast.
Farewell to the world…to that swindler
Who makes us a victim, to those who have power.
We toil in vain hoping to live better.

ACT II

Scene 1

Herdsmen   Come Kati, come Kuuti, - Hurry up you big dogs.
The wolf is ready to render our lamb lifeless.
Stop! You bastard! Grab him! Grab him!
Oh Kuti! You let him take her. Oh it's a shame!
This son of a thief! How do you let him come!

Dogs   Haaw! Haaw! Which way did he slip away?
Search! Smell his footprints! Hurry! Block his way!

Stout dog   Haaw ! Haaw! Butchi… Kutchi .. Come on!
I got him!…. Feel happy everyone!
Early in the morning, I saw that lamb
Standing by himself, being left alone.
I just stood on my guard, keeping an eye on him.
He then took the path going to the stream.
I then heard a wail, just a while later.
I rushed as fast as I could, upon seeing a wolf,
Saved him in an instant, before he was cut down.
The wolf was so tough; he fought me so hard,
Had I not been the one, the lamb would be dead.
It took all my breath to throw him down.
Seizing him by the throat, I killed him alone.

(*Wagging his tail, he boasts. Starts to strut back and forth.*)
The lamb's mother (*Smelling her son*)
    Biaa- Miaa... hurrah! Good news! My son is here!
    What would become of me, hadn't the dogs been near?
Lamb Alas! My mother... what makes you so happy?
    When the wolf has chopped off my leg completely.
    I can't move an inch. Come here beside me,
    Let me have your breast, I am badly sick.
    Listen mother please, I tell you frankly,
    Not only one leg, if I lost both of them
    My hands also gone, crippled I become
    If I am destined to die, I let whatever comes.

Scene 2

Sheep When we live peacefully, chewing our grass
    Why are creatures so envious?
Snake: Sitting under the stone, I've heard what you said.
    I talk with you straight, libelling is not good.
    If someone's statement has lost its true meaning
    It would remain, despite excuses, just a useless thing.
    It is customary to speak with parables.
    A sheep is just foolish, picks trivial things,
    He held a grudge, when offended once,
    A stone being a stone causes one to stumble.
    Water by its nature flows down hill.
    Whatever gets in its way, it sweeps away all.
    When first seen, the earth, stone and water,
    To discern good from bad, they've had an order.
    Knowing no one closely, never have ill-feeling,
    But everyone, surely, gets a little envious?
    They are so skilled, and know how to disguise.
    I don't know their way, mine is obvious.
    Eve and that Adam were punished for nothing,
    Fired from heaven, due to my spiteful doing.
    I had seen them both, being God's true courtier,
    Went ahead purposely, and put them in grave error.
Sheep It is just amazing, very surprising,
    How such a story gets one listening!
    Disclosing your deed, talking of your shameful act
    Are you not afraid, how others will react?
Snake Why should I be ashamed, when I am a hero?
    You want me to let my brave deed go?
    Oh, let me tell you, you just listen to me,
    You think your bashful act, will save you completely?
    Every time I see something become good,
    Unless I see it lost or destroyed,

I never can sleep, nor have a peaceful mind.
I simply can't, when I see good-hearted people.
Sheep Like a hot fire, your talk gets one burnt.
What good it does to you, just to hurt someone?
Snake What benefit do you get from your fairness?
Except getting knocked by the big and small ones?
If everyone was not jealous of each other
We would have been limitless, perfect creatures.
Whatever idea that appears sincerely
Fairly undertaken, straight forwardly,
Till it becomes fit, till it gets perfect,
It just goes astray with some impediment
Where does then mischief go, to be able to survive?
It is foul play which has kept it alive.
Now let me tell you the whole thing clearly,
I also advise you to listen actively.
If in our career, there had not been disorder,
Had not death been part of us, the big destroyer,
How would you ever come to accept that God exists ever?
Do not be confused, rather take care,
When God allows mishaps, from the very start,
It is not to harm us, but to get us to be alert.
Sheep For God's sake! Stop it, I've had enough.
You've told me half-truth, half-lie, a mixture of stuff,
What can be done now? You've had your lecture.
How we are delighted, this being our nature,
To get a chance to talk, we often desire,
We compliment you for your jealousy
We wish also to die, living sincerely.
Shepherd My sheep ! Are you here? Let me count you.
To see if one is lost without leaving a clue.
One, two, three …Oh God! I have been wounded!
By a snake! Just driving my sheep, I am poisoned.
You disgraceful bastard! Now die! Yes die!
Here … I've medicine which keeps me alive.

ACT III

Scene 1
(The sheep awaking from their sleep talk to each other)
1st sheep Using his wisdom God has created
And filled with rich beauty this world.
Various creatures, with soul and soulless.
The sun, the moon … countless stars,

In good combination, fitting one to the other.
Created He, hot air and wind, including water.
But ... Each one has its opposite, its destroyer.
2nd sheep Furthermore, to keep it from totally vanishing
He made the forces equal, to get them balancing.
3rd sheep Even with poison, there is medicine that makes it nothing.
4th sheep For us luckily, time has gone by.
Here is the daylight, come it is dry.
A Crow *(Sitting on the tree)*
Qua! Waa ! Hoping to get something from those sheep over there,
Till I get lucky, let me wait just here.
Unless I get rubbish, suddenly by sheer luck,
I am feeble creature, I can't grab by force and am not able to attack.
To live being honest does not fit my nature.
I also get tired looking for rations, running forever.
A pregnant sheep *(with violent pain)* Oh! Ah :.......please; you sheep, plead with St. Mary,
I am in agony ...oh!.oh, oufff...here comes the baby.
Lamb Mee ... Mee ... Mee ... Mee ...Wow!
Unexpectedly, all around me, I see a sudden change
In all places ... Light is shining covering every edge.
It is just marvelous! Everything that I see
In such a magic place, how did I come here really?
Living until today, ignorant of all these things.
Where have I been hiding, not knowing such things?
Pleased with everything, nothing to choose from
I just get confused, all being well made
It seems a nightmare ... a dream or, as just as if one were drunk.
Let me check again, have a close look.
Examine each of them and, let me judge what they are.
Is there someone near me who is an observer?
Why then my heart throbs, I am seized by sudden fear.
I think there is someone watching, hidden somewhere.
Mother sheep Beea ... Don't weaken! Hold on my baby.
Here ....take my breast, adapt to the odour of my body.
Oooof! I just got relieved from the afterbirth, hiding in my belly.
Crow Waa! Waa! I got finally, my heart's desire
The fat placenta has fallen over there.
Why waste my time, I go and eat my lunch,
I then leap about, no need to search for any food.

ACT IV

Scene 1

Fox *(Looking up, sitting under the tree)*
   Welcome Mr Crow ... long life for ever,
   Among the big birds, that I saw here and there,
   To whom God has given such a charming body.
   It is just a wonder, seeing your beauty,
   God has never been short of craft and deep knowledge.
   When he made beauty, he ran to your cage.
   If one tells the truth, one need not fear darkness.
   Your feathers, your fingers; they look like silk;
   Just like your body, you are sweet-voiced.
   You deserve to be king of the birds.
   Now if you would let me, can I hear you singing?
   You would entertain me more than anything else.
Crow *(Opening his mouth)* Haa ... Hii ...Hii.
   Your talk is pleasing, I am touched by it.
   Oh ! What a wonder! Alas, what foolishness!
   When I opened my throat, to let him hear me right
   All the meat dropped out which had been in my mouth.
Fox *(Picking up the meat)*
   Farewell my good friend, but just remember,
   Once I have got the meat, why should I bother with you?
   I have never seen you. Shout as much as you can.
   I go and poke about where the sheep are playing.
   They are just like you, and will always be like that.
   They never get suspicious; I fool them as I want.

Scene 2

Goat *(Moving among the sheep)*
   Hello, sheep! How are you?
   Have you any news, which you have heard lately?
   Forget it. Let me share mine with you. Listen attentively.
   The rats had discovered all the hidden knowledge
   And got organized, seeing the advantage
   Then for their new union, they wanted a leader.
   They chose to be in agreement, avoiding conflict, discussing together.
   They have got such a system, from those overseas,
   And my friend python has told me all this.
Sheep Haa! Haa! What a funny tale you've told us today.
   Ha! Haaa! Kingdom of Rats! Nobody will believe that.
   Who the hell had the guts to get them this level?
   As to being able to form a state, who wrote the constitution?
   When we first heard it, we thought it a joke

Because rats had no law, or a good social system,
Never knew agreement, or had any rules.
In the state of their judgeship, getting citizenship
No one really needs
Please put this aside. It is a lot to discuss
To form government, let alone for rats.
We know it is harder for human beings.
By the way those rats have a special career
To destroy one's house, is their unique nature.
They are clever at distraction.
They have never been productive, except at smelling filth.
It could be good things, or something attractive,
Or a special dress, or a bolt of clothe that they easily move.
They love to damage it; cut it into pieces,
That is what they are best at, all the rest is just false.
To think of those rats having a union or a state formation,
Is like wishing to farm, without yoking oxen.
So, neither of their state, nor of their leader,
Do I believe, whatever you tell me, they never existed.
And, who excels the cat as boss of the rats?
It is a sealed case, no one ever competes.

Goat Why?
How come you've missed the story till today?
The strange happening concerning Mr Cat.
The rats held a forum, everyone was present.
Wait till I tell you all, you will laugh with all your heart.
Wurye[1] they call him, and he is a huge one.
Unexpectedly the cat had dropped by inside their city.
He cunningly saw they were off-guard. Thinking all was fine,
Holding his breath, creeping stealthily,
He killed ruthlessly a whole army of rats.
The rest stood shocked, checking the cat's advance.
Elders soon gathered, and held their meeting,
As to how to trick *Wurye*, the big cat.
After discussing everything they came to a decision,
But *Wurye* had no clue what they were doing.
One brave male rat with a strong voice
Spoke thus, giving new advice.
"Unless we kill today, this beast of white- eye,
Nothing will save us, whatever we try.
Now, avoiding too much talk, let's march together,
And encircling the cat, kill him forever."
Then one cowardly rat, upon hearing such talk,
Wanted to run away from its place.
"Keep to yourself this kind of advice
You all know the saying, I give it as an example,

'When a rat wishes death, she runs like hell,
As she gets near the cat, she smells him in the mouth'.
The rats may wage a campaign, wanting to kill a cat,
This was just a talk, we change now to a real act.
Well, you go for yourself, holding your death warrant
But I am a coward, I don't want to lie.
Let alone kill the cat, getting myself near him.
Standing in the distance, if I watch his white eye
As I smell his odour, I will stay who I am."
Then the real advisor, the third rat, got up.
Even among them, there are some who are very sharp.
"Your deliberation has been just fruitless.
Listen, taking advantage of a situation is often marvelous.
To lead your life as such, you don't need a bonesetter
If one is careful enough, why should one worry?
I had one thought earlier, to bring a small bell,
To put round his neck, or tie to his tail,
Taking precautions. If that measure is taken
Who will be afraid of him, as if he were a lion?
Better now be ready, find a bell quickly,
Then onto the cat's neck, tie it very slowly.
Once we have done that, though we harbour fear,
When the bell rings, we can clearly hear.
Then all of our rats, will change their direction,
By jumping in their holes, they save their skin."
All the rats who were there shouted as a chorus
"Fine ! Fine!", they said, "What wonderful advice."
This makes our council over and done with.
They soon made the bell, without making a fuss,
Be that as it may, having thought of the best scheme.
Tying now the bell onto *Wurye's* neck, to fulfil their dream.
No one could come forward. No one could stay firm.
Having passed the whole day consulting each other
They came to their wits' end. Upon reaching here
All rats had been asked, all made excuses,
All shunned tying the bell, what a daring council!
With jokes, derision, mockery and laughter,
No plan could be fulfilled, nobody could excel.

Sheep What a funny story! I never heard such a thing.
Really, the rat's arrogance has been limitless and huge.
It has never been easy for a rat to kill a cat.
Is not like getting into a small granary with grain in it.

Goat Don't be surprised at the rat's plans.
You will be more astonished when you hear the rest.

Sheep What more could be there, stranger than this?
I have found this story amazing.

Goat Yes, there is a story exceeding what you heard.
Mr Monkey as a Judge, was yesterday appointed.
Sheep Ha! Ha! Ha! Hee! Hee!
Oh, this is too much! I can't have any more!
My heart is aching, don't kill me with laughter!
Think of anyone arguing his case, the Judge being a monkey.
Instead of lying, please talk wisely.
Goat Listen. Fox and Hyena, having quarreled one day,
To appeal for justice, went to the judge monkey
Hyena sued the fox, for committing a theft.
The fox denied the charge, saying he was not dishonest.
Each called their witness, brought their surety,
Made a legal wager, each bet with their honey.
The monkey in the end rendered his judgement.
Please wait all of you, you never heard this before.
"For what we have here, we do not lack what is needful.
No one lives peacefully if we are all arguing.
The young and the old! All love to dispute!
You! ... And you! I know both of you
You deserve punishment, I don't care who is who
Listen, Mr Hyena, you are a damned liar.
In the absence of a theft, you shout for a robber.
Well, you are a cunning fox, you are famous for it.
There is no need to doubt you, if there is thieving your name comes first.
If I had to be ruthless like friends who work as judges,
Both of you would be sentenced to our prison cage
Well ... I can't help it; I have to act as one.
Submit five salt² each, for the judge in person."
Sheep My goodness!
How on earth could there be, such kind of order.
A monkey is not born to act as a judge.
Goat Judgeship has been honoured during our forefathers' time,
Anyone who did wrong got what he deserved.
But then gradually, as the system declined badly,
Monkey became a Judge in our country.
If two country fellows accuse one another
The Judge looks for a sin, to shout at both opponents,
Forgetting to judge them with court procedure,
He takes a bribe openly without being private.
Sheep Be that as it may what else has occurred?
Why don't you tell me Tiger's famous deed?
Goat Have a good day, I am busy.
It is getting dark, I have to take a long journey.
You have had enough, I talked too much today.
Oh, what looks like a dog is coming this way.

Scene 3

Fox As soon as day broke, it turned out well,
   I got my breakfast, crow had dropped down the hill.
   Lamb would be just fine for my lunch.
   Or I would gladly snatch a sheep that had lost its way.
   There they stand, all the sheep together,
   I think they don't watch me, grazing over there.
   They seem restless, how do I trick them?
   As I made my move, they would all run together.
   Once they start running, no sheep tries to stop,
   All sheep are foolish, they are beyond help,
   As the saying goes,
   "If a sheep runs, if a fool gets serious,
   They cannot be stopped, till a further crisis."
   I am just standing here without making progress.
   I'd better think of some trick, controlling my temper.

THE END

NOTES

1. Puss.
2 Salt: first of the four 'grades' in judicial betting.

Book Reviews

Jane Taylor (ed.), *Handspring Puppet Company*

New York & Parkwood, SA: David Krut Publishing, 2009

ISBN 978-0-9814328-3-0 (pb.), 978-0-9814328-5-4 (hb.), (ZA) R480 (pb.), R650 (hb.)

It was with great anticipation that I received this new publication, as prior to this only Carolyn Christov-Bakargiev's catalogue, *William Kentridge* (1998), for the Société des expositions du Palais Beaux-Arts de Bruxelles, and the texts of *Ubu and the Truth Commission* (1998) and *Tall Horse* (2006) have been published on Handspring's work over almost thirty years. Notably the latter two publications included photographs, thus acknowledging the centrality of the visual in the work of Handspring, and perhaps explaining why, despite their international reputation, published material on this company has been so sparse. It is thus not surprising that the most noticeable things about this collection are the extraordinary photographs, sketches and stills from various productions. These visually exemplify the extraordinary interaction between puppets, puppeteers and back projections. The visual material alone would make this book outstanding, and worth purchasing, but the six articles and Jane Taylor's introduction make it exceptional.

I was surprised that this was not presented as a history of the company since it traces the company's work from *Episodes of an Easter Rising* in 1985 to *War Horse* in 2007. Rather, six articles, written by South Africans, each offer a specific perspective on the company, its approach to puppetry and what makes it distinctive.

Appropriately Jane Taylor, as an editor, and close friend and associate of the company: as author of *Ubu and the Truth Commission* and the libretto for *Zeno at 4 a.m./Confessions of Zeno*, introduces the collection with a provocative analysis of the meaning of puppets in contemporary theoretical terms. She explores the boundary between human beings and objects, here the puppets, in relation to the post-structuralist question of how we create meaning in relation to subjectivity. She begins by discussing the implications of surrogacy in relation to the issues raised in *War Horse*, whose success at the National Theatre in London has brought the company to the attention of the international theatre world. This is an important question when one bears in mind that, beginning with the hyena in *Faustus in Africa*, Handspring have projected identifiable human values and strategies onto animals without anthropomorphising them. This offers a way to look at acculturation and how one might cross borders, literally and metaphorically. She discusses the way *Woycek on the Highveld* uses a baby to illustrate how puppets may evoke the idea of an emergent personhood; and how Woycek is used to offer us a mirror and distance from which to recognise our own humanity and explore our existential dread, longing, fear and fury. She concludes by exploring how the 'dispersed body' of the puppet is part of the reason for an implicit anxiety that puppetry often invokes. Taylor explores why this is so, and how the Handspring Puppet Company 'has been responsible for a massive transformation of popular attitudes to this rather esoteric medium' (36).

The next article, 'Thinking through puppets', written by Handspring's master puppet designer, maker and performer, is a very detailed and generous reflection by Adrian Kohler on the evolution of his conceptualisation and creation of the various Handspring puppets from his student days at the Michaelis School of Fine Art in Cape Town in the early 1980s to the present. In this article that is almost half of the book, he reflects on the various influences: people, performances and styles, that have effected this evolution through the twelve productions he discusses. As I read this article I was struck by the way the company thought through and negotiated the integrity of the puppets in relation to space, back projection, the puppeteers, various complex texts and the socio-political contexts in which they were creating the performances. Kohler also helps his reader to understand how the magic of puppetry is achieved, how the puppeteer 'breathes' life into the puppet and the article demonstrates an incredible breadth of theatrical context – from children's puppet shows, to work with classic European texts (*A Midsummer Night's Dream*, *Woycek on the Highveld*, *Faustus in Africa*, *Ubu and the Truth Commission*), to opera (*Il Ritorno d'Ulisse*), as well as the intercultural collaboration with the Malian Sogolon Puppet Company with *Tall Horse*. Finally Adrian Kohler traces the processes involved in realising *War Horse* from the novel, through to the actual creation of working life-size equestrian puppets. One of the greatest legacies of this production has been the extent to which it has legitimised puppet theatre, a term avoided almost at any cost in the UK, owing to a perceived negative stigma.

Adrienne Sichel, a journalist with a national profile as a theatre and dance critic, explores Handspring's 'Escaping the Puppet Ghetto'. This article traces various audience's insights into Handspring's work, exploring the performance traditions that inform the work. As someone profoundly interested in dance on the African continent, Sichel specifically engages with the way Handspring creates dialogue between contemporary cosmopolitan performance and the African arts.

The articles are interrupted half way through with a dialogue between Jane Taylor and William Kentridge, the visual artist who has had a profound impact on Handspring Puppet Company since *Woycek*. Kentridge discusses the collaborative process and how this has aided the company's development of unique theatrical strategies in meeting the challenges of combining puppetry and animation, and how both his and their work has been transformed by the collaboration.

The fifth response evidences the full range of eclectic collaborations of Handspring. Lesego Rampolokeng's essay, in the form of a rap poem, takes us towards his edited and 'disrupted' reading of Goethe's *Faust,* which became the text for *Faustus in Africa*. Rampolokeng juxtaposes this European canonical text to images of the colonised African, and his 'literary prostration' before this giant. Interspersed with this struggle for an African voice, burdened historically, are images of the puppets, 'their visuals stun … & then along is supposed to come The Word' (217). However, although he says that he 'feel[s] finest bashing my senses against the walls. alone. / kentridge's images flickered, came alive … & hands sprung wood animate' (219), and inspiration is born. This is a powerful, visceral and creative reflection on the problems of collaboration, canonicity and history.

The penultimate article by Gerhard Marx looks at 'The function of malfunction in the work of Handspring'. Marx is an artist, theatre director and film-maker who collaborated with *The Chimp Project*, his first engagement with animation, which he has extended very successfully in his own work. Marx returns to some of the issues Jane Taylor raised in her introduction around understanding an object in relation to its materiality as well as its power as a signifier. The malfunction explored relates to the 'body outside the body', the puppet which is both a tool and a subject itself. Again, Marx engages with ideas Taylor explored, here in relation to Heidegger and Baudrillard in the effect of the overlapping of the verb and the material solidity of the noun, which becomes invisible until it malfunctions at which time the relationship between the subject and object must be renegotiated. Marx's comparison of the 'black box' of theatre and the 'white cube' of the exhibition gallery in relation to these puppets that are both sculptural objects and performers, and/ or props is a stimulating provocation.

Appropriately the final article returns us to the Company itself, with Basil Jones discussing 'Puppetry and Authorship', and the reasons for authorial rights for the puppets, both in design and performance, apart from the author of the text. He discusses both micromovement, the performance of life, and the macromovement, the mimetic choreography of the puppet performances. He argues how and why the design of the puppet is an act of authorship insofar as it provides the semiotic grammar for the puppet, 'a meta-script', Jones argues.

This final article takes me back to my introduction, and the question about publication in relation to this company's work. Jones refers to the fact that plays traditionally come into the public domain through published texts, and the link between this and ownership suggests why we view the author as the owner of the play. However, as he rightly argues, theatre is intrinsically about collaboration, as is evidenced through the articles in this book. Thus ownership cannot be singular, nor can the word represent a performance, much less a puppet performance.

This book is a tribute to how Handspring Puppet Company has challenged traditional western approaches to theatre, demonstrating the 'process which reveals the workings of the play's thoughts', in Basil Jones words, and thus 'embody the deepest meaning'.

REFERENCES

Burns, Khephra (performance script, 2006) *Tall Horse*. In *Journey of the Tall Horse*, Mervyn Millar. London: Oberon Books.
Taylor, Jane & The Handspring Puppet Company (1997) *Ubu and the Truth Commission*. Cape Town: University of Cape Town Press.

Yvette Hutchison
Warwick University

Osita Okagbue, *African Theatres and Performances*
London: Routledge, 2007, 200 pp.
ISBN10: 0-415-30453-9, £58.50

Osita Okagbue's book is a panegyric on African indigenous performance forms, a homage to their social relevance as theatrical practices, and a recognition of their resilient stamina for resisting change and the attempt of forces of modernisation to marginalise or consign them to the past as theatrical relics. In this study he teases out in four samples he has chosen the theatrical features of African indigenous events as modes of community entertainment.

The book begins with an engaging and scholarly introduction in which Okagbue delimits the scope of the study and establishes his critical procedure. But he has first to deal with what he calls 'some misconceptions about African performance and theatre'. The first (reversing the order in which he discusses them) is the error of designating indigenous forms as 'traditional' with the implied connotation of antiquated irrelevance, while honouring written/literary drama with the epithet 'modern'. He contends that this theatrical tradition is a living form constantly updating itself by absorbing elements of contemporary reality into its dramatic arsenal. The Igbo masquerade theatre, for instance, has appropriated the atom bomb and the computer into its dramatic vocabulary. Both the oral theatre and the written drama constitute what he calls 'the performance landscape in Africa' (9).

A more serious issue is the futility of evaluating indigenous performances using 'dramatic criteria'. These criteria revisit the Aristotelian concepts of what is or is not drama. Western pioneer scholars of African drama (Molly Mahood, Ulli Beier, and Ruth Finnegan) using such concepts came up with the stunning conclusion that drama in the Aristotelian sense never existed in Africa. African scholars reacting to this claim expended enormous intellectual energy proving that African indigenous performances were drama. Ugonna and Amankulor went to the extent of establishing elaborate dramatic structures for the Igbo and the Ekpe masquerade performances respectively. Okagbue thinks that all this energy is wasted labour because African indigenous performances are not drama. Both schools of critics (the pioneers and their African counterparts) were led by a curious error of terminology to confuse performance/ theatre with drama. They used the terms drama, theatre, and performance interchangeably as if they meant the same thing. A distinction needed to be made between those three terms, he argues (8). Establishing this distinction is one of this study's main contributions to scholarship.

The work of theatre and performance theorists such as Richard Schechner, David Kerr, and Andrew Horn helped Okagbue to make differentiations between drama, theatre, and performance. Schechner's important work, *Performance Theory* (1977), is highly commended for recognizing a 'generic distinction' between drama, theatre, and performance, and for helping to 'rescue discourses of drama, theatre and performance from prolonged...hegemony of Aristotelian tragic drama' (6). Schechner states that 'drama is the domain of the author, the composer, the scenarist, and the shaman; theatre, the domain of the performer; and performance, the domain of the audience'. His model makes three key propositions:

i. Both drama and theatre are types of performance.
ii. Drama is a kind of performance.
iii. Not all theatres or performances are drama (6).

The third proposition is important to Okagbue as he is looking at the works presented in the study as theatres and performances (he deliberately avoids designating them as drama). Performance is seen as a collaborative venture and interaction between three key elements: space, performer, and spectator (52). The burden of the study is to examine the nature of the interaction between these three elements within a performance process. We can hear the echo of Schechner in the following bold declarations:

i.   African indigenous performances such as the ones examined in the study are not and do not aspire to be drama.

ii. There can be no similarity between the Igbo masking theatre and Greek or Western models of drama.

iii Every performance, every theatre event, doesn't have to be drama (5).

Armed with insights from Schechner, Okagbue goes on to analyse four indigenous performances as theatres and performances. These include the Mmonwu masquerade theatre of the Igbo; the Bori ritual theatre of the Hausa; the Jaliya *griot* art of the Mandinka; and the Koteba satirical theatre of the Bamana in Mali. Each performance is examined under the following sub-headings (1) cultural and social background, (2) the occasion for performance, (3) training of actors, (4) staging techniques, (5) design and costume, (6) audience participation, (7) function and social relevance. The discussion of the Mmonwu masquerade theatre is the most detailed because it is the performance culture the author is most familiar with.

His conclusion provides the following benchmark for validating African performance:

1. performance occurs when performers meet and engage with spectators in a designated space;

2. indigenous African performances are usually improvisatory. They rely on the improvisational skill of the performers and the willingness of spectators to contribute;

3. performance takes place in an open-air space to allow easy mobility to both performer and spectator;

4. performance is usually part of community events such as festivals, feast days, group celebrations, times of communal crises, and periods of significance to individuals (births, initiations, weddings and funerals). Festivals are the most frequent context (179-82).

The Introduction is the best part of the book. Okagbue has done a great service to indigenous performance forms in Africa. His work will help to reinstate this theatre tradition in the popular psyche as a serious art form with serious social relevance. It is to be noted, however, that the argument against designating indigenous theatre as 'traditional' in order to elevate it to the same status as written drama is hard to sell. Also it is somewhat puzzling that the author chose to ignore the rich culture of performance theatre among the Yoruba of Nigeria. No mention is made even in passing of this rich cultural heritage or of scholars who have worked in the area.

Obi Maduakor
Tyndale University College, Toronto

Three Memoirs of Nigerian and Ghanaian Theatre

Ademola O. Dasylva, *Dapo Adelugba on Theatre Practice in Nigeria*
Ibadan: Ibadan Cultural Studies Group, 2007, 328 pp.
ISBN 978-978-48100-3-6. $85, Naira 1000

Bode Sowande, *Just For The Fun of It: An Anecdotal History of Odu Themes Theatre*
Ibadan: BookBuilders Editions Africa, 2008, 308 pp.
ISBN 978-978-8088-65 (pb). £6.25, Naira 1500

James Gibbs, *Nkyin-Kyin: Essays on the Ghanaian Theatre*
Amsterdam & New York: Rodopi, 2009, 238 pp.
ISBN 978-90-420-2517- 2. €53.

The first edition of *Dapo Adelugba on Theatre Practice in Nigeria* was published in 2003 after many years spent by Ademola Omobewaji Dasylva conducting a series of interviews with Dapo Adelugba, long-time head of Theatre Arts at the University of Ibadan, Nigeria, and a major theatre director, actor, writer and critic. This is in many ways an informal collection, sometimes repetitious, which forms an enormously important chronicle of nearly half a century of Nigerian theatre, from the time the young Adelugba entered Ibadan as a student in 1958, to his retirement in 2004 (from Ibadan: he moved in 2005 to Ahmadu Bello University). This rich, informative, often anecdotal and very personal view of theatre in and beyond Ibadan, is a fascinating reference for anyone interested in the history of Nigerian theatre, and the personalities – playwrights, actors, directors, academics – involved in it. For me this collection has especial significance: I knew Dapo Adelugba when he was a student, worked with him in the UI Travelling Theatre, and have subsequently enjoyed and benefited from so much of his work, and from his friendship. Dasylva has assiduously pursued Adelugba's career, conducting interviews which are in the best sense 'live', with Adelugba's distinctive voice – that of one of the major figures in contemporary Nigerian theatre – clearly and trenchantly heard.

The anecdotal is also forefronted in Bode Sowande's *Just For The Fun of It*, a history of his work in Nigerian theatre and the repertory company – Odu Themes – he created. Sowande's contribution as a playwright and producer is sometimes obscured in chronicles of Nigerian theatre behind the critical attention paid to others. But it should not be. In his major plays – *Farewell to Babylon, Flamingo, Tornadoes Full of Dreams* etc. – Sowande engages positively with social and political issues of contemporary Nigeria, and does so with a talent for storytelling and theatrical energy that is mirrored in his work as director and actor. In this splendidly free-wheeling chronicle, Sowande recalls the trials and triumphs of Odu Themes, offering us insight into the ingenuity and often the personal risk of maintaining a vibrant theatre company through Nigeria's troubles. The volume is illustrated by Sowande's own recollections of his life and times, of productions and personalities, of hazardous encounters with police and the military, and – helpfully (because this kind of visual record is precious) – a range of production photographs. The title *Just For The Fun of It* captures the warm enthusiasm of Sowande's engaging memoir which is generous to the other artists and players on the great stage of Nigeria, but modestly underplays his radical engagement and the professional contribution he has made.

James Gibbs' authority as a commentator (and activist) on Ghanaian theatre is well-established, and in *Nkyin-Kyin*, a collection of eleven essays – written, as he tells us, over a period of thirty years – he offers a fascinating range of topics. The essays are gathered under four headings, 'Outsiders and Activists', 'Intercultural Encounters', 'Plays and Playwrights', 'Players and Playmaking', all prefaced by a hugely informative contextualising Introduction 'Theatre in Ghana'. As this implies we have records and discussions that take in the pioneering work in 'Drama for Development' (in the 'Gold Coast') by Alec Dickson (best known for establishing the VSO organisation in the UK), the work of Efua Sutherland (for whom he also provides a full bibliography of primary and secondary sources), Ama Ata Aidoo, Joe de Graft and others, critical responses to specific plays and productions, historical chronicles and observations on filmmaking in Ghana. There is also a valuable description of the contribution to Ghanaian theatre of a particularly remarkable 'outsider', the Haitian poet-playwright Félix Morisseau-Leroy. As is typical of the author, he does not hesitate to engage with critics whose views he feels need challenging, but this is a richly informed and committed selection of essays which, even though Gibbs disclaims any attempt 'to provide a comprehensive history of Ghanaian theatre', forms a lively chronicle of plays, personalities and projects in Ghanaian theatre from the 1940s onwards.

Martin Banham
University of Leeds

Kathy A. Perkins (ed.) (2009) *African Women Playwrights*
Urbana and Chicago: University of Illinois Press. 364 pp.
ISBN 978-0-252-07573-5 (pbk), $25

African Women Playwrights by Kathy A. Perkins is an anthology of the work of nine female playwrights from seven African countries south of the Sahara. It is the author's second anthology of African theatre and women and like her first, *Black South African Women: an anthology of plays,* benefits from her professional and research experiences with African artists in the USA and in Africa.

In an introduction that provides a very useful context and rationale for the playwrights and plays included in the volume, Perkins addresses some of the big issues affecting African theatre and women playwrights: the under and misrepresentation of women in African theatre; the relatively few plays that engage with issues affecting women; the still fewer plays by African women that speak about such issues from their own perspectives as artists; the challenges that face women writers such as access to education, opportunities to write, get published, and performed.

The playwrights are representative of different generations but all are accomplished and still very active. They are award-winning authors who write in more than one literary genre and creative medium including music, film, and radio.

The nine 'plays' that form the collection are significant as literary pieces and as performances. They include seven full-length stage plays, one radio play and 'an excerpt from a novel'. However, the anthology is much more than a simple collection of plays. Following the winning formula of Perkins' first anthology, it includes brief biographies of the playwrights and their interviews with the author which cover a variety of issues ranging from the artistic to the political. Direct quotations from these interviews punctuate her introduction as well as preceding each play, thus giving further space for the writers' voices beyond the plays themselves. Individually the interviews serve to situate each play in its specific socio-political, cultural, and artistic context.

The plays are a celebration of women's artistry, their strength, and their individuality as well as their commonality. They are plays that are concerned with the visibility and centrality of women. Through characters and situations, they address issues that 'are wide ranging, contemporary and often controversial…', including women's health, women's oppression, women's rights and the more general themes of poverty, racial identity and 'cultural differences'. All are socially relevant plays which aim to simultaneously inform, educate, challenge, and empower their audiences to action. They cover a variety of cast size and performance styles including the realistic, the multi-media and the dramatic narrative.

The anthology opens with the 'classic' fable-like play, *The Dilemma of a Ghost* by the veteran Ghanaian writer and one of Africa's first published female playwrights, Ama Ata Aidoo. It 'explores cultural differences and misunderstandings between Africans and African Americans', which according to the author, 'still resonate more than four decades after the play's original publication'. The domestic setting of this first play continues in *Over My Dead Body* by Violet Barungi from Uganda which explores amongst other things the right of women to higher education. On a similar note *She No Longer Weeps* by the Zimbabwean writer, Tsitsi Dangarembga examines women's rights in a patriarchal society and the celebration of one young woman's journey to emancipation.

What may at first seem a strange choice to include in the volume is *Better Days Come in Bitter Ways*, by Nathalie Etoke from Cameroon. But this is a beautiful and humorous piece of storytelling told in first person narrative. Originally written in French, it is a translated excerpt of a monologue from a novel, *Le Rêve de Weli* (Weli's Dream), exploring some of the social factors that force young, intelligent women into prostitution. *Homecoming* is a radio play by Kenyan writer, Andiah Kisia (Chika Okigbo) based on the Rwandan genocide.

From South Africa comes Sindiwe Magona's *Vukani!* (*Wake Up!*), one of two AIDS plays included in the volume. The other is *In the Continuum* (the ninth and last play). As Perkins herself points out, given the statistics and the devastation it wreaks on women's lives directly and indirectly, AIDS is understandably a popular topic with dramatists. Both plays explore the issue in interesting and innovative ways. On the one hand, *Vukani!* '…details the complex interaction between democracy and cultural values, mores, and rituals' in post apartheid South Africa. This is reinforced by its questioning, interactive style aimed at encouraging debate between characters as well as audiences. *In the Continuum* on the other hand offers a cross cultural exploration of AIDS and is jointly written by Danai Gurira and Nikkole Salter (from Zimbabwe and the United States respectively). In contrast to *The Dilemma of a Ghost*, this is not a play about cultural differences but one about exploring the 'devastating parallels between AIDS stricken African and North American black women…'. Described by the author as 'two emerging actresses / playwrights', both wrote and portrayed the multiple roles in what can best be described as a complex piece of duo storytelling set in two environments.

The anthology succeeds in demonstrating that African women's playwriting often reflects their mastery of the art of storytelling. It is an art that is versatile and dynamic and this is evident in the increasing number of plays that are derived from real life testimonies and portray contemporary experiences. The South African Malika Ndlovu's

(Lueen Conning) solo piece, *A Coloured Place* and *Edewede (The Dawn of a New Day)* by the Nigerian writer Julie Okoh are two examples included in the volume. *A Coloured Place* combines personal experiences with interviews conducted by the playwright to explore the issue of racial identity in apartheid and post apartheid South Africa from a woman's perspective. The resulting sense of immediacy and realism of the content is undercut by an innovative use of multimedia. Similarly derived from interviews, *Edewede* relies on a more traditional form of audience participation to explore cultural practices and values that oppress women and place their health at risk, such as female circumcision.

African Women Playwrights showcases women's talent and creativity. It is a collection of women writers speaking out to other women, to their entire communities and beyond with each drawing inspiration from different sources in their societies. However, as with any anthology there's the problem of whom and what is included or excluded. Perkins bases her selection on what she describes as urban-based female writers, the majority of who 'spend most or all their time in Africa'. With the exception of Cameroonian Nathalie Etoke who writes in French, they are from English-speaking African countries. The author makes up for what is excluded by providing a list of published and unpublished plays by African women at the end of the volume.

Although the almost textbook-like form of the anthology may not necessarily appeal to everyone, there are very few weaknesses of note (with the exception of the reference to the world renowned Nigerian novelist Chinua Achebe as Ghanaian in the Introduction). The anthology provides a range of known and new plays from established and emerging African women playwrights in one accessible, cost effective volume. It will be of great interest to a wide spectrum of academics and practitioners including teachers, students and researchers of African theatre, Gender / Feminist Studies, post colonial and intercultural theatre. Each play breathes life and shouts out to be performed and as such the anthology will appeal equally to directors, actors and their audiences.

Jumai Ewu
University of Northampton

Mieke Kolk (ed.) *Performing Gender in Arabic/African Theatre*
University of Amsterdam, 2009, 239 pp.
978-908-1516-011-3. Digital document

This volume is number four in a series of publications arising from a partnership over a number of years between Mieke Kolk of the Institute of Theatre Studies at the University of Amsterdam and Sudanese theatre academics and practitioners; each book deriving from the proceedings of a succession of conferences held in Khartoum. The explanation is necessary because it helps the reader understand the reason for the uneven quality of the content of the text. The 2007 conference brought together academics from Africa, Europe and the US and covers a range of artistic production; mainly theatre, but also dance, song, film, art and the novel. It is divided into four sections, but since I failed to find much internal logic to these I will review, as I think the reader is likely to encounter, the book, according to a series of connections around genre and place of production. For me some of the most interesting articles, because the area is still under-reported in English, came from the writers speaking about performance in a Muslim context, mainly within Africa, but extending to a fascinating discussion of a dance performance in Iran. Time and again writers speak of the severe restrictions on all forms of performance, but most particularly on anything involving the display of the female performing body. Hubertus Mayr, in his article 'Dancing with the Veil: Letters from Tentland', speaks of how the Islamic government describes the female body as a 'source of sin and shame' (208), to explain the huge difficulties encountered by a female dance project which had to be passed by no less than 10 censors and was later recalled summarily from a foreign tour. The group chose to perform veiled in nylon tents and behind a translucent curtain emphasising what is seen as both literal and psychological veiling of the female form. A subsequent attempt to build on the project with a group of diaspora Iranian women was forbidden permission to perform in Iran.

A more overt challenge to veiling is described in a short report on an art exhibition by artists of Moroccan descent currently living in the Netherlands; 'Between two homes, Moroccan artists in migration', by Paula van Zijl. While many of the artists refused to be drawn in to a political or nationalist agenda the article focuses on an installation by Aziz Bekkaoui, *Times Burka Square*, where dancers performed in burkas and audience members were invited to also put on the garment, whether male or female. However, Bekkaoui complicated what might have appeared a simple denunciation of demands for women to cover themselves by showing photographs of beautiful women dressed in burkas but posing in the style of western advertising imagery. The artist says he is asking questions about not just the burka but also about how Western advertising tries 'to make all women look the same, with their perfect teeth, hair, lips and clothing' (232).

Two further strong articles elaborate the obstacles faced by women performers in Islamic states. Natasja van't Westende's article, ' "God Gave Me A Good Voice To Sing", Female Wedding Singers in Great-Khartoum, Sudan', discusses the opprobrium and double standards experienced by wedding singers. To have a professional wedding singer is seen as an integral part of many wedding ceremonies in the area. These women are generally of low social status, and they sing, play instruments and help the bride choreograph a series of dances, some of which may be sexually explicit, for an all female audience – prior to the establishment of *sharia* law in 1983 these performances had often been for both sexes. The article explains both the strict laws controlling these events, and how they are often broken, but it focuses particularly on the perspectives of six wedding singers and how they seek to negotiate issues of self-esteem and justification of a profession which while widely patronised is simultaneously derided as shameful. Finally in this group comes an overview piece by Nehad Selaiha, 'Voices of Silence: Women Playwrights in Egypt'. As with the other writers she describes a background of repression of women's voices and creativity by the Islamic state, and then gives short, clear annotated details of the 10 Egyptian women playwrights so far produced by that nation. Several have written either only one play and/or only had that play published but not performed, and the majority are not heaped with any great praise for their technique, but Selaiha picks out two playwrights for especial recognition, Nehad Gab and Fetaheya El-Assal.

Two articles in this volume I found particularly moving, both on Theatre for Development. In her discussion of a project she carried out with women who had been involved in the recent Sudanese civil war, 'Theatre for Change in South Blue Nile: Participatory Workshops', Nora Amin describes how she worked with 15 women to help them shape and perform their narratives of key events that happened to them during that conflict. The article concludes with the scripts of three of these stories; stories told with great simplicity and dignity of almost unbearably horrible events – a husband and child blown up while travelling on a donkey by a roadside bomb while the children travelling ahead and the narrator and a further child travelling behind are untouched – a woman's struggle to gain adequate treatment after being shot in the thigh – and the tale of the escape of a woman who had just given birth from marauding troops after she had been shot in the foot. Jessica Kaahwa's project was also with those affected by war, in this case a mixed group of refugees, Ugandan, Sudanese, Congolese, Rwandans, Burundians, Kenyans and a solitary Ethiopian, all taking shelter in a large camp in western Uganda.'Gender Performance in a Refugee Camp: Prospects and Challenges', explains how a chance meeting led Kaahwa to a camp where access is strictly controlled and she could only work by using the subterfuge that there was insufficient public transport for her to quickly leave the area. The story she tells focuses, unusually for this volume, on masculine gender issues, for while women are able to maintain their 'traditional' roles as nurturers and therefore even in extremely taxing conditions seem to retain their sense of identity and self-esteem, the men, denied a public social role and a position as breadwinners, are sunk deep in depression, purposelessness and a loathing of acceptance of the hated role of refugee. Kaahwa persuasively argues that social roles are key to sense of identity in this context, and that the denial of ability to perform masculinity is deeply damaging to the men concerned. Frustratingly the writer gives almost no information as to the theatre work she undertook in the camp, so this remains a sociological rather than a theatrical study.

The final article I focus on is also predominantly about masculinity, and in a related but more densely theorised manner than Kaahwa's article seeks to explore the position of the performative in constituting gendered and national identities, this time in Arab states. Michiel Leezenberg's 'The Postcolonial Performative: Constitutions of Gender and National Identity in (post) Ottoman Drama' explores in particular whether British theorist Judith Butler's ideas about performance constituting gender can usefully be applied to Arab gendered identity and theatre analysis. This thoughtful, exploratory article concludes with an analysis of language in two plays which Leezenberg postulates demonstrate ambivalence and undercutting of national stereotypes of the performance of masculinity, and a destabilising of the myth of a uniform Arab identity.

Other articles in *Performing Gender* include two on the portrayal of women by leading Cameroonian playwrights, and one each on gender in plays from Nigeria and Zimbabwe. Issues of migration, interculturalism and cross-culture work are raised in relation to the US and Egypt, South Africa and the Netherlands, and African youth in the Netherlands, and Osman El-Badawi opens up a new area for theatrical analysis in his study of priestesses and possession amongst the Nuba people of Sudan. Some of these latter articles, as was the case in the earlier volumes in this series, would have benefitted greatly from a strong editor, and one at least able to ensure the use of English was of a consistently acceptable standard for an academic publication. However, there is much of interest in *Performing Gender*, and some work which opens up new areas of study, both geographically and conceptually.

Jane Plastow
University of Leeds

Index

Printed and bound by CPI Group (UK) Ltd, Croydon, CR0 4YY

13/04/2025

14656524-0001